AF519581

Development Communication and Media Debate

MRIDULA MENON

KANISHKA PUBLISHERS, DISTRIBUTORS
NEW DELHI-110 002

KANISHKA PUBLISHERS, DISTRIBUTORS
4697/5-21 A, Ansari Road, Daryaganj
New Delhi-110 002
Phones : 2327 0497, 2328 8285
Fax : 011-2328 8285
E-mail : kanishka_publishing@yahoo.co.in

Development Communication and Media Debate

Edition–2007

PRINTED IN INDIA

Published by Madan Sachdeva for Kanishka Publishers, Distributors, 4697/5-21A, Ansari Road, Daryaganj, New Delhi-110 002, Typeset by Sunshine Graphics, Delhi, and Printed at Nice Printing Press, Delhi.

Preface

Mass communication began with the invention of the steam-driven press in the early nineteenth century. This was followed by the high-speed rotary press, the linotype machine and photoengraving, which were accompanied by the appearance of the land-line telegraph, the oceanic cable and the land-line telephone.

Our generation has seen the development of moving—then moving and talking—pictures of wireless transmission used for telegraph, telephone and voice broadcasting; of airplane transport; of offset and colour printing. Together they have changed the character of mass communication, adding to the printed word, the broadcast word and the moving image and bringing the remote corners of the world within a few hours of one another. This book deals with Development Communication and Media Debate. Every effort has been made to make this book valuable for the readers and students.

In compiling and editing this book, we have taken support from various sources. Moreover, we have greatly helped by our friends and colleagues whom we would like to express our deep gratitudes for their sincere help and suggestion, without which the work would have been incomplete.

MRIDULA MENON

Contents

1

Media and Communications Revolution

Instruments of Change

The new instruments which technology has given the media have enormously increased the range, variety and speed of mass communications. They have also contributed to the growth of huge business corporations. The development of new techniques and growth in the size of units are not peculiar to the press. They have occurred in almost all industries. Moreover, the changes in the press are closely related, partly as cause and partly as effect, to the technological and industrial changes elsewhere. The technical-industrial development in other areas made possible the new machinery of mass communication which permits, and even requires, operation on a continental scale. The minutely timed reactions of the new industrial society depend, in turn, on the service supplied by the vast network of the agencies of mass communications.

Technological Revolution

Mass communication began with the invention of the steam-driven press in the early nineteenth century. This was followed by the high-speed rotary press, the linotype machine and photoengraving, which were accompanied by the appearance of the land-line telegraph, the oceanic cable and the land-line telephone.

Our generation has seen the development of moving-then moving and talking-pictures, of wireless transmission used for telegraph, telephone and voice broadcasting; of airplane transport; of offset and colour printing. Together they have changed the character of mass communication, adding to the printed word the broadcast word and the moving image and bringing the remote corners of the world within a few hours of one another.

We are now in the midst of this technological revolution. It is far from completed. The war put into military use a new series of inventions. Their possibilities have not been fully realized, partly because of delays resulting from reconversion from war work and partly because of the need for further experiment. Technological advance creates its own inertia because investment does not disappear so rapidly from the balance sheet as new inventions render the equipment obsolescent. The investments of users of existing machinery and the vested interest of skilled employees slow down change.

The fullest use at lowest prices of radio telegraph was retarded, and still is retarded, because of the huge investment in ocean cables and land lines; direct international radio voice broadcasting from the United States languished for want of interest by advertisers until the war compelled its exploitation and proved its value to the American people. Linotype machines which can do the job of four or five ordinary machines are held back by the opposition of the unions; apprenticeship rules are holding back improvements in engraving. It is admitted that frequency modulation (FM) radio has been delayed not only war priorities but also by AM (standard broadcasting) owners and by the unions. It remains to be seen whether similar delays will be encountered, for similar reasons, by television and the facsimile newspaper.

But full utilization of these inventions is clearly in the offing, and their potential influence is enormous.

A world-wide voice broadcasting network over which the deliberations of the United Nations as they take place could be transmitted to every citizen on the planet is mechanically possible at the present time. Such a network has been recommended by the United States National Commission for U.N.E.S.C.O.

Air mail and air express are technically at the point where films or periodicals can be delivered anywhere on the inhabited earth in two or three days. Light plastic plates of magazine pages can be flown to printing plants anywhere so that a complete periodical may come off the press on five continents forty-eight hours after it has been assembled in the originating office.

Through new processes of book manufacturing the people of the world can be supplied with the best literature of all countries at twenty-five cents a copy or less. Experimental work on printing presses is expected to reduce the cost of manufacture still further, particularly for the smaller plants.

Frequency modulation radio is now mechanically ready for general use. It is expected to replace the standard broadcasting systems, except for high-powered clear channels reaching sparsely settled areas. FM's technical superiority over AM is that it gives better tone, free from static. FM provides an opportunity for more stations, each serving its local community on equal terms as to volume and makes possible new and more widely distributed station ownership.

An even newer device, pulse-time modulation, though not yet clearly established as a means of broadcasting to home receivers, will undoubtedly make it possible within a few years to broadcast more than one program simultaneously over one channel. It will cut down the cost of broadcasting any programme and at the same time increase the variety of programmes available to a community at a given time.

Of immediate importance are the advances which the war produced in long-distance wireless transmission. Speeds up to eight hundred words a minute (as compared with average cable speed of forty to sixty words a minute) have been attained and interruptions resulting from atmospheric conditions are slowly yielding to the ingenuity of the engineers. Four-colour facsimile, by which text or photographs or both are transmitted by wireless, has reached the point where whole pages of book and periodicals with their illustrations are now being instantaneously sent in any language halfway round the earth.

The war also gave impetus to multiple-address press transmission, by which news is distributed by wireless, not from point to point, but from a single originating station to receivers in an entire region. Just how radically this reduces costs appears from an application to the F.C.C., of a subsidiary of the International Telephone and Telegraph Company, recently approved. The cost to the users of this multiple-address press system will be a cent and a half a word. This is four to ten times cheaper than any previous service. It is as cheap for the obscure editor in a distant outpost of civilization as for the metropolitan publisher in a European capital. It is as cheap—and it is of the same quality. Within the next decade or two this kind of service will be a major means of communicating news across national borders. Only national regulations and the habits of press associations prevents its general adoption today.

The facsimile newspaper is equally practicable now. Such a newspaper would go to press at the local radio station at 5.00 A.M., say, would be broadcast from FM transmitters, and would drop, automatically folded, from the home radio receiver ready for the family breakfast table. It can be distributed more quickly and more frequently than the standard newspaper. No expensive power presses will be required to print it and no newsstands, news dealers, trucks, trains, or airplanes to distribute it. The farmer and the city dweller will have access to news of the same quality.

The facsimile newspaper need not be expensive. John V.L. Hogan, one of the ablest experts in the facsimile field, estimates that receivers may come down to the price of radio phonographs, say \$100-\$400. The paper, to be provided by the reader, at present costs four cents for a four-page facsimile edition. But Hogan estimates that it eventually may cost only a penny—actually cheaper than the printed newspaper.

Television is more familiar to the layman, but his conception of it does not altogether reflect the importance of the invention. Television is not just a better or different form of radio. It is a combination of radio and motion picture which adds new dimensions to mass communication. The form, colour and sound of events will sooner or later be re-enacted by television before enormous household audiences all over the world. People in remote parts of the globe will be permitted the same face-to-face observation of each other that is now limited to the citizens of small communities.

The speed, quantity and variety of mass communication will continue to increase. Long since, the volume and variety of words and images have exceeded the capacity of any individual consumer to assimilate them. The press has an increasing responsibility for the organization and selection of the material it distributes. But the citizen, who has always had to shift the material he has received, will now have a more complicated task than ever.

We cannot assume that the mere increase in quantity and variety of mass communication will increase mutual understanding. It may give wider currency to reports which intensify prejudice and hatred. Nevertheless, the new instruments exist and will be used in any case. The cure for distorted information would seem to be more information, not less—the full and responsible use of the new instruments of communication to get before the peoples of the world a true picture of one another and of what goes on among them.

Organizational Features

These technological changes have in one sense resulted in a greater diversity of communication. Information and discussion are now supplies through different channels by different managements. Television and the broadcast newspaper may introduce still further diversity of ownership and management, for it is not certain that these new instruments will become the property of those who control the old ones.

But the outstanding fact about the communications industry today is that the number of its units has declined. In many places the small press has been completely extinguished. The great cities have three or four daily newspapers each, smaller cities may have two; but most places have only one. News-gathering is concentrated in three great press associations and features are supplied from a central source by syndicates. There are eight majors in motion pictures, four national radio networks, eight to fifteen giants among magazine publishers, five to twenty-five big book houses. Throughout the communications industry the little fellow exists on very narrow margins and the opportunities for initiating new ventures are strictly limited. The detailed picture of concentration in each medium is as follows :

Newspaper Concentration

For a considerable period (since 1909) the number of daily English-language newspapers has fallen at a fairly constant rate. At the same time there has been a growth in literacy, in total population, and in total circulation. The peak of 2,600 dailies reached in 1909 has been steadily reduced to the present 1,750. Dr. R.B. Nixon, who has done the most recent research on this subject, reported in the *Journalism Quarterly* for June, 1945, that only 117 (approximately one out of twelve) of the cities in which daily newspapers are published now have competing dailies. He also found that in ten states of the Union no cities have competing dailies; in twenty-two states no cities have competing Sunday newspapers. Altogether 40 per cent of the estimated total daily newspaper circulation of forty-eight million is non-competitive. Rival newspapers exist only in the larger cities.

Twenty-five hundred of the 16,000 and more weekly newspapers of the nation disappeared between 1910 and 1920, another 1,300 between 1920 and 1930 and 1,750 more in the next decade. Fewer than 10,000 now survive.[1]

Magazine and Book Concentration

A few big houses own the magazines of largest circulation.[2] The eight leading publishers include the so-called "Big Five": Curtis, with the *Ladies' Home Journal, Saturday, Evening Post, Country Gentleman,* and the new *Holiday;* Time, Inc., with *Life Time, Fortune,* and *Architectural Forum;* Crowell-Collier's, with *Colliers, American,* and *Women's Home Companion;* Hearst, with *Good Housekeeping, Harper's Bazaar, House Beautiful,* and the new *Junior Bazaar;* and McCall's , with *McCall's Magazine* and *Red Book.* To these should be added the *Reader's Digest,* which had at the end of the war an estimated domestic circulation of 8,500,000, plus Spanish, Portuguese, Swedish, Arabic, Danish and Finnish editions totalling another 1,500,000; all but the last of these had the largest circulations in their languages. Among the giants must be included also the Capper group of farm periodicals and the separately owned *Farm Journal,* which together have a circulation over six million. Very recently the Coronet-Esquire group, with a reported circulation of four million for *Coronet,* has jumped into the higher brackets.

Thirty years ago there were nearly two dozen major women's magazines and a group of six large magazines which was just emerging. Now the six largest in a reduced field have nearly nine-tenths of the total circulation.

Though there is still a lively interest in new ventures in magazines and the attempt to launch one is frequently made, the advantages in promotion possessed by the big groups give their publications a head start in the race for readers.

In book publishing the competitive area is comparatively broad. Now book houses appear frequently, and some rapidly achieve financial success. Approximately two hundred houses provide 90 per cent of the books published in the United States each year. More than a quarter of the annual titles are produced by the ten largest publishers.

There is a Big Five in trade or general publishing. They are headed by Doubleday-Doran, which printed forty million volumes in 1945, with gross receipts somewhere near thirty million dollars. The next four, Macmillian, Pocket Books, William Wise, and Harper's, do not approach this size. (The Book-of-the-Month Club could be included in this group.) In the textbook and subscription book field a small number of still other publishers do a large percentage of the total business which equals or exceeds the trade publication total.

In the field of technical books McGraw-Hill deserves special mention. It accounts for approximately 25 per cent of such books and, in addition, dominates the field of business and industrial magazines. The importance of these magazines, and hence of concentration in this area, should not be underestimated.

Radio Competition and the Networks

The situation in radio is distinguished by the fact that the number of stations which can broadcast without interference is limited by nature and the further fact that the maintenance of competition among these stations is enjoined by law. The result is that the number of stations at present is just over a thousand, of which only twenty-five are Class IA clear channel stations, and that single ownership of more than one in any locality or more than eight in all is effectively prevented by the Federal Communications Commission. In spite of these facts, however, the prevalent trend in the communications industry has dominated radio. The broadcasting networks which provide programmes to the stations are outside the regulative power of the F.C.C., except as they own stations subject to regulation, or except as regards their contracts with affiliated stations. Over the last twenty years, four great networks have emerged—the National Broadcasting Company, the Columbia Broadcasting System, the American Broadcasting Company, and the Mutual Broadcasting System. The natural tendency of national advertisers to gravitate toward the networks has induced nearly eight hundred of the thousand stations to become affiliated with the chains.

Motion Picture Concentration

The eight major motion picture companies are Loew's (M-G-M), RKO, Warner Brothers, Paramount, and Twentieth Century-Fox, which five produce distribute and exhibit pictures; Columbia and Universal, which produce and distribute alone; and United Artist, which distributes for a group of independent producing companies and exhibits in England. Approximately a fifth of the theatre capacity of this country has been affiliated with the five producing companies among the eight majors. The theatres in the best city locations with the largest audiences, the highest admissions, and the longest runs have been controlled by the eight major companies.[3]

Chains

Large individual units in a single medium are not the only types of Big Press that have grown up. Another kind of development, especially in the newspaper field and in motion pictures, is the ownership of more than one newspaper or other mass medium in one or several cities by a single person or corporation. These are technically called chain ownerships.

The number of papers controlled by national chains has actually declined in recent years, the papers included in the Hearst chain having dropped from twenty-six to seventeen in the ten depression years, and those in the Scripps-Horward chain from twenty-three to eighteen. At present only a dozen chains among newspapers extend beyond seven dailies, and all but three or four are limited to a single region.

The number of regional chains or, more properly single ownership of papers in two to a dozen different communities has, however, increased. In 1935 there were 63 such combined ownerships, and in 1945, 76. Fourteen were cases of single ownership of 8 or more papers. The 76 chains—national, regional, and local—own 375 dailies altogether, or 25 per cent of all English-language dailies. In addition, there are 174 localities in which there are partial combinations of separately published newspapers through joint use of the single printing establishment, so that a Republican and a Democratic newspaper run peacefully through the same press but at different times of day.

Whatever the tendency is, the fact remains that the local and regional chains, together with the Hearst, Scripps-Howard, and McCormick-Patterson ownership groups, control more than half (53.8 %) of the total newspaper circulation of the nation. Fourteen newspaper owners control 25 per cent of the daily circulation, with less than fifty owners controlling nearly half the total Sunday circulation.

Local News Monopolies

Monopoly, in the strict sense of single control of all current information coming into an area, does not exist in the communications industry. The nearest thing to it—and it is too near for comfort—is unitary ownership in a single locality. This does exist. Ninety-two per cent of the communities in this country, all but the bigger cities, have only one local newspaper. In a hundred small communities the only newspaper owner also owns the only radio station. This creates a *local* monopoly of local news.[4] Joint newspaper-radio ownership is increasing. About a third of the radio stations in the United States are controlled by newspapers, and the applications for FM licenses so far received exceed this ratio.

Communications Empires

The Commission doubts that any regional or national monopoly of communications by a single owner is possible. Mr. Hearst at the top of his fortunes, not many years ago, had accumulated twenty-six news-papers, thirteen magazines (mainly with large circulation), eight radio stations, a newsreel company, a substantial interest in a motion picture feature producting company, a leading feature syndicate, and one of the three press associations, for a total of an estimated thirty million readers and a huge motion picture and radio audience. But at this peak Hearst's organization was in brisk competition with rivals in each medium. It was a communications empire of great size and influence; but it was no monopoly. And it has visibly decreased in size in recent years.

The Luce interests, the Cowles interests, and the Marshall Field interests, are powerful combinations in the various media. The Radio Corporation of America, if not an empire in the Hearst sense, was at its moment of greatest extent a mass communications principality of extraordinary scope.

The Luce interests have owned, at one time or another, a weekly news magazine (*Time*), a weekly picture magazine (*Life*), two monthly magazines (*Fortune and Architectural Forum)*, a documentary motion picture producing company and a radio programme ("March of Time"), and interest in a metropolitan radio station (WQXR) and a radio network (A.B.C.)—the two latter now sold. The Cowles brothers own four midwest newspapers,four radio stations and a weekly picture magazine. The Radio Corporation of America, which is a leading manufacturer of radio and sound and colour equipment, owns the National Broadcasting Company, had a substantial interest in RKO-Radio Pictures, Inc., and is one of the two leading American companies handling the international radio telegraph business to and from the United States.

Big money made in other fields is now going into communications. The Atlas Corporation has recently bought *Liberty Magazine* , with a circulation of a million and a half, and has a substantial interest in RKO-Radio Pictures, Inc., and Walt Disney Productions, as well as three movie-fan magazines. Marshall Field owns two metropolitan dailies, four radio stations, a farm journal and a Sunday newspaper magazine supplement used by more than forty papers. He also has a controlling interest in a large book publishing house and its related reprint house. Edward Noble used money from the sale of Lifesavers to buy the

Blue network. The Pew interests (Sun Oil) control one of the biggest farm journals, a group of trade papers including *Iron Age*, and *Pathfinder* magazine with a large circulation in small town and rural areas.

News Agencies, Features and Syndicates

The press associations and some one hundred and seventy-five companies offer feature services with nation-wide coverage, so that, as compared with fifty years ago, an increasing sameness appears in news stories, photographs, cartoons and columns. Even editorials are mass-produced for certain categories of papers. Almost all of the ten thousand weekly news-papers still surviving, for example, have for a long time used the services of the Western Newspaper Union a manufacturer of editorials, features and columns, owned by John H. Perry, the so-called "Boiler Plate King." Nearly three thousand of them use an eight-page paper provided by Western Newspaper Union, four of the pages of which are pre-written, pre-edited and pre-printed by syndicate. Perry is also developing a chain of small papers including seven dailies, fourteen weeklies and four radio stations. He owns the principal trade magazine for the weekly press and has an interest in plants producing printing machinery which he sells to his clients.

Of the 1,750 remaining general English daily newspapers in the United States, 95 per cent, serving all but one-fifth of 1 per cent of the total daily circulation, take the services of one or more of the three major press association—the Associated Press, United Press and International News Service. This standardization is made more uniform still by the fact that International News Service is owned by interests identified with Hearst, United Press by interests identified with Scripps-Howard and the Associated Press by a limited and until recently self-limiting, group of newspaper publishers. (Radio stations and news magazines are now admitted to associate membership without a vote.)

The same interrelationship within an interrelationship appears in the syndicate news and photo feature business which sells photographs, comic strips, feature columns and the like, thus providing a central control of content far more extensive than any control through ownership. Perry's Western Newspaper

Union is itself one of the country's biggest newspaper syndicates in terms of papers served. Of the five or six biggest syndicates, among the hundred- and-seventy-odd now operating, King Features is connected with the Hearst interest: United Features and Newspaper Enterprise Association, with the Scripps-Howard interests. Associated Press operates one of the largest and most complete feature services. Large syndicates are owned or controlled by metropolitan newspapers: the *Chicago Tribune* and the *New York Daily News* (jointly). One of the largest of all the syndicates, the *New York Herald Tribune*, the *DesMoines Register* and *Tribune*, the *Chicago Sun, PM*, the *New York Evening Post*, and the *Chicago Times*.

Monopolistic Practices

The main causes of the trend toward concentration in the communication industries have been the advantages inherent in operating on a large scale using the new technology. High labour costs have also contributed to the elimination of the smaller, marginal owner.

Other forces are at work as well. They are *personal* forces; they have nothing to do with technological change. They exist, and always have existed, in all branches of the economy, and the communications industries are no exception. These forces are those exaggerated drives for power and profit which have tended to restrict competition and to promote monopoly throughout the private enterprise system. As in other industries, the means employed in specific instances have varied all the way from complicated economic pressures down to the simple instruments of physical violence.

Hearst and McCormick fought an epic newsstand war in Chicago early in the present century, which involved not only the destruction of papers but also the shooting of employees. These battles, and the private armies which fought on either side, were a factor in promoting the gang warfare which has distressed the city since. Violence as a curb on competition has not, however, been confined to Chicago. The New York paper, including the *Times* and the *Herald Tribune*, had newsstand fight in the thirties; and *PM* faced serious difficulties in finding a place on the newsstands.

Potential competitors have divided territory as Hearst, Gennett, and Block did in upstate New York and as motion picture theatres have done elsewhere. Small publishers are now complaining that giant concerns, such as Time-Life and Curtis, have pre-empted paper stocks and printing facilities under long-term contracts. In recent litigation the Associated Press was compelled to give up a practice which the Supreme Court found monopolistic, since it permitted one publisher to deny the Association's service to a competitor. Antitrust actions, now on appeal, against the eight great motion picture companies are designed to separate the control of production from exhibition, a combination which is claimed to amount to monopoly. These companies have produced 80 per cent of American feature films and distributed 95 per cent of the films reaching the public

Cost of New Ventures

Monopolistic practices, together with the cost of machinery and the momentum of big, going concerns, have made it hard for new ventures to enter the field of mass communications.[5]

Although there is no such thing as a going price for a great city newspapers, it is safe to assume that it would cost somewhere between five and ten million dollars to build a new metropolitan daily to success. The investment required for a new newspaper in a medium-sized city is estimated at three-quarters of a million to several million; for a small-town paper, $25,000—$100,000. Radio stations have been sold at figures well over a million dollars, though such prices must include, in the words of Commissioner Durr, "something [the sellers] do not own and have no right to sell; namely, the use of a radio channel." The equity needed for a new feature motion picture producing company would probably be at least $100,000, but this is merely a shoestring; one cannot sensibly initiate a producing unit without a contract with one of the major distributors. A publisher should not start a magazine aimed at the mass market unless he is prepared to lose two or three million dollars at the outset. On the other hand, a book publishing house might be established for as little as $100,000.

Our survey of the instruments and the organization of the communications industry leaves us with certain questions. To what extent has the reduction in the number of units of the press reduced variety? Has the reduction in the number of units cut down the opportunity to reach an audience on the part of those who have something to say? Has the struggle for power and profit been carried to such a point in this field that the public interest has suffered? Have the units of the press, by becoming big business, lost their representative character and developed a common bias—the bias of the large investor and employer? Can the press in the present crisis rise to its responsibility as an essential instrument for carrying on the political and social life of a nation and a world of nations seeking understanding? If not, will its irresponsibility deprive it of its freedom?

These questions require an examination of the actual performance of the press today.

References

1. The approximately 100 foreign-language dailies and 150 Negro dailies and weeklies have shown neither marked increase nor decline.
2. There is a top group of magazines, a dozen to fifteen, each of which has a circulation of 2,000,000 or more and second group of seventy to eighty with circulations over 100,000.
3. Other large and well-established companies dealing in production and distribution are Monogram, Republic, and PRC. There are a number of other"satellite" producing companies which distribute their pictures through one or the other of the majors.
4. There are cases of significant concentration of newspaper and radio ownership in some *regions,* such as that of Frank E. Gannett, whose chain of papers does not extend outside upstate New York. His hegemony, powerful as it is, falls far short of giving him an actual monopoly in that region.
5. This is especially true in the newspaper, magazine and radio network fields; not so much so in book publishing and radio station ownership.

2

Changing Dimensions of Mass Communications: An Indian Perspective

Introduction : The Parameters

In the context of broadcasting, the application of space technologies can be classified in two distinct areas:

— Distribution and assembly of programme signals.
— Direct Broadcasting–Satellite service (DBS) to community or home receivers.

The Indian experience in both of these areas dates back to 1975 when with the help of a borrowed satellite-ATD-6, Doordarshan in association with the department of science, launched a massive experiment in the application of space technology for TV programme distribution and DBS in community viewing mode. This experiment—popularly known as SITE—has already been extensively described. Encouraged by the success of the SITE experimental project, it was decided to use the domestic satellite system-INSAT I—to support the television service to the extent possible. The configuration of the space segment, therefore, included two relatively high power transponders capable of transmitting two television channels with a countrywide coverage zone. These two transponders on the INSAT-IB platform are currently being used for:

(i) The National Programme Service
(ii) The Area Specific Services directed to certain States and Educational Television (ETV).

After the initial introduction of TV services in the INSAT system, pressing demands for regional programmes led to the allocation of an additional low power transponder for TV use. This transponder is currently being used to support regional language services in the States of Andhra Pradesh and Maharashtra. Later this year, another satellite in the INSAT I series is due to be launched. Initially conceived purely as a stand-by platform, it has now been decided to utilise some of the capacity of that satellite to support three other regional services, one each for the North East region and the states of Karnataka and Orissa. INSAT II series of satellites in the early 1990's. The enhanced capacity of the INSAT II generation of satellites will enable additional services to be derived.

Although the INSAT transponders dedicated to television service are potentially capable of yielding signals which can be directly received at community viewing posts, the predominant utilisation is currently in the area of distribution to rebroadcast centres. This has been necessitated largely by the need to minimise the cost of reception: Direct reception of satellite signals as will be discussed later in this paper, requires the use of comparatively more expensive receiving apparatus.

The INSAT system is also being utilised for the distribution of radio programmes from the point of origination to the rebroadcast centres. This has enabled simultaneous dissemination of centrally originated programmes from all stations operating in the AIR network. Enhanced capacities will become available for the networking of AIR transmitters with the launching of INSAT IC and subsequently the INSAT II series of Satellites.

We have now arrived at a stage where a long-term view must be taken of the role that communication satellites would have to play in the future in the field of broadcasting . Because of the rapidly changing technology scenarios, it is becoming extremely difficult to make firm decisions. Nevertheless, the factors which will determine the possible choices are becoming visible. These are discussed in the following sections:

Distribution of TV Programmes

With the advent of space technology, it has become possible to distribute and assemble TV programme signals over large territories using a comprehensive satellite network, the availability of satellite systems has given rise to the following possibilities:

- If the receiving earth stations are hooked on to terrestrial transmitters, programmes can be distributed in real time without loading the terrestrial communication network.
- If a system is to be designed where TV programmes are assembled from different parts of the country for deferred transmission, this can be achieved fairly economically.
- News and cultural programmes can be exchanged between various programme production centres for live or deferred transmission.

In comparison with the classical TV distribution modes based on the use of coaxial cables or microwave circuits, the satellite mode offers the following advantages:

- A satellite covers a large territory simultaneously and with uniform quality. On the other hand, the classical distribution system yields only a point-to-point linkage. As a rule, satellites do not requiie the provision of additional equipment in the space with the addition of receiving points. Reception is unlimited.
- Satellite distribution requires only earth stations on the ground. These are usually located in the vicinity the programme production centres so that no long rearward links are required for programme transmission. The number of personnel required for the operation of a link is thus considerably less than in the case of a terrestrial system. Minimisation of human intervention consequentially leads to greater reliability.

— Satellites ensure the simultaneous transmission of a number of programmes. In a terrestrial system this is possible only when optical fibre links are used.

— The launching of a satellite and construction of earth stations takes only a few years instead of decades needed for the construction of a classical terrestrial system of equivalent capability.

— Yet another advantage of the satellite distribution system is that the earth station can be relocated more or less instantly and access to the satellite can be secured from new locations within the coverage zone. This is evidently not possible in a terrestrial system where the terminals are firmly anchored to pre-determined locations.

In addition to the above, preliminary economic analysis has indicated that a satellite-based distribution would cost substantially less than a terrestrial distribution system of equivalent capability and similar flexibility in effecting connections between various centres. Furthermore, the Doordarshan network as it has come to exist is—as explained in the following section-uniquely suited for the satellite mode of programme distribution and has in actual fact resulted from the availability of a domestic satellite platform. If a nationally-owned satellite platform was not available, the configuration of the network of Doordarshan would perhaps have been radically different.

Characteristics of Doordarshan Network

The initial step in designing a TV network is the identification of the number of separate programme production centres required for all linguistically and culturally homogeneous regions and the number of transmitters to be associated with them. The general principal to follow is that within a homogeneous region only one mandatory programme production centre with a co-located transmitter will exist. All other transmitters in the region will be relay transmitters. Differences in target population such as urban/rural distinctions might, however, exceptionally necessitate separate production facilities even within a homogeneous region.

Having thus identified the programme production centres and their zones of coverage, the number of transmitters, and the required investment on them, will depend on the priorities of TV coverage and on the optimisation of system parameters such as location, power and antenna height. These are critical variables. Another important factor to be considered is the availability of a telecommunication infrastructure to effect linkage between the programme production centres and the relay transmitters.

These consideration require that in constructing a transmitter network, lower priority must be given to areas which are underpopulated or have an underdeveloped telecommunication infrastructure. Furthermore it is necessary to select the transmission parameters which will yield maximal coverage. In most situations the best solution will be a network of reasonably high power transmitters associated with high antenna towers and located in areas of high population density. A supplementary set of lower power transmitters will usually be necessary to extend coverage to pockets beyond the reach of the principal transmitters due to topographical reasons and to small settlements.

These principles did not come to be wholly applied to the development of the Doordarshan network. In the early eighties when the Government embarked upon a massive TV expansion programme, INSAT had been established and the status of the terrestrial telecommunication infrastructure was not seen as a key factor in locating the transmitters. Furthermore, even though it was recognised that a network consisting; for the most part, of low power transmitters was not the most efficient in terms of obtainable coverage, such a network was nevertheless established because it provided the most expedient solution.

Optimum Distribution Arrangement

Given the profile of the TV network as it has developed during the current decade, it would appear that the most efficient distribution system will be a hybrid system with a satellite facility as a mandatory component because of the following reasons:

— The transmitters are widely scattered and many of them are located where the terrestrial telecommunication facility will probably take decades to develop.

- Gathering of programme material from locations removed from the major urban centres will in any event, necessitate the use of a satellite system (as in SNG operations, described later in this paper).
- Where a domestic satellite exists, as is always likely to be the case in India, a TV distribution capacity can be achieved only by an incremental investment.
- The cost of substitution of the satellite links by terrestrial links will be excessively high.
- The connectivity requirements are very complex. The State-level programme production centres are required to be linked with all transmitters within their coverage zones. Connection of all transmitters is also necessary with Delhi for the purpose of the national channel. In addition, there is a need for programme distribution across the regions. The complexity will increase with the introduction of a second TV channel already foreseen in the Eighth Plan period. Microwave links, most of which have the capability of carrying only one video channel, are not likely to be fully responsive to this complexity. Optical fibre links which can carry several video channels, would be a viable alternative to a satellite distribution system but in the present state of development, these are far too expensive.

Nevertheless, there is a need to develop a supplementary terrestrial distribution system in order to:

- provide service security that will result from diversity of the distribution media;
- provide additional linkage to meet unplanned needs (this is highly desirable because experience has shown that demands have often exceeded the existing possibilities);
- enable smaller production centres on a terrestrial root to contribute to a programme pool even though these centres may have been established primarily to generate programmes for local consumption.

Satellite News Gathering

The above discussion relates fundamentally of the distribution of television programmes to various terrestrial station for rebroadcast purposes. An equally important function of a television organization is to gather programme material at a central location, specially for the purposes of news telecasts. This has given rise to a new kind of news gathering operation which has come to be known as Satellite News Gathering (SNG).

A SNG system is conceived as a highly portable satellite uplink operating in the Fix Satellite Service (FSS) of such small size and weight that it is capable of being transported in a scheduled airline helicopter, automobile or even being hand-carried to the site of a fast breaking news event. Such an equipment could be set up and operated by a crew of no more than two people within a reasonably short time (for example, one hour). A complete fly-away SNG system would be packaged in shock resistant flight cases, each having total dimensions (length+width+height) of less than 80″ in order to meet the IATA regulations for ordinary baggage on scheduled flights. This system would also enable the transmission of TV associated sound and two-way technical co-ordinated messages.

The effective use of SNG would require worldwide agreement on uniform technical approaches and uniform operating procedures which are currently being examined by the International Telecommunication Union (ITU).

SNG operations can not evidently be supported by the terrestrial distribution networks because these require a signal to be injected into an existing base band station on an established route.

Direct Broadcasting–Satellite Service (DBS)

DBS implies the emission of television signals from a satellite platform which are strong enough to be received directly by relatively simple receivers either at community viewing posts or in individual homes. DBS has become entirely viable in the recent years and it is conceivable that satisfactory reception can be obtained with a receiving antenna size of less than one metre. DBS has not only provided an innovative means to serve an entire country all at once but has also made it possible to develop new services which would be difficult to realise by terrestrial means.

The method traditionally adopted by broadcasters to enlarge coverage has depended on increasing the number of terrestrial transmitters and their judicious location in the midst of major population concentrations. However, this method has not always succeeded as is evident from the fact that even in a country like Japan which has approximately 7,000 TV stations, including 6,000 transmitters, a very large number of households are still unserved by the terrestrial system. Furthermore, the construction of terrestrial TV stations has invariably expanded from largely populated cities and towns to less populated rural communities. Because of this, in the later phases of expansion, the effective increase in coverage can be quite small even though a large number of terrestrial stations are constructed. The cost efficiency in such a case is low because the per capita construction cost rises steeply as coverage is extended to the thinly populated areas. An additional factor to be kept in view is that terrestrial systems may be simply incapable of providing coverage in territories having harsh geographical features. It must also be remembered that the construction of a huge network of terrestrial transmitters is a time-consuming process and does not provide an adequate solution where coverage may have to be obtained in the quickest possible time.

DBS provides a one shot solution but its principal disadvantage is that its establishment requires a large investment concentrated in a very short period of time.

The other major disadvantage is that the cost of reception tends to be higher; this imposes an economic burden on the viewer. This additional burden can be significantly reduced if the receivers are manufactured in large quantities. It has been estimated in at least one study that if a DBS service is to be established economically, the minimum goal for viewership must be one million.

The key to large scale introduction of DBS lies in establishing a viable number of viewers. As a step towards achieving this, it is highly desirable to design a system that will enable reception by existing domestic receivers with the adoption of reasonably inexpensive adaptors. In order to benefit from the full flexibility that can be built into DBS, these adaptors in principle have the capability of receiving, apart from the television picture signal, additional sound signals not necessarily related to the TV signal and data signal such as teletext, sub-titles, still pictures and telesoftware, service information signals such as the signals that may be transmitted to describe the characteristics of the service signals or signals intended to be used to adjust the receiver circuits for proper decoding of the picture and other service components. Where the television is scrambled, as in the case of Pay TV, the adapters should also be capable of recognising additional data signals which may be transmitted and distributed to the de-scrambling keys. Such an adaptor is bound to increase the cost of a DBS receiver. It may, therefore, be desirable in such cases to conceive of an initially minimum-option adaptor which only performs the basic function of delivering the base band picture signal together with its associated sound signals.

Another possibility of reducing the receiver cost is to increase the power radiated from the satellite so that a relatively strong signal is available at the receiving location. Radiating higher power from the satellite would however mean substantially larger investments in the space segment.

While the appropriate choice of technological solutions can result in substantially reducing the costs of DBS receivers, most broadcasters have come to believe that the cost can be reduced to the affordable levels only when a reasonably large demand for receivers is generated so that the scale of production is sufficiently large. It can be stated, however, that such a demand is not likely to arise unless DBS is designed not merely as a substitute for a terrestrial broadcasting system but also to offer new and unique services which cannot easily be achieved through the terrestrial system. In other words, a viewer can be expected to invest in a suitable DBS receiver only if he is able to receive some value added services.

Several new services not easily realisable in terrestrial systems have been proposed for DBS. Of these, I will mention the most important, namely, High Definition Television (HDTV).

HDTV is a system which would be able to produce a picture quality superior to that of the present day 35mm film. It offers the following advantages in comparison with the conventional TV systems:

— a picture resolution both in vertical and horizontal directions, twice that of the existing TV systems.
— better colour reproduction.
— a larger aspect ratio (5.33: 3) as for wide screen film projection.
— larger screen display for more relaxed viewing.
— better picture contrast.
— better reproduction of rapidly moving scenes without objectionable blur.
— stereophonic sound.

The central feature of HDTV is a higher scanning rate (1125 or 1250 lines) than the existing TV systems (625 or 525 lines). Because of this, it is necessary to provide a channel band width which is substantially larger than the band width assigned to a terrestrial TV channel. It is, therefore, impossible to transmit an HDTV signal from a terrestrial network. DBS provides a unique solution. HDTV has made rapid progress in the recent past and the first feature film produced in HDTV for cinema release "Julia and Julia" of RAI (the Italian television network) has been successfully released in Europe and USA.

Other countries in Europe have also unveiled a new HDTV campaign and launched a joint project named URICH to finalise the transmission and production standard. There are presently no uniform world wide standard for HDTV but at least two candidate systems are under consideration of the International Radio Consultative Committee (CCIR). It can be expected that as soon as such a standard is finalised, there would strong demands for the introduction of HDTV even in the developing countries.

Prospects of DBS

The Satellite Instructional Television Experiment (SITE) and the subsequent operationalisation of the INSAT satellite has universally been acknowledged as a pioneering effort in the field of DBS. In fact, the utilisation of INSAT has been recognised as the first genuine exercise in DBS. However, the limitation of the INSAT derived television service is that it operates on the community viewing mode and satisfactory reception is only possible with antenna size of less than approximately 2.5 metres. Way back in 1977, it was realised that in order to achieve an effective direct broadcasting service in the individual reception mode, it would be necessary for us to exploit the Ku (12 GMZ band where it is possible to derive regional beams of a polar flux density high enough to provide reception with an antenna diameter of less than one metre. We, therefore, sought and obtained frequency assignments for a Ku band facility at the World Administrative Radio Conference which was convened that year by the International Telecommunication Union. The ideas generated in that conference provides for the parking of Indian transponders. If this plan is implemented, it would be possible to achieve altogether 12 satellite beams each supporting as many as four television channels. In principle, this plan would make it possible for us to create a space segment capability that would cater both to regional programmes as well as national programmes. However, the implementation of a Ku band satellite receiver work is beset with the difficulty that, the radiated power being high, the raw power consumed by each transponder would be of the order of approximately 300 Watts. Since the power generated on board is limited by the size of the solar panel it would be difficult to accommodate more than five transponders in each spacecraft. The full implementation of the 1977 plan would, therefore, need the launching of several satellites which is a very expensive proposition. Careful consideration would, therefore, have to be given to techno-economic factors before a firm decision is made. The difficulty is compounded by the fact that the Ku band signals are prone to considerable losses in the tropical regions where rainfall is high. Because of this, a significant reduction in the radiated power and a corresponding increase in the number of transponders which can be accommodated in a spacecraft is not conceivable. In the circumstances, a practical solution may lie in initiating direct broadcasting service with only a small number of channels and then progressively enhancing it to fully implement the provisions of the 1977 Plan. As stated earlier, the key factor to be considered in making this decision is the cost of reception. It may be stated in this connection that where as DBS provides a highly efficient solution for the expansion of TV coverage, a judicious balance must be struck between efficiency and equity. A service that benefits only the prosperous segments of the country's population, would hardly be worthwhile.

Use of Satellites and Sound Broadcasting

Based on several studies that were carried out in the late 1970s, several administrations, including India submitted proposals concerning the possible introduction of satellite broadcasting service to the World Administrative Radio Conference convened by the ITU in 1979 to review the radio regulations including the table of frequency allocations. These proposals put forward the concept of a satellite sound broadcasting service directed to portable and vehicular receivers. Technical studies have concluded that current satellite technology is capable of providing the service in a frequency band near 1,000 MHz. The conference was unable to make a suitable allocation to the service, but it authorised the next World Administrative Radio Conference to make an appropriate decision. This conference is scheduled to take place in autumn this year. It is not however, certain that a favourable decision would be taken because of two major problems viz., the requirement of rather high radiated power from the satellite to serve the vehicular receivers with a high degree of reliability and the difficulty in sharing the frequency band with certain terrestrial telecommunication services to which the frequency band in question is currently allocated. The proposals which were submitted to WARC 1979 were based on the use of FM sound transmission techniques which would permit the reception of satellite sound broadcasts by the addition of a low cost frequency converter to a conventional VHF/FM receiver. However, since this requires a rather high satellite power, technical studies are currently being carried out for the use of advanced digital systems which would not only reduce the power requirement of the satellite but also facilitate shared use of the frequency band between the broadcasting satellite service (sound) and the terrestrial services to which the frequency band is presently allocated. It has also been claimed that these techniques would also lead to more efficient use of the frequency. Spectrum techniques would however necessitate the acquisition of new receivers. The prospect of introducing DBS (sound) will become clearer only after this year's World Administrative Radio

Conference. But as of now, it seems most likely that the decision to make a frequency allocation will be deferred until the current studies are concluded.

In the meanwhile, at least one country, viz., the Federal Republic of Germany has decided to introduce a 16-channel sound broadcasting system using one of the transponders on the German satellites-TV-SAT. This transponder will replace Ku band television channels for which the administration of Federal Republic of Germany secured a frequency assignment in the 1977 plan. It has been claimed by FRG that this service will produce an improvement of quality to the level already being achieved in compact disk and digital tape recorders. This conclusion has been derived from field tests performed with the help of operating satellites such as OTS, ECS1 and INTELSAT V as well as laboratory simulators. .

Indian experience in the field of satellite radio is presently confined to the distribution of programmes rebroadcast by terrestrial radio stations. If the concept of DBS (sound) becomes realisable with the allocation of a frequency band by the competent World Administrative Radio Conference, it would be especially beneficial to India where because of the vastness of the territory to be covered and situational proximity to the equator, the satellite solution is the most suitable.

An attempt has been made to survey the Indian experience in the use of satellites to support television and radio services and the various considerations that need to be kept in view in making plans for the future. It has been concluded that satellites would open up exciting possibilities for the expansion of coverage and for the introduction of new services. For the distribution of programme signals for rebroadcast purposes, satellite technology undoubtedly provides the most efficient solution. However, before the introduction of DBS in the individual reception mode, it, will be essential to ensure that the cost of reception is reasonably low. This would ensure that this service is truly beneficial to the society as a whole.

Electronic Media : Power and Purpose

Radio and Television are much too powerful as instruments of conditioning the people's mind to be given the kind of "autonomy" many starry-eyed idealists seem to be dreaming of. Secondly, "autonomy" means different things to different men; and for the more naive, it seems to be coterminus with "independence." Can India afford a radio-television system which with "independence", can arguably become oblivious of social concerns?

To begin with, let us look at the awesome power of the electronic media, especially in the sensitive field of the nation's integrity in which India is right now so vulnerable. Half the work of the Pakistan-backed secessionists in Kashmir is being done by the radio and television broadcasts beamed with unerring accuracy at the people from "Azad" Kashmir and Pakistan proper. Indeed, two senior Indian correspondents who were allowed to visit "Azad" Kashmir recently found the whole place a primitive wilderness except for the radio and television facilities.

This is of a piece with the pattern obtaining all around the world. The Sri Lanka Tamil campaign for secession never really got off the ground until they instituted "Voice of Tamil Eelam"; and when this "Voice" did get itself heard, we know how Indian soldiers had to go to fight and die in Sri Lanka in the effort to save the island nation's integrity. Similarly, if the African National Congress seems to have achieved a breakthrough in its battle against apartheid, it owes this to a large extent to the "Radio Freedom" broadcasts beamed to South Africa from neighbouring frontline states.

Role of Media : A Historical View

The electronic media have made major contributions to every war or liberation movement since World War II. The uprising which toppled Marcos in the Philippines, the Cuban revolution of President Fidel Castro and the liberation of Algeria all came about only when physical effort was supported by a powerful blitz to capture the minds of the people. The Sandinista triumph over the Somoza dictatorship in Nicaragua was powerfully aided by a radio blitz and the fall of the Sandinista regime is attributed even more to the propaganda war waged by the U.S.-aided groups from neighbouring EL Salvador and Honduras.

If the Lebanese cauldron continues to be on the boil for the umpteenth year now, a major reason is that each faction has its own radio. One of the first things that the Awami League did when General Tikka Khan's legions cracked down on the Bangladesh people was to set up a radio and news agency. And, let us not forget that both the Hungarian uprising of 1956 and the Czechoslovak uprising of 1968 were triggered off by incendiary and persistent broadcasts from "Radio Free Europe" and "Radio Liberty", which were both started in the beginning of the cold war by the USA. Finally, many have forgotten that President Gorbachev admitted right at the beginning of his programme of perestroika and glasnost that the decades-old Soviet effort to jam broadcasts from the cold warriors on the other side of the fence had been futile. He reasoned that if the Soviet state could not stop this campaign to create discontent and disaffection in the communist world, it had no alternative but to grant more freedoms to the people and to restructure itself.

Can the Indian Union afford to leave this powerful medium in the hands of people whose main concern cannot be the political, military and social security of the country?

Freedom and Fear

No state in the world has done this so far. The much trumpeted British Broadcasting Corporation may have the freedom to broadcast whatever it thinks to be the truth about India or Ismailia, Trinidad or Timbuctoo, but where British interests and security are concerned, it cannot have that freedom. The Battle of Britain during World War II was fought jointly by the Royal Air Force and the BBC. During the infamous Anglo-French Suez Expedition in 1956 in collusion with Israel, while all the world decried the cowardly deed the BBC dutifully broadcast the official propaganda. This happened during the Falkland war also. It might have been all right for Britain to leave the Red Dean of Canterbury looking after the church. But would he have been allowed, for instance, to run the BBC?

Indeed, the clamour for a New World Information Order is the result of realisation by the Third World countries that the media reflect the concerns of their societies, the concerns of those who run the media organs. Ironically, opponents of the Third World's demand for a more equitable World Information Order trot out the same reasons which those who want "independence" for All India Radio and Doordarshan do. They echo the proponents of the "free flow" theory according to which information should be allowed to flow freely like water from the high-information mountains to the low-information valleys and plains.

To say all this is not to pooh-pooh the need for genuine autonomy. That is, autonomy to radio and TV experts to run these two media professionally. But, just as wars are too serious a matter to be left to generals, radio and television must be run professionally subjects to ultimate social control.

Social Control

How this social control is to be exercised is, however, subject to debate. The control which the previous regime exercised had much in it worth condemning. The present regime has been more restrained. But this is not for want of trying by individual wielders of power. It is most likely the consequence of the situation that a more strident effort to control radio and TV might result in the fall of the Government itself.

The Prasar Bharati Bill 1989 is a hurried model put before the nation. Unfortunately, in the name of "autonomy" it seeks to institutionalise the control of whoever is ruling at the Centre. Section 22 (1) in Chapter IV of the Bill gives the Central Government power to give "such directions as it may think necessary" to the proposed corporation "in the interest of the security of the state or preservation of public order". The direction may require the corporation not to make a broadcast on a particular matter, or to make a broadcast on "a matter of public importance specified in the direction". In the latter case, the Corporation is free to announce that a particular broadcast is being made in pursuance of a Government direction. But there is no mention in the Bill of a notice to listeners or viewers if a particular broadcast is not allowed to be made. Further, all employees of the proposed corporation will be "public servants" with, for instance, the same immunities as policemen.

This is something going against professional autonomy. What is more, it would tend to formalise and institutionalise what has so far been done unofficially, that is, by giving instructions over the telephone or an official or politician parking himself in the radio or TV newsroom. The only occasion when such officially-sanctioned media management was possible was the Emergency. I wonder if the authors of the Bill realise this.

Professional Autonomy

It is not as if omission of autonomy for the professionals who run radio and television has been done by oversight. The Bill provides for a Chairman of the Board of Governors, an Executive Governor, a Governor (Personnel) and a Governor (Finance). There is no mention either of a Governor (Editorial) or a Governor (Engineering), the two areas which make the electronic media what they are. It is like handing over the control of a newspaper to the people manning the management, personnel and finance departments.

Those who work in the print medium would vouch that something like this has progressively been happening, and that explains the transformation of many formerly respected organs of public opinion into news sheet un-shamedly trying to take a stance depending on which side their bread is buttered. The point is, if radio and television are to be just another incarnation of such proprietor-dominated and commercially-minded media, where is the need to finance them from public funds?

Media Reform : Approaches

For over two decades—beginning with the Chanda Committee report in 1966 and continuing through the reports of the Verghese Committee (Akash Bharati) in 1978 and the Joshi Committee (an Indian Personality for Television) in 1985—expert committees set up by the government have made a case for organisational restructuring of broadcasting so as to give it greater autonomy. Once again, talk of media autonomy is in the air. One is entitled to hope that actual action will follow the pronouncements, this time around. A few points—generally accepted, but often ignored—bear reiteration in this connection:

(*i*) Autonomy, in our context, does not necessarily imply functional freedom. Any number of "autonomous" institutions bear ample testimony to this. Such institutions are generally subject to the same rigidities as government Departments, are often dominated by petty bureaucrats from the concerned Ministry, are sometimes prey to interference by politicians, are prone to be treated as "dumping grounds" for unwanted persons, and are generally the antithesis of true autonomy.

(*ii*) There are—on the other hand—examples (admittedly few) of government Departments/agencies working with great freedom, flexibility and innovation.

(*iii*) Interference—overt or covert—in media may come not only from government, or from other politicians, but also from other individuals and "interest groups."

(*iv*) Sycophancy is as much of a danger as censorship.

(*v*) Independence and freedom for the electronic media have meaning only if they are practised down to the local level. Internal decentralisation and devolution of authority is as crucial as the external (Macro-level) restructuring.

(*vi*) The massive investments made in the electronic media have justification only when the media are used for public service purposes. In this context, the "returns" garnered through advertising revenue are trivial compared to the potential gains in quality of life and in GNP that are possible through appropriate programmes.

(*vii*) Huge investments have been made in recent years in expanding the theoretical reach (*i.e.*, signal coverage) of the electronic media. In order to derive the full benefit of this, it is now necessary to make matching large scale investments in dispersed programme production facilities and in community reception facilities. It is only through the latter (community reception in schools, panchayats etc.), that one can provide access to the media for the disadvantaged.

(*viii*) The electronic media should not—intentionally or inadvertently—erode the very premise of our nationhood, *viz.*, unity in diversity. Any push towards homogenisation is not only undesirable, but will be counterproductive.

(*ix*) In a vast, diverse and heterogenous country, meaningful communication requires the use of local languages local characteristics and local idiom. Programmes must be specific to the soil, water, weather and resource conditions prevailing. Without becoming, parochial most of the programming must, therefore, be local, while keeping open the windows to the outside world.

(*x*) Programme planners and programme makers must be sensitive to the socio-cultural environment and the realities of their intended audience. Sensitivity to issues like gender equality, environment, exploitation, etc., is as important as aesthetic sensitivity. This implies special efforts in both recruitment and training.

(*xi*) While efforts and investments in educational TV have been increasing, these are completely over-shadowed by the large-scale commercialisation of TV. A consumerist culture has been actively promoted, and the developmental role of TV has taken a back seat. Radio has been greatly neglected.

(*xii*) The response to new developments—especially to VCR's and cable TV—has been unplanned and *ad hoc*. New innovations-programme feeds from various locations, vast reach through satellite, teletext services, etc.—have been exploited primarily for news and commercial purposes, rather than for developmental goals.

Guidelines

It is within this general context, and based on the experience of radio and TV operations in the country, that the following guidelines/mandate is suggested for the electronic media.

1. Radio and TV will be public service media, with their primary role being development and nation-building.

"Public service" will obviously include news, information and sheer entertainment, all of which are part of the real needs of the people. However, media will not lose sight of the primary goal of development (through programmes that disseminate information, create awareness, promote social change, improve education and skills, etc.) and nation-building (involving the promotion of diverse languages, cultures and thoughts, but with the underlying current of unity and by providing a broader national perspective to local, national and international events.

2. Radio and TV will serve as "active" rather than passive media. They will promote and reflect debate on vital issues.

Thus, the media will not put out the view on various issues, but will seek to reflect diverse viewpoints and to generate debate on important issues. They will thus provide a platform for debate, rather than serve as a mouthpiece of the government.

3. Radio and TV will operate at local, state and national levels, with all three levels being given equal importance.

In the long term, there will be three distinct channels, with viewers having a choice. In the immediate future, these levels may have to operate in a "time-sharing" mode. "Equal importance" implies that at each level there is independent decision-making authority of equal status (thus the State-level programmers cannot dictate terms to the local level). The decision of what to broadcast and what not to will be left to each level—except that a mandatory "National programme" (not synonymous with "network programme") of not more than 60 minutes in the day and 90 minutes in the evening/night will be broadcast by all transmitters. Satellite uplink stations will be immediately set up in all States, so as to create the State-level network, and programme production facilities will be set up in a phased manner at all existing transmitters, enabling local broadcasting.

4. There will be separate autonomous bodies for radio and TV. These will be financed by government and will be accountable (for policies, not for day to day operations) to Parliament. The policies will be laid down by a Board of Governors for each of the media, to whom the Chief Executive will report.

5. Within each media, there will be separate wings/units for developmental programmes, for educational programmes, for news, for sports and for culture. Other wings/units may be added as necessary (*e.g.*, for children's programmes).

6. Programme making by other organisations—especially by voluntary groups and activist agencies concerned with issues of relevance to the disadvantaged—will be encouraged. Appropriate slots will be provided for broadcast of such programmes.

7. Selection and scheduling of programmes for broadcast will be done on a professional basis.

Ribbon-cutting and inaugurations, etc., by dignitaries will generally not qualify for broadcast. Programmes that have excessive violence, promote superstition or debase tastes through vulgarity will not be aired. Due time will be kept aside (at the right time of the day) for children's programmes, and also for other important groups like youth and women.

8. Local broadcasting—through both radio and TV—will be given maximum emphasis.

A lot of resources have been invested in generating and disseminating "national/network programmes". However, in vast areas of the country the relevance and comprehensive of these is minimal. While these need to be continued (through on a more limited scale—see 3 above), emphasis now needs to shift to the local level, where it is possible to use media for concrete and immediate benefits. While radio is finally poised to go local in a big way, in the case of TV the only real example is probably in Kheda district of Gujarat.

9. At the local level, radio and TV will co-ordinate closely with each other and with developmental agencies (both government and voluntary), so as to maximise their effectiveness.

10. Radio and TV will move beyond mere information transfer and try to motivate and even mobilise people.

While the mass media are well-suited to information dissemination, innovative use can turn them into instruments for motivating and even mobilising people. This can turn development into a people s programme, with the government playing a facilitative role.

11. Radio and TV will be used for "horizontal" and "reverse flow" rather than merely "top-down" communication.

While the mass media are ideally suited for one-to-many communication, they can be used for generating a dialogue within the audience. Conveying the experiences of the group to another, such "horizontal" communication is the essence of people-oriented development. The media can also be used as a means of feedback from the people to policy and decision-makers. Much positive experience of such uses of TV (as also of attempts at motivation and mobilisation—see 10 above) exists in the Kheda Communications Project of DECU/ISRO. Such use of media presupposes the creation of local broadcasting, and the Kheda model will be replicated in a large number of places.

12. Sensitisation and training of programme and managerial personnel in radio and TV is recognised as being crucial. A large-scale and planned, effort will be undertaken in this field, on a continuing basis. Present training instructions will be rejuvenated and new ones set up, if necessary.

13. Communication research will be made an integral part of the broadcasting effort and will be carried out through a well-organised in-house set-up and also through outside agencies.

14. Operational guidelines will be laid down to reduce the consumerist orientation of the broadcasts and to promote positive values, the negative portrayal of women, the exploitation of children and of the female form will be constrained by strengthening codes, for both advertisers and programme makers.

15. National programmes will be given a truly national character. The Delhi-centric orientation of the media will be done away with.

16. New technological possibilities will be fully exploited, especially for developmental and educational broadcasts.

Possibilities such as talk-back systems (one-way-video, two-way-audio) will be used for training of development functionaries in the field, teachers etc. Teletext and data transmission systems will also be used for educational/development purposes and for the benefit of farmers (*e.g.*, market price information). Unique satellite features, such as an "anywhere to everywhere" broadcast capability (through transportable TV/Radio uplinks, conversion of TVRO's and RN terminals into uplink facilities) will be used to bring in diversity and real life into the programmes and to get out of the Delhi-centric syndrome.

17. The internal structuring and management systems of radio and TV will be such as to ensure professionalism, foster creativity and innovation, and provide motivation for excellence. This would require flexibility and decentralisation, combined with accountability.

18. An Ombudsman will be set-up for radio and TV to look into complaints of various types, including bias, distorted reporting or harmful programmes.

19. Active consultative committees—with appropriate

representation from audience groups—will be set up for each station. These will have a major say in the type of programmes produced and will also determine which of the networked programmes (from State and national level) are to be broadcast by the local station. (The national programme will, of course, be mandatory, as mentioned in 3 above).

20. The "success criteria" will be relevance, effectiveness and credibility of programmes rather than the amount of advertising revenues.

This paper only seeks to highlight, for discussion, the major issues involved and to point out that mere macro-level structural changes (*e.g.*, creation of autonomous corporations) will not by themselves be the magic wand that provides instantaneous solutions. If commercial, mercenary or "opiate" interests are not to dominate the electronic media—which may, in fact, be easier with an autonomous/corporate structure—it is necessary to mandate the role of the media first.

3

Media and Politics: A European View

Dissatisfaction with the Media and Politics

In 1992, as more and more East German state security service (Stasi) files were made accessible to and leaked to journalists, Germany was swamped with a flood of stories about Stasi connections. Right in itself, the attempt to learn from the past and not to suppress for a second time inhuman atrocities carried out by a German dictatorship threatened to turn into a witchhunt. Documents which appeared from nowhere and whose reliability was extremely suspect were taken at face value and treated as if there were no taint of the Stasi clinging to them. The hunt for actual and suspected informal collaborators developed into a type of pillorying journalism which hit both innocent and guilty, but was in any case full of premature judgements. And so a few journalists brought many of their profession into disrepute. The politicians affected hit back, issuing blanket condemnations of the media.

Scarcely had the wave of Stasi exposures died down when in 1992/93 a new wave broke. Prime ministers and ministers who had used official notepaper to extol the products of a cousin by marriage, who had travelled free in jet planes belonging to industrialist friends, whose memory had failed them before commissions of inquiry or who assumed responsibility for slip-ups in the search for wanted persons disappeared from the political stage in a storm of media indignation. During this wave of resignations, which included that of the general secretary of a trade union found guilty of insider dealing, the Federal Republic appeared to be submerged in a maelstrom of iniquity reminiscent of ancient Rome. Certain sections of the population turned their backs on politics in disgust. Antipathy towards politics and politicians spread, but the people against whom it was directed were quick to identify those responsible for the sorry state of affairs: the media. Politicians argued that the media had in their self-righteous way vastly exaggerated, characterised relatively minor shortcomings as outrageous, and blown them up into scandals. The journalists in turn tried to brush aside criticism of and displeasure with the media by commenting that they had only been fulfilling their obligation to inform the public. This led Hermann Bolventer to conclude, correctly, in the RHEINISCHER MERKUR of 28 May 1993: *"Under the pretext of exposing shortcomings what actually happened was an economisation and commercialisation of journalism."* Since 1993 the old topic of

Confidence in Leading Politicians

Federal Republic of Germany, population over the age of 16

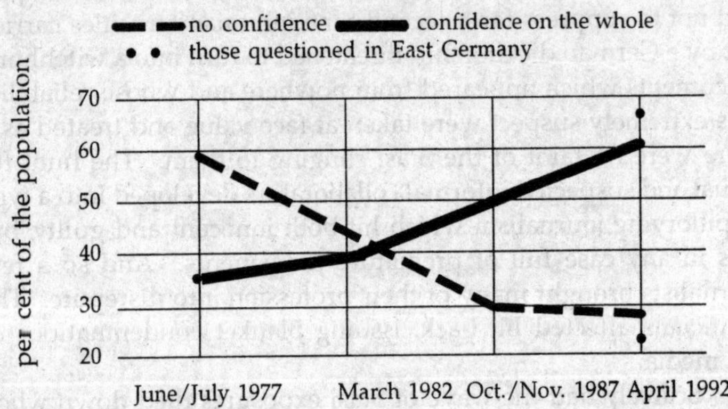

(*Source*: Allensbach, published in BERTELSMANN-BRIEFE, No. 120/ 1993).

Media Image of Objectivity
Statement: truthfulness
... reports truthfully and represents things as they really are

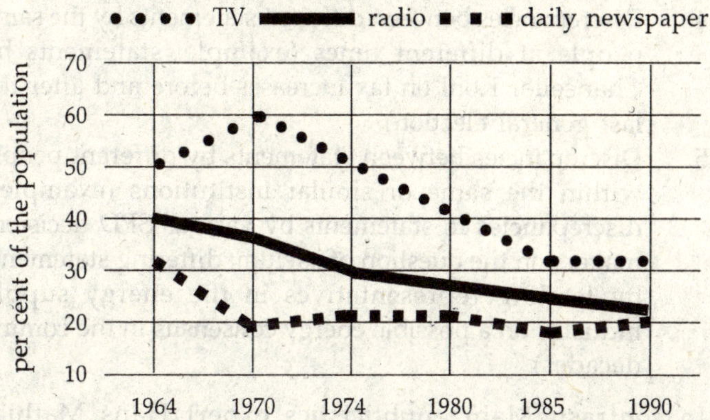

(*Source*: Kiefer, published in BERTELSMANN-BRIEFE No. 129/1993).

connections between the media and politics and between journalists and politicians has been back on the agenda. Each side accuses the other of having contributed toward the loss of confidence and authority.

However, the current discussion ignores the fact that for the past few decades in West Germany, and of late increasingly in East Germany, public confidence in leading politicians and belief in the veracity of the media have continually declined, as the two charts show.

Bamberg communications specialist Gunter Bentele names five "discrepancies in public communications" which in his opinion can at least partially explain the loss of confidence in the political system:

"1. Discrepancies between information and the underlying facts (examples: lies, information which glosses over the facts, cf the chemicals accident at Hoechst in Frankfurt at the end of February 1993).

2. Discrepancies between verbal utterances on the one hand and actual behaviour on the other (examples: stalling tactics, diversionary manoeuvres, certain types of symbolic politics)

3. Discrepancies between different types of behaviour or action by the same authorities (example: contradictory administrative actions, differences between different states).
4. Discrepancies between different statements by the same people at different times (example: statements by Chancellor Kohl on tax increases before and after the last general election).
5. Discrepancies between statements by different people within the same or similar institutions (examples, discrepancies in statements by various SPD decision-makers on the question of asylum: differing statements by leading representatives in the energy supply industry on a possible energy consensus in the coming decades)."

In contrast, Mainz publicistics expert Hans Mathias Kepplinger offers the following thesis. The way politics is portrayed in the mass media is a cause of the antipathy to politics and political parties. His reasons for this pretty one-sided apportionment of blame are as follows:

"Until the mid-1960s the majority of journalists saw themselves as neutral mediators. Since then a growing number have regarded themselves as involved critics who both criticise and consider it their task to give expression to the criticism of others. This development was linked with a change in the concept of criticism. In former times a journalist who did not publish a report until he had ascertained its accuracy was considered critical. Nowadays a journalist is regarded as critical if he reports on negative facts or describes them in a negative way.... By reporting more and more frequently on negative events and more and more seldom on positive ones, they consciously or unconsciously gave the impression that new developments magnify rather than minimise existing problems.

"The development outlined had two significant consequences. On the one hand, it promoted a negative view of the world. Things seemed increasingly to be turning out for the worse. On the other hand it reinforced doubt in the problem-solving capacity of the political and financial system. Those responsible seemed to be less and less in a position to overcome the problems waiting to be tackled. These two aspects characterise what is nowadays a widespread attitude in Germany: an aggressive self-pity accompanied by vagabond fears for the future. Some examples of this are the dying of the forests and the missile modernisation debate, the discussion on technology and the tendency to regard expenditure on the new federal states as the cost of unity rather than investment in the future. The reason for this, in view of the actual conditions of life before and after German reunification, is to be found less in reality than in the portrayal of reality" [BERTELSMANN-BRIEFE, No. 129/1993].

Interactions

An ideal vision of the media is that they promote topics, needs and opinions of the citizens to those active in politics, who in turn communicate their plans and decisions to the public via the media. Thus both sides are dependent on each other—the journalists on the politicians because they need them as a source of information, and the politicians on the journalists, because they are essential for relaying their intentions, ideas and decisions. The Swiss communications specialist Ulrich Saxer has worked it out as follows: "Nowadays the political process has become a thoroughgoing process of communication carried out by politicians and journalists in symbiosis, though to the public they often still appear as antagonists.... Both groups have to convey a semblance of distance because media manipulation by politicians is considered undemocratic, and visibly dependent media lack credibility. The normative expectations of the mutual relationship control it so to speak as a front-stage drama, while other relationships are being cultivated backstage." [Ulrich Saxer: Beziehungsspiele statt Streikultur? (Relationship Games Instead Of Conflict Culture?), in Beziehungsspiele—Medien und Politik in der offentlicher Diskussion (Relationship Games—Media And Politics In Public Debate), Gutersloh, 1993).

An increasing significance in the political communications process is ascribed above all to TV, which has changed politics and the way it is presented and mediated. Passau political scientist Heinrich Oberreuter refers to a "mediatisation of politics," meaning "the subjugation of politics to the autonomous laws of the media" (in: Frank E. Bockelmann (Ed.): *Medianmacht und Politik*

(The Power Of The Media And Politics), Wissenschaftsverlag Volker Spiess, Berlin 1989). Some signs of this are:

— as far as the public are concerned politics is becoming a spectacle, stylised by dramatic requirements (excitement, brevity, simplification), with a preference for what can be visualised, personalised and ritualised.
— politicians are forced into over-hasty statements and actions. Frequently, the dramatic requirements of TV (for example the argument: "otherwise we won't make today's TAGESSCHAU") replace political leadership. What counts is not what is necessary but what goes down well.
— a gulf emerges between politicians' actions and their appearance on screen; the hope is that this gulf will be bridged as theatre and harping on topics become political reality and communications planning replaces political planning.

Symbolic Activity

"More and more often symbolic activity is replacing what we have up till now understood as politics, replacing the conflict of opinions, the development of an informed public opinion and political decision-making. Symbolic politics first manifest themselves where politics is unable to change things and where it cannot live up to the expectations it has aroused. We read and hear about, or indeed see, pseudo-events which only take place so that they can be reported on. These pseudo-events keep the important news and critical thoughts from the public. Together with the competition for circulation and viewer ratings, the pressure grows on journalists day after day to make something important out of insignificant trifles, to detect conspicuous goings-on, to sniff out or even to produce supposed sensations" [Reinhard Hoppner, SPD leader in the Saxony-Anhalt state assembly, in SAGE UND SCHREIBE No. 4/1993].

Ulrich Saxer has alerted us to the dangers of this development: "The opportunities opened up primarily by the visual media, radio and TV, for the personalisation of politics, are readily used by politicians for excessive self-presentation, during the course of which many in particular convey the appearance of possessing more positive power to shape events than is in fact the case. In this way, expectations of the ability of democratic politics to deliver are disappointed time and again."

Relationship Games between Journalists and Politicians

Whereas at press conferences journalists and politicians face each other as opponents, that is, keep their distance, they seek proximity to each other in 'background' conversations. Confidential talks of this kind can aim,

— to clarify hitherto hidden contexts (for example, a trip abroad by a head of government, officially described as a routine visit, is actually intended to avert a crisis),
— to publicise plans so as to find out what response they elicit (flying a kite).
— to win understanding for their own interests.

The problem facing a journalist after every background conversation is to find out whether its purpose was to enlighten or disinform, initiate or use him. He has to weigh up when and to what degree he might by way of exception even break a confidence, maybe because he values the public's entitlement to important information more highly than the interests of the informant. For every journalist the temptation to become the servant of an individual or group is particularly great once he has been taken into the confidence of a politician who supplies him with special information and overwhelms him so generously with invitations to dine out that it takes the bite out ot his next commentary ("crony journalism").

The proximity of Bonn correspondents to the powers-that-be has often been the subject of criticism: After 17 years' experience of what it was like, Hans Peter Schutz wrote:

"(In Bonn) they are all sitting on top of each other, politicians, Press people, lobbyists and civil servants. They rub up against each other, sometimes they find each other awful and sometimes just great. There is only one thing which none of them likes: for politics to be described as it really is. For then it would become evident that the protagonists very often float on the hot air they have themselves produced" [in: JOURNALIST, No. 7/1993].

On the other hand, during the 1992/93 wave of resignations journalists proved that they can keep their distance from the politicians. At that time there was even talk of notching up victims: apparently journalists were behaving like Wild West heroes who used to notch up every successful shooting on their revolver stocks and display them to their rivals and an astonished public in the evening in the saloon. To be fair, one has to add that the politicians were not entirely uninvolved in bringing about their own downfall. In a statement published in May 1993 the German Press Council emphasised that "the public debates about possible peccadilloes of prominent politicians which have recently led to consequences were certainly not caused by inadmissible Press reports about the private lives of the people affected." For example, Oskar Lafontaine, Prime Minister of the Saar, enraged over the publication of details about his connections with the red light milieu, had demanded an extension of the law on protection of the personality.

The reaction of the German Press Council: "There is no need for legal initiatives to discipline the media. Every step in this direction would entail grave harm for the democratic development of this country."

Wrong as it is to criticise the media and journalists wholesale, it is true that in order to boost circulation and viewing figures, individual organs of the Press and TV magazines do try to turn politicians' peccadilloes into affairs of state.

In doing so, they set the moral yardstick so high that the question is raised as to whether the exemplary role of politicians obliges them to live up to it in all situations of life, and what standards, journalists apply to themselves. In this context communications specialist Ulrich Saxer as right in raising some concerns: "As far as responsibility for shaping democratic politics is concerned, journalists shift this one-sidedly onto politicians, even though journalism is always boasting about its public duty. For example, politicians are always expected to exercise consistency of judgement, journalists hardly ever. Whereas politicians are held responsible for contradictions, including moral ones, journalists can adapt flexibly time and again to changed situations. And whereas for politicians in an election it is really a question of sink or swim, journalists can from time to time pass unjustified criticism on politicians without it being particularly professionally harmful." Of course the image of hordes of journalists hunting down politicians does not always correspond to reality. Politicians are not entirely at the mercy of the media. They do not have to put up with slander and character assassination and they do have an entitlement to their private and intimate lives and—if these are seriously violated—to damages. In contrast, only express legitimisation through the public interest can in individual cases protect a journalist who commits such violations.

Media Criticism = Court Criticism?

"Anyone who is accused by the media must be permitted to defend himself and to admonish journalistic lapses. However, acceptance of this appears to be not as self-evident as one would think. The language alone is telling. The reports on my critical statements were not printed under the headline 'Lafontaine criticises media' but 'Lafontaine upbraids the media.' Consciously or unconsciously, analogies were drawn between a third and fourth power, and words were selected to hint at the inadmissibility of my action. The message is that criticising the media should be judged in a similarly negative way to criticising the courts.

The less a free Press is controlled from outside, the more it has to be able to accept harsh criticism from outside. If there is one profession where it is inappropriate for members to stick blindly together in professional solidarity, it is journalism. Journalists must exercise mutual control and practise mutual criticism: a mutual watchdog function." [Oskar Lafontaine in a speech to journalists at the "Initiative Tages-zeitung" conference in Magdeburg on 27 April, 1993].

The saying that competition is good for business is normally true. However, it can also endanger business. In many newspaper and magazine offices and TV studios the fear that a competitor could be first on the market with his story leads editorial staff to succumb to the pressure of topicality at the cost of investigative thoroughness. A type of jet-flame journalism, coupled with bragging announcements, has come into fashion. Now a new sow is trotted out not every day, as it used to be, but every hour, accompanied by a great hue and cry. Recently it has become increasingly obvious that politicians have a powerful hand in pushing this accelerating carousel for information and what passes for information.

Despite some accurate references to individual journalistic lapses, it is wrong to conclude that the media have abused their power, destroyed social consensus with their criticism and prevented responsible people from engaging in professional politics.

It is the basic function of the media to inform and to contribute to the development of informed opinion. When a state audit office ascertains that West German state politicians in East Germany have drawn excessive salaries, the Press must sound the alarm. This it did in the late autumn of 1993, leading to the fall of the Saxony-Anhalt state government in Magdeburg. Now, in the words of WOCHENPOST, there are "some Wessi punters fewer at the gaming tables of power." In December 1993, critical statements in the media, plus some from politicians in his own party, led Saxon Justice Minister Steffen Heitmann to stand down from his candidature for the Presidency, which the Chancellor had persuaded him to accept. Subsequently the Saxon Environment Minister, Arnold Vaatz, referred in an interview with the FRANKFURTER ALLGEMEINE ZEITUNG to "irresponsible character assassins" and "masterminds of crime"—a further indication of how strained relations between politics and media in Germany have become.

4

Indian Media System and Search for Identity

Introduction

The Indo-Soviet Conference in Moscow (23-26 May 1988) was an enlightening experience. It was not a first interaction with media professionals in the Soviet Union but on several counts it was the most stimulating one.

The communication group of the conference was, quite predictably, interested in *Glasnost i.e.*, the unfolding of the process of "openness" in the Soviet Union, but some basic issues of communication, conceptual as well as operative, were deliberated upon within the conference and outside it.

One such issue was the differing perceptions of the media role. What role do the media, print and electronic, have in society? Is it confined to serve the "public's right to know", *i.e.*, to report "fairly and objectively" happenings and events of interest to the people? Or does it go beyond, to inform and educate the people and be an "instrument of social change"? More importantly, should the media attempt to reinforce or strengthen political, social and cultural structures? Can the media be called upon to act as a unifying force? What are the potentials of each medium if some such objectives are to be assigned to the media system as a whole?

Answers to these and other related questions are not simple and no conclusions could be arrived at. It was, however, recognised that there is a wide divergence of opinion around the world.

The western media system, *e.g.*, apart from "seeking truth", informing people and serving as a watchdog, has a responsibility to support the capitalist system. In other words, as a Western commentator has said, "objectivity is a mechanism for ensuring the *status quo*, an instrument to guarantee the preservation of institutions and of the social order."

Not Simple

In the socialist countries, particularly the Soviet Union, the media role and responsibility are being reappraised. But even as understood up to now, the term "media as an instrument of propaganda" in fact means education for the people in order "to help them behave wisely so that the social order will be safeguarded."

The three roles for the newspapers identified by Lenin *i.e.*, "collective propagandist", "collective agitator" and "collective organiser" are in essence all educative.

This is not an occasion to analyse the meaning of the three roles. But let it be said that first of all this definition was given by Lenin in a certain context which has undergone a fundamental change. Secondly, as it happens, Marxist terminology is given an entirely different interpretation by the western media.

I have made this somewhat sketchy description only to bring in for discussion the perception of media role in developing countries, in general, and In India, in particular. I may begin with a general statement which can, of course, be challenged. Which is that in the developing countries the media are required to act as a unifying and not a divisive force. They are to be instruments of information as also of social change and social justice. The media are meant to support a participatory system of communication. In this context it can happen that the viability of the nation may have precedence over freedom of the media.

The last point is highly sensitive and controversial. Who is to decide about the viability factor and to what ulterior motive? It is a difficult question to answer but in a democratic set up it is assumed that the verdict should finally rest with the people.

In another context India's first Prime Minister, a passionate defender of liberty, Jawaharlal Nehru has said: "we cannot imperil the safety of the whole nation in the name of some fancied freedom which puts an end to all freedom." But he also made an emphatic statement in favour of media freedom when he said, "I do think that basically it is dangerous to suppress thought and the expression of thought in any way, because this may, besides suppressing a particularly good thing, produce many kinds of evil which stunt the growth of a social group."

Viability Factor

In the past few weeks the freedom of the press has been a topic of intense concern in our country. A legislation concerning defamation proposed by the Government has provoked uprecedented resentment from the entire press and political parties in the opposition. Without going into the details of the legislation one can make a general statement that the press in this country has acquired the maturity and the strength to take a firm stand with a view to safeguard its freedom. Another point to be mentioned is that, by and large, the media—print as well as electronic—have given a high priority to cultural and social obligations.

Let me, briefly, refer to the role of the electronic media, All India Radio and Doordarshan. The two media are under the central government's control (unlike the press). In view of their reach and impact the electronic media have been assigned a special role in "nation-building". I am using the term nation-building advisedly and in its larger meaning, which includes political awareness, economic development and social and cultural belongingness. For the benefit of the Soviet friends participating in this seminar a few bare but relevant facts may be mentioned.

Besides English we have 15 major languages, all with rich and varied literature, recognised in our Constitution. Then there are a number of "minor" languages and a few thousand dialects (1600 according to one estimate). In certain areas, people communicate with each other only through their dialect.

Language and Dialects

Secondly, of the nearly 800 million population, over 75 per cent live in villages. Thirdly over 40 per cent of the total population has been classified as living "below the poverty line." Finally, not more than 40 per cent of the people can read and write.

Also, we are a secular state *i.e.* there is no state religion but there are several religious faiths with their own beliefs and practices. We still have a caste system which is often responsible for many social tensions.

Thus, besides being a developing country with a democratic political system, India is truly a multi-religious, multi-lingual, multi-ethnic and multi-structured society. There are diversities as well as challenges which make the task of nation-building peculiar. The electronic media acquire a special role in the process.

Simply put, the electronic media are required to inform, educate as well as entertain with a view to creating awareness among the people about the nation's potential for development and its problems. They are to help people to widen their horizon through their own participation in programmes of economic development and social change.

Let me quote from the official document of the Seventh Five Year Plan. Says the document: "the major thrust of the Plan relating to the mass media will be to raise the level of the people's consciousness and enrich their cultural and social life and make them better informed citizens. It will assist in stepping up the pace of development of programmes and sensitise the people towards national and international events of importance. Besides entertainment, programmes covering sports, culture and fine arts will be provided. There will also be target group oriented programmes *i.e.*, for the youth, for women for children and for the weaker section."

Further the media will act as a vehicle of education and extension and so, narrow information gaps faced by the people from different walks of life. It will assist in enlarging the scope of formal education through special schemes like "open universities". This may read like an omnibus definition but the underlying thrust is for development and integration.

The emphasis on national integration, however, does not mean cultural homogeneity. Nor does it mean that the electronic media should reinforce the social *status quo*. On the other hand, the regional and local cultural and art forms which are important expressions of the heritage of the people have to be preserved and strengthened, but within the national ethos. Thus pride in regional and local cultural expressions including languages, literatures and art forms has to prosper through the media alongside national belongingness.

Underlying Thrust

It has for example, been our experience that any attempt to impose a language or to give precedence to a particular art from through the electronic media meets with strong, even violent, resistance. That is why the radio stations (81 full-fledged and a few local centres) devote a major part of their transmission to broadcasting in the language and dialects of the people within the range of the station. There is a national channel which can be listened to in any part of the country but it remains an alternative for the listeners.

The experience of television expansion has been somewhat different. The number of centres independently planning and producing programmes is much smaller, only 18 yet, but the number of transmitters covering nearly 70 per cent of the population is more than 260. Therefore, many of the transmitters carry programmes from the Delhi centre through our satellite. A part of the transmission from Delhi is also meant for the entire network.

As a visual medium, TV should be expected to transcend the language barrier. It has also a greater potential for creating and developing national symbols and images. In many distant and remote areas the medium has succeeded in creating national awareness. People living in mountain-locked valleys such as Kashmir have, for example, acquired a national "vision".

Yet it cannot be said that the medium has escaped strong resistance or criticism from other language and culture groups. In fact, it goes to the credit of the TV professionals that they have, by and large, succeeded in a balancing act of regional pulls and national goals.

Social tensions, to which a brief reference has been made earlier, has been a more challenging task for the electronic media.

As government-controlled media, they have often erred of the side of extreme caution. Politicians with local compulsions and bureaucrats responsible for law and order have often inhibited the media treatment of social problems and tensions. This in turn, has seriously jeopardised media interaction with the community and interfered with the media role for social justice and social change.

Severe Criticism

But on that account the two electronic media have often been subjected to severe criticism by the people and in Parliament. It may also be added that in dealing with some very sensitive situations such as communal riots or caste conflicts, AIR and Doordarshan have made some valiant efforts to project actualities and to probe causes. Acts of terrorism in certain parts of the country are a comparatively new challenge to the media. Media coverage in this regard has been seriously debated. The question is of striking a balance between presenting the truth and risking possible violent reaction. But then the media, whether in the west, in the socialist countries or in developing countries have all to face such issues now and again within their own political and social system.

In conclusion one more observation may be made. The media system in India is somewhat peculiar with the press entirely free and the electronic media under government control. This dichotomy, seemingly irreconcilable, has in a way helped the electronic media to function with much greater freedom and responsibility than any other government-controlled broadcasting system.

This is not to defend the existing system. In fact, most of us have been asking for a change. But as the Soviet experience shows, much depends upon the vigour of public opinion.

Varadan Committee

A summary of the report of the Varadan Committee set up by the Government of India on how to face the challenge of foreign broadcasts coming via satellite and Cable TV is presented here.

Broadcasting has generally been perceived the world over as a powerful medium for social and cultural change. It is also an effective instrument for economic and educational development. The role played by broadcasting in the lives of individuals and families is significant. Almost effortlessly, members of a family gain immediate access to information, entertainment and knowledge in the familiar environment of their homes. Many others gain access through friends, neighbours or community sets.

With the advancement of technology the topicality, quality and variety of programmes have become very remarkable. It is a familiar sight to see a vegetable vendor in a city street or a farmer tilling his land in a village tuning in to his or her favourite programme on the transistor radio. Television too has become ubiquitious in the cities and is rapidly percolating to towns across the length and breadth of the country. Radio listening or TV viewing has become an integral part—practically a habit—of modern life.

The fact that these programmes simultaneously reach a large section of people inevitably creates a psychological bond amongst those exposed to a particular kind of programme such as music, sports, plays, etc. This can and has been a ready foundation for building up common values amongst members of a society. The reach and potential power of these electronic media is immense. No country in the world whatever its economic condition, can afford to ignore the crucial part played by radio and television in the minds and feelings of its people.

Radio was introduced in India early this century. Doordarshan, which was started on an experimental basis in 1959, was separated from AIR and established as an independent entity in 1975. Doordarshan and All India Radio have, over a period of time, developed and enviably good network covering almost the entire country. While this gives scope for expression of regional diversities, the media very often in the day hook up the entire nation to a feast of classical music, illuminating talks, an engaging play or the speech of the Head of the Nation.

The introduction of commercial advertisements has clearly demonstrated the reach and impact of these two media. There are far more programmes and sponsors for these programmes on Doordarshan than can be accommodated. Simultaneously, foreign

TV stations have started beaming programmes through satellites which can be picked up directly by dish antennae in different parts of the country. While the relevance of these programmes to our views as they are at present telecast may be questioned, this development has some disturbing implications. No country can afford to sit back passively and let some foreign agency decide what kind of programmes should be broadcast to the people of the country. At the same time, it is neither desirable nor feasible to stop these transmissions or ban their reception.

The organisations which beam down these programmes through satellites have vast resources at their command and are able to telecast some visually very impactful programmes such as the Gulf war or the attempted coup in the USSR, etc. It is a moot point whether the highly glamorous entertainment programmes of these channels, which are somewhat irrelevant to the ethos of an Indian viewer, will lead to steady viewing in this country. Even so it is a fact that the very novelty and glitter of these programmes have excited perceptible interest among Indian viewers. The possible diversion in the long-term of advertisement revenue from the existing Indian channels can cause concern. But the Indian viewer of television and listener of radio deserves more choices.

Limits to Competition

At the sametime, there are counsels for caution against unrestrained proliferation of broadcasting channels. Broadcasting in India has essentially been informed by developmental and public interest objectives. This is very important in a country where there is large-scale poverty and illiteracy.

The electronic media have proved to be very powerful in their impact, and in the Indian context, broadcasting rights in the hands of unscrupulous elements could lead to very undesirable effects on society. Moreover, establishment of additional channels would involve substantial investments and these can only come from the investible resources of the country. The question or according priority to the further development of the broadcasting system would, therefore, have to be carefully considered in the context of the planned economic development of the country.

Is ad Cake Big Enough?

Already advertising on the electronic media has come to stay. It is expected that new channels in non-governmental hands would be sustained only by advertisement revenue. However, at this stage it is not known whether the advertisement market in the country can prove to be so elastic as to sustain all these new channels. Many eminent public men and sociologist have also cautioned against the deleterious effects on Indian society of advertisements on the electronic media which are overtly consumerist in their content.

Another area for caution is the possibility that these channels may, in a particular situation, fall into the hands of unscrupulous and anti-national elements. Even in normal times it is not unlikely that, in wrong hands, such broadcasts could become tools for harmful propaganda and dissemination of wrong information. The Committee, after a careful study of various broadcasting systems in the world, and also based on its discussion with many specialists in the field, recommend the following set of guidelines:

(*i*) The licence will fully conform to the advertisement codes which are now applicable to All India Radio and Doordarshan and to future modifications therein.

(*ii*) News, current affairs and other programmes on this channel will not be such as to offend the religious sentiments of any group.

(*iii*) The programmes, including news and current affairs, should not in any way be prejudicial to the sovereignty and integrity of India; security of the state; friendly relations with foreign states; public order; decency or morality or of such nature as will be likely to involve defamation or contempt of court or incite the commission of any offence.

(*iv*) The programmes shall conform to the same principles in relation to programme content as may be specified by the Central Government from time to time, in exercise of powers under the provisions of sub-section (2) of Section 5B of the Cinematograph Act, 1952.

(*v*) The programmes should not infringe the provision of the Copyright Act.

(*vi*) The programmes should endeavour to use the talent available in the area of broadcast to the extent possible. At any rate not more than ten per cent in terms of time of the programmes broadcast in this channel can be imported from abroad.

(*vii*) The channel must carry at least for twenty per cent of its broadcasting time programmes considered by the Broadcasting Council to be socially relevant and necessary for development purposes.

(*viii*) The channel shall carry such programmes of importance to the nation as may be directed by the Government from time to time. This would include Addresses to the Nation by the President and the Prime Minister.

(*ix*) The programmes broadcast by the channel should not be the means for furtherance of the interests of any political party.

(*x*) During election time, in respect of broadcasts by or about political parties, the channel shall conform to the guidelines issued by the Election Commission.

(*xi*) While dealing with any matter of controversy, the programmes shall present all points of view in a fair and impartial manner.

It is obvious that there has to be an arrangement under which the programmes put out by the licenses are continuously monitored to ensure that they do not violate these guidelines. Suggestions regarding such an arrangement will be dealt with later.

Quality Rating

Since one of the primary objectives of providing for competition in broadcasting is to bring about a general improvement in the quality of programmes, the Committee considers it necessary that there should be an arrangement by which a credible and autonomous body assesses continuously the quality of the programmes put out by the existing and the new channels. Periodical publication of the result of such assessment can itself be expected to have a wholesome influence on these channels. In addition, the committee recommends that whenever the quality goes below a certain threshold as decided by this authority, the concerned channel should be warned about it for necessary corrective action. When the time comes for renewal of licence the track record in terms of quality would certainly be one of the criteria for appropriate decisions.

Broadcasting Council

The Prasar Bharati Act, 1990, contains a provision (sections 14 & 15) regarding the setting up and functioning of the Broadcasting Council, the council shall consider complaints against any particular programme broadcast by the Prasar Bharati Corporation and give its recommendation. The Prasar Bharati Board is to consider these recommendations and take appropriate action.

The Prasar Bharati can also be directed by the Broadcasting Council to broadcast it recommendations with respect to a complaint. These provisions are intended to ensure that a forum for redressal is available to an individual or institution in respect of programmes broadcast by the new channels which we are discussing. We recommend, therefore, that the provisions regarding the Broadcasting Council are appropriately taken out of the Prasar Bharati Act and placed as part of the legislation for the purpose of the new broadcasting system.

We recommend that there may be a single statutory/ autonomous body known as the Broadcasting Council of India to perform the functions listed hereafter in respect of the management of the new broadcasting system. This body will also perform prescribed functions in respect of Prasar Bharati as provided in the Act. Hence this suggestion does not amount to creating a new statutory body apart from what will be otherwise created under the Prasar Bharati Act.

(a) Licensing:

We have as against the option of government issuing licences for a new channel, already recommended that a body known as the Broadcasting Council of India should be vested under the law with the powers to do so.

(b) Monitoring of Programmes:

We have recommended that the new channels shall be governed by certain guidelines regarding their programmes. We have also suggested that there should be an arrangement for monitoring the programmes to ensure that they conform to guidelines. We recommend that the Broadcasting Council of India can be that agency. They can work out appropriate modalities for monitoring the programmes and sending warnings to erring channels whenever the guidelines are violated. We also recommend that when such violations recur frequently and the Broadcasting Council of India for reasons to be recorded in writing considers such violation wilful and avoidable, it may then cancel the licence.

The Committee notes that there are provisions in the Prasar Bharati Act for a Parliamentary Committee to ensure that the Prasar Bharati carries out its functions in accordance with the provisions of the Act and to submit a report thereon to Parliament. The Government for certain specific defaults of the Prasar Bharati can also submit a report to Parliament. Parliament can recommend appropriate action against the Board including supersession. The committee feels that these provisions should be adequate to ensure that there is equity as between Prasar Bharati and the new channels in respect of penal action for lapses.

(c) Quality:

We have already recommended that in order to bring about healthy competition between the channels, an authority with credibility can monitor the programmes and evaluate their quality. We recommend that the Broadcasting Council can do this function. Such evaluation will include both the existing media (and the Prasar Bharati when formed) and the new channels to be set up. The findings of this authority may be published periodically.

Sub-section (i) of Section 4 of the India Telegraph Act, 1885, empowers the Government to licence any person for operating a telegraph. This provision has been interpreted to mean that Government can give new broadcasting licences. However, in practice, this provision has been rarely invoked. Since, for the first time, Government has announced its intention to enable non-governmental agencies also to operate broadcasting systems and since this new policy would require a comprehensive legal frame for proper implementation, we recommend that a new policy would require that a new legislation be enacted to govern the setting up and operation of broadcasting channels in India.

The new law and the rules framed thereunder may provide for the following matters:

— Setting up of the Broadcasting Council of India and prescribing the qualifications, conditions of service, etc., of the Chairman and members thereof.
— Specifying the functions of the Broadcasting Council.
— Laying down the eligibility criteria for applicant for broadcasting licences.
— Laying down the guidelines that would govern the programmes put out by the new channels.
— The Broadcasting Council monitoring programmes and sending out warning etc.
— Punitive action in case of persistent violation of guidelines.
— The Broadcasting Council evaluating the quality of programmes put out by the existing and new channels on the basis of criteria to be specified.
— Periodical publication of the results of the evaluation of programme quality.
— Renewal of licences, etc., based on the performance of the channel including the quality ratings.
— Allocation of frequencies to the existing and new channels by the appropriate authorities in the government and adherence to stipulated technical parameters for ensuring national radio frequency management.
— Control and/or management of all broadcasting by the government in the event of war or natural calamities.
— Consequential amendments to Prasar Bharati Act, the Indian Telegraph Act or any other Act as may be necessary.

Summary

The Committee recognise the importance of introducing competition in the electronic media. Following the advent of trans-border television, it is necessary to improve the quality of programmes on Doordarshan and AIR in order to retain audience interest and protect advertising revenue. It is equally important to provide additional outlets to the creative talents in different fields like music who are presently constrained due to the limited time a available. Competition would also strengthen the democratic fabric of the nation and help better in meeting the cultural aspirations of different regions.

There are however some sound reasons for caution. The country does not have unlimited resources and the priority for establishing additional broadcast channels must fit in with the broader national requirements. There is also a need to guard against the dangers of unrestrained commercialism which may follow the establishment of additional channels financed solely through advertising.

The dangers of control of these media falling into the hands of unscrupulous or anti-national elements also should not be discounted. The Committee has taken these factors into account while making its recommendations.

In regard to the approach to the new broadcasting system the following recommendations have been made:

Subject to viability of operations, preference should be given to setting up new TV/radio channels in different parts of the country for regional broadcasts. These transmitters can, over a period of time, link up suitably either by forming a consortium or by entering into suitable arrangements amongst themselves. Such a link-up would provide an inter-regional network.

(*a*) Simultaneously, the second Doordarshan channels in the four metropolitan cities can be leased out to suitable licensees.

(*b*) Also simultaneously, additional radio channels including FM stations wherever available may be similarly leased out.

These actions under this option should be taken only after suitable legislation is passed.

The option to permit one agency or consortium to set up a series of transmitters in the country will, in the opinion of the committee, rank only next to the option of permitting a number of licensees to set up different TV/radio transmitters in the country.

The Committee does not recommend leasing out of a particular chunk of time from an existing TV/radio channel.

The option of a licensee leasing a transponder on a satellite for satellite-driven direct broadcast would perhaps be appropriate for developmental or educational telecasts. The committee notes that as of now there is no such spare space segment available. As and when one becomes available, the Government can take an appropriate decision.

The Committee feels that in view of the sensive nature of the choice, the selection of agencies for grant of licence should be performed by an independent agency in a transparent manner. It feels that the organisations eligible to receive licences should be public limited companies with major interest groups concerned with broadcasting represented in management and with open access to share holding. Such organisations should be willing to abide by guidelines to be prescribed by the Government regarding their functioning. Certain cross-media restrictions are recommended in order to avoid monopoly over information sources. Preference may be given to public bodies like universities, co-operative institutions etc., if they apply for licences.

The Committee has suggested that the Broadcasting Council of India to be constituted through a legislation, amending the relevant sections in the Prasar Bharati Act, be entrusted with the functions of licensing, monitoring of programmes and quality rating.

The Committee has recommended that a new legislation be enacted to govern the setting up new broadcast channels.

5

Media and Press Freedom

The Principles

Freedom of the press is essential to political liberty. Where men cannot freely convey their thoughts to one another, no freedom is secure. Where freedom of expression exists, the beginnings of a free society and a means for every extension of liberty are already present. Free expression is therefore unique among liberties: it promotes and protects all the rest. It is appropriate that freedom of speech and freedom of the press are contained in the first of those constitutional enactments which are the American Bill of Rights.

Civilized society is a working system of ideas. It lives and changes by the consumption of ideas. Therefore it must make sure that as many as possible of the ideas which its members have are available for its examination. It must guarantee freedom of expression, to the end that all adventitious hindrances to the flow of ideas shall be removed.[1] Moreover, a significant innovation in the realm of ideas is likely to arouse resistance. Valuable ideas may be put forth first in forms that are crude, indefensible, or even dangerous. They need the chance to develop through free criticism as well as the chance to survive on the basis of their ultimate worth. Hence the man who publishes ideas requires special protection.

The reason for the hostility which the critic or innovator may expect is not merely that it is easier and more natural to suppress or discourage him than to meet his arguments. Irrational elements are always present in the critic, the innovator, and their audience. The utterance of critical or new ideas is seldom an appeal to pure reason, devoid of emotion, and the response is not necessarily a debate; it is always a function of the intelligence, the prejudice, the emotional biases of the audience. Freedom of the press to appeal to reason may always be construed as freedom of the press to appeal to public passion and ignorance, vulgarity and cynicism. As freedom of the press is always in danger, so is it always dangerous. The freedom of the press illustrates the common place that if we are to live progressively we must live dangerously.

Across the path of the flow of ideas lie the existing centers of social power. The primary protector of freedom of expression against their obstructive influence is government. Government acts by maintaining order and by exercising on behalf of free speech and a free press the elementary sanctions against the expressions of private interest or resentment: sabotage, blackmail, and corruption.

But any power capable of protecting freedom is also capable of endangering it. Every modern government, liberal or otherwise, has a specific position in the field of ideas; its stability is vulnerable to critics in proportion to their ability and persuasiveness. A government resting on popular suffrage is no exception to this rule. It also may be tempted—just because public opinion is a factor in official livelihood—to manage the ideas and images entering public debate.

If the freedom of the press is to achieve reality, government must set limits on its capacity to interfere with, regulate, or suppress the voices of the press or to manipulate the data on which public judgment is formed.

Government must set these limits on itself, not merely because freedom of expression is a reflection of important interests of the community, but also because it is a moral right. It is a moral right because it has an aspect of duty about it.

It is true that the motives for expression are not all dutiful. They are and should be as multiform as human emotion itself, grave and gay, casual and purposeful, artful and idle. But there is a vein of expression which has the added impulsion of duty, and that is the expression of thought. If a man is burdened with an idea, he not only desires to express it; he ought to express it. He owes it to his conscience and the common good. The indispensable function of expressing ideas is one of obligation—to the community and also to something beyond the community—let us say to truth. It is the duty of the scientist to his result and of Socrates to his oracle; it is the duty of every man to his own belief. Because of this duty to what is beyond that state, freedom of speech and freedom of the press are moral rights which the state must not infringe.

The moral right of free expression achieves a legal status because the conscience of the citizen is the source of the continued vitality of the state. Wholly apart from the traditional ground for a free press—that it promotes the "victory of truth over falsehood" in the public arena—we see that public discussion is a necessary condition of a free society and that freedom of expression is a necessary condition of adequate public discussion. Public discussion elicits mental power and breadth; it is essential to the building of a mentally robust public; and, without something of the kind, a self-governing society could not operate. The original source of supply for this process is the duty of the individual thinker to his thought; here is the primary ground of his right.

This does not mean that every citizen has a moral or legal right to own a press or be an editor or have access, as of right, to the audience of any given medium of communication. But it does belong to the intention of the freedom of the press that an idea shall have its chance even if it is not shared by those who own or manage the press. The press is not free if those who operate it behave as though their position conferred on them the privilege of being deaf to ideas which the processes of free speech have brought to public attention.

But the moral right of free public expression is not unconditional. Since the claim of the right is based on the duty of a man to the common good and to his thought, the ground of the claim disappears when this duty is ignored or rejected. In the absence of accepted moral duties there are no moral rights. Hence, when the man who claims the moral right of free expression is a liar, a prostitute whose political judgments can be bought, a dishonest inflamer of hatred and suspicion, his claim is unwarranted and groundless. From the moral point of view, at least, freedom of expression does not include the right to lie as a deliberate instrument of policy.

The right of free public expression does include the right to be in error. Liberty is experimental. Debate itself could not exist unless wrong opinions could be rightfully offered by those who suppose them to be right. But the assumption that the man in error is actually trying for truth is of the essence of his claim for freedom. What the moral right does not cover is the right to be deliberately or irresponsibly in error.

But a moral right can be forfeited and a legal right retained. Legal protection cannot vary with the fluctuations of inner moral direction in individual wills; it does not cease whenever a person has abandoned the moral ground of his right. It is not even desirable that the whole area of the responsible use of freedom should be made legally compulsory, even if it were possible; for in that case free self-control, a necessary ingredient of any free state, would be superseded by mechanism.

Many a lying, venal, and scoundrelly public expression must continue to find shelter under a "freedom of the press" built for widely different purposes, for to impair the legal right even when the moral right is gone may easily be a cure worse than the disease. Each definition of an abuse invites abuse of the definition. If the courts had to determine the inner corruptions of personal intention, honest and necessary criticisms would proceed under an added peril.

Though the presumption is against resort to legal action to curb abuses of the press, there are limits to legal toleration. The already recognized areas of legal correction of misused liberty of expression—libel, misbranding, obscenity, incitement to riot, sedition, in case of clear and present danger—have a common principle; namely, that an utterance or publication invades in a serious, overt, and demonstrable manner personal rights or vital social interests. As new categories of abuse come within this definition, the extension of legal sanctions is justified. The burden of proof will rest on those who would extend these categories, but the presumption is not intended to render society supine before possible new developments of misuse of the immense powers of the contemporary press.

The Principles in the Present Situation

The principles we have attempted to state are those general truths which are valid as goals for all civilized societies. It must be observed that freedom of the press is not a fixed and isolated value, the same in every society and in all times. It is a function within a society and must vary with the social context. It will be different in times of general security and in times of crisis; it will be different under varying states of public emotion and belief.

The freedom we have been examining has assumed a type of public mentality which may seem to us standard and universal but which is in many respects a product of our special history-a mentality accustomed to the noise and confusion of clashing opinions and reasonably stable in temper in view of the varying fortunes of ideas. But what a mind does with a fact or an opinion is widely different when it is serene and when it is anxious; when it has confidence in its environment and when it is infected with suspicion or resentment; when it is gullible and when it is well furnished with the means of criticism; when it has hope and when it is in despair.

Further, the citizen is a different man when he has to judge his press alone, and when his judgment is steadied by other social agencies. Free and diverse utterance may result in bewilderment unless he has access—through home, church, school, custom—to interpreting patterns of thought and feeling. There is no such thing as the "objectivity" of the press unless the mind of the reader can identify the objects dealt with.

Whether at any time and place the psychological conditions exist under which a free press has social significance is always a question of fact, not of theory. These mental conditions may be lost. They may also be created. The press itself is always one of the chief agents in destroying or in building the bases of its own significance.

If we now fix our problem in space and time and look at the press in the United States today, we see that the conditions of our society and of the press in our society require new applications of the principles we have stated.

The aim of those who sponsored the First Amendment was to prevent the government from interfering with expression. The authors of our political system saw that the free society they were seeking to establish could not exist without free communication. As Jefferson put if: "The basis of our governments being the opinion of the people, the very first object should be to keep that right; and were it left to me to decide whether we should have a government without newspapers or newspapers without a government, I should not hesitate a moment to prefer the latter. But I should mean that every man should receive those papers and be capable of reading them."

Our ancestors were justified in thinking that if they could prevent the government from interfering with the freedom of the press, that freedom would be effectively exercised. In their day anybody with anything to say had comparatively little difficulty in getting it published. The only serious obstacle to free expression was government censorship. If that could be stopped, the right of every man to do his duty by his thought was secure. The press of those days consisted of hand-printed sheets issuing from little printing shops, regularly as newspapers, or irregularly as broadsides, pamphlets, or books. Presses were cheap; the journeyman printer could become a publisher and editor by borrowing the few dollars he needed to set up his shop and by hiring an assistant or two. With a limited number of people who could read, and with property qualifications for the suffrage—less than 6 per cent of the adult population voted for the conventions held to ratify the Constitution—there was no great discrepancy between the number of those who could read and were active citizens and those who could command the financial resources to engage in publication.

It was not supposed that any one newspapers would represent all, or nearly all, of the conflicting viewpoints regarding public issues. Together they could be expected to do so, and, if they did not, the man whose opinions were not represented could start a publication of his own.

Now was it supposed that many citizens would subscribe to all the local journals. It was more likely that each would take the one which would reinforce his prejudices. But in each village and town, with its relatively simple social structure and its wealth of neighbourly contacts, various opinions might encounter each other in face-to-face meetings; the truth, it was hoped, would be sorted out by competition in the local market place.

Those circumstances which provided variety and interchange of opinion and easy individual access to the market place of ideas have changed so radically as to justify us in saying that this country has gone through a communications revolution.

Literacy, the electorate, and the population have increased to such a point that the political community to be served by the press includes all but a tiny fraction of the millions of the American people. The press has been transformed into an enormous and complicated piece of machinery. As a necessary accompaniment, it has become big business. There is a marked reduction in the number of units of the press relative to the total population. Although in small communities we can still see a newspaper plant and product that resemble their Colonial prototypes, these are no longer the most characteristic or the most influential agencies of communication.

The right of free public expression has therefore lost its earlier reality. Protection against government is now not enough to guarantee that a man who has something to say shall have a chance to say it. The owners and managers of the press determine which persons, which facts, which versions of the facts, and which ideas shall reach the public.

This is one side of the shield—the effect of the communications revolution on the right of the citizen to publish his beliefs. The other side is the effect of the communications revolution on the press as the agency through which the members of a free society receive, as well as exchange, the judgments, opinions, ideas, and information which they need in order to participate in the management of that society. The press has become a vital necessity in the transaction of the public business of a continental area.

In local affairs there is still a chance for face-to-face observation to get in its work. Many private groups, formal and informal, throw an extensive web of alternative communication over the country or over parts of it. But there is obviously less opportunity for direct observation and news by word of mouth in a metropolitan region, in a great nation, or in a world society than there is in a village, a small state, or a single country. For the most part the understanding of the leaders and people of China, Russia, England and Argentina possessed by the citizens of New Hampshire, Kansas, Oregon and Alabama will be gained from the agencies of mass communication. Hardly less is the dependence on these agencies of midwest farmers for their understanding of a strike in Detroit or a change in the discount rate by the Federal Reserve Board in Washington.

The complexity of modern industrial society, the critical world situation, and the new menaces to freedom which these imply mean that the time has come for the press to assume a new public responsibility.

Through concentration of ownership the variety of sources of news and opinion is limited. At the same time the insistence of the citizen's need has increased. He is dependent on the quality, proportion and extent of his news supply, not only for his personal access to the world of event, thought and feeling, but also for the materials of his duties as a citizen and judge of public affairs. The soundness of his judgment affects the working of the state and even the peace of the world, involving the survival of the state as a free community. Under these circumstances it becomes an imperative question whether the performance of the press can any longer be left to the unregulated initiative of the few who manage it.

The moral and legal right of those who manage it to utter their opinions must remain intact; this right stands for the valid kernel of individualism at the heart of all social life. But the element of duty involved in the right requires a new scrutiny; and the service of news, as distinct from the utterance of opinion, acquires a new importance. The need of the citizen for adequate and uncontaminated mental food is such that he is under a duty to get it. Thus his interest also acquires the stature of a right.

To protect the press is no longer automatically to protect the citizen or the community. The freedom of the press can remain a right of those who publish only if it incorporates into itself the right of the citizen and the public interest.

Freedom of the press means freedom from and freedom for. The press must be free from the menace of external compulsions from whatever source. To demand that it be free from pressures which might warp its utterance would be to demand that society should be empty of contending forces and beliefs. But persisting and distorting pressures—financial, popular, clerical, institutional—must be known and counterbalanced. The press must, if it is to be wholly free, know and overcome any biases incident to its own economic position, its concentration, and its pyramidal organization.

The press must be free for the development of its own conceptions of service and achievement. It must be free for making its contribution to the maintenance and development of a free society.

This implies that the press must also be accountable. It must be accountable to society for meeting the public need and for maintaining the rights of citizens and the almost forgotten rights of speakers who have no press. It must know that its faults and errors have ceased to be private vagaries and have become public dangers. The voice of the press, so far as by a drift toward monopoly it tends to become exclusive in its wisdom and observation, deprives other voices of a hearing and the public of their contribution. Freedom of the press for the coming period can only continue as an accountable freedom. Its moral right will be conditioned on its acceptance of this accountability. Its legal right will stand unaltered as its moral duty is performed.

Freedom and Responsibility

If the freedom of the press is freighted with the responsibility of providing the current intelligence needed by a free society, we have to discover what a free society requires. Its requirements in America today are greater in variety, quantity and quality than those of any previous society in any age. They are the requirements of a self-governing republic of continental size, whose doings have become, within a generation, matters of common concern in new and important ways. Its internal arrangements, from being thought of mainly as matters of private interest and automatic market adjustments, have become affairs of conflict and conscious compromise among organized groups, whose powers appear not to be bounded by "natural law," economic or other. Externally, it has suddenly assumed a leading role in the attempt to establish peaceful relationships among all the states on the globe.

Today our society needs, first, a truthful, comprehensive, and intelligent account of the day's events in a context which gives them meaning; second, a forum for the exchange of comment and criticism; third, a means of projecting the opinions and attitudes of the groups in the society to one another; fourth, a method of presenting and clarifying the goals and values of the society; and, fifth, a way of reaching every member of the society by the currents of information, thought and feeling which the press supplies.

The Commission has no idea that these five ideal demands can ever be completely met. All of them cannot be met by any one medium; some do not apply at all to a particular unit; nor do all apply with equal relevance to all parts of the communications industry. The Commission does not suppose that these standards will be new to the managers of the press; they are drawn largely from their professions and practices.

A Truthful, Comprehensive and Intelligent Account of the Day's Events in a Context which Gives Them Meaning

The first requirement is that the media should be accurate. They should not lie.

Here the first link in the chain of responsibility is the reporter at the source of the news. He must be careful and competent. He must estimate correctly which sources are most authoritative. He must prefer firsthand observation to hearsay. He must know what questions to ask, what things to observe and which items to report. His employer has the duty of training him to do his work as it ought to be done.

Of equal importance with reportorial accuracy are the identification of fact as fact and opinion as opinion, and their separation, so far as possible. This is necessary all the way from the reporter's file, up through the copy and make-up desks and editorial offices, to the final, published product. The distinction cannot, of course, be made absolute. There is no fact without a context and no factual report which is uncolored by the opinions of the reporter. But modern conditions require greater effort than ever to make the distinction between fact and opinion. In a simpler order of society published accounts of events within the experience of the community could be compared with other sources of information. Today this is usually impossible. The account of an isolated fact, however accurate in itself, may be misleading and, in effect, untrue.

The greatest danger here is in the communication of information internationally. The press now bears a responsibility in all countries, and particularly in democratic countries, where foreign policies are responsive to popular majorities, to report international events in such a way that they can be understood. It is no longer enough to report the fact truthfully. It is now necessary to report *the truth about the fact*.

In this country a similar obligation rests upon the press in reporting domestic news. The country has many groups which are partially insulated from one another and which need to be interpreted to one another. Factually correct but substantially untrue accounts of the behaviour of members of one of these social islands can intensify the antagonisms of others toward them. A single incident will be accepted as a sample of group action unless the press has given a flow of information and interpretation concerning the relations between two racial groups such as to enable the reader to set a single event in its proper perspective. If it is allowed to pass as a sample of such action, the requirement that the press present an accurate account of the day's events in a context which gives them meaning has not been met.

A Forum for the Exchange of Comment and Criticism

The second requirement means that the great agencies of mass communication should regard themselves as common carriers of public discussion.[2] The units of the press have in varying degrees assumed this function and should assume the responsibilities which go with it, more generally and more explicitly.

It is vital to a free society that an idea should not be stifled by the circumstances of its birth. The press cannot and should not be expected to print everybody's ideas. But the giant units can and should assume the duty of publishing significant ideas contrary to their own, as a matter of objective reporting, distinct from their proper function of advocacy. Their control over the various ways of reaching the ear of America is such that, if they do not publish ideas which differ from their own, those ideas will never reach the ear of America. If that happens, one of the chief reasons for the freedom which these giants claim disappears.

Access to a unit of the press acting as a common carrier is

possible in a number of ways, all of which, however, involve selection on the part of the managers of the unit. The individual whose views are not represented on an editorial page may reach an audience through a public statement reported as news, through a letter to the editor, through a statement printed in advertising space, or through a magazine article. But some seekers for space are bound to be disappointed and must resort to pamphlets or such duplicating devices as will spread their ideas to such public as will attend to them.

But all the important viewpoints and interests in the society should be represented in its agencies of mass communication. Those who have these viewpoints and interests cannot count on explaining them to their fellow-citizens through newspapers or radio stations of their own. Even if they could make the necessary investment, they could have no assurance that their publications would be read or their programmes heard by the public outside their own adherents. An ideal combination would include general media, inevitably solicitous to present their own views, but setting forth other views fairly. As checks on their fairness, and partial safeguards against ignoring important matters, more specialized media of advocacy have a vital place. In the absence of such a combination the partially insulated groups in society will continue to be insulated. The unchallenged assumptions of each group will continue to harden into prejudice. The mass medium reaches across all groups; through the mass medium they can come to understand one another.

Whether a unit of the press is an advocate or a common carrier, it ought to identify the sources of its facts, opinions and arguments so that the reader or listener can judge them. Persons who are presented with facts, opinions and arguments are properly influenced by the general reliability of those who offer them. If the veracity of statements is to be appraised, those who offer them must be known.

Identification of source is necessary to a free society Democracy, in time of peace, at least, has a justifiable confidence that full and free discussion will strengthen rather than weaken it. But, if the discussion is to have the effect for which democracy hopes, if it is to be really full and free, the names and the characters of the participants must not be hidden from view.

The Projection of a Representative Picture of the Constituent Groups in the Society

This requirement is closely related to the two preceding. People make decisions in large part in terms of favourable or unfavourable images. They relate fact and opinion to stereotypes. Today the motion picture, the radio, the book, the magazine, the newspaper and the comic strip are principal agents in creating and perpetuating these conventional conceptions. When the images they portray fail to present the social group truly, they tend to pervert judgment.

Such failure may occur indirectly and incidentally. Even if nothing is said about the Chinese in the dialogue of a film, yet if the Chinese appear in a succession of pictures as sinister drug addicts and militarists, an image of China is built which needs to be balanced by another. If the Negro appears in the stories published in magazines of national circulation only as a servant, if children figure constantly in radio dramas as impertinent and ungovernable brats—the image of the Negro and the American child is distorted. The plugging of special colour and "hate" words in radio and press dispatches, in advertising copy, in news stories—such words as "ruthless," "confused," "bureaucratic" —performs inevitably the same image-making function.

Responsible performance here simple means that the images repeated and emphasized be such as are in total representative of the social group as it is. The truth about any social group, though it should not exclude its weaknesses and vices, includes also recognition of its values, its aspirations, and its common humanity. The Commission holds to the faith that if people are exposed to the inner truth of the life of a particular group, they will gradually build up respect for and understanding of it.

The Presentation and Clarification of the Goals and Values of the Society

The press has a similar responsibility with regard to the values and goals of our society as a whole. The mass media, whether or not they wish to do so, blur or clarify these ideals as they report the failings and achievements of every day.[3] The Commission does not call upon the press to sentimentalize, to manipulate the facts for the purpose of painting a rosy picture. The Commission believes in realistic reporting of the events and forces that militate against the attainment of social goals as well as those which work for them. We must recognize, however, that the agencies of mass communication are an educational instrument, perhaps the most powerful there is; and they must assume a responsibility like that of educators in stating and clarifying the ideals towards which the community should strive.

Full Access to the Day's Intelligence

It is obvious that the amount of current information required by the citizens in a modern industrial society is far greater than that required in any earlier day. We do not assume that all citizens at all times will actually use all the material they receive. By necessity or choice large numbers of people voluntarily delegate analysis and decision of leaders whom they trust. Such leadership in our society is freely chosen and constantly changing; it is informal, unofficial and flexible. Any citizen may at any time assume the power of decision. In this way government is carried on by consent.

But such leadership does not alter the need for the wide distribution of news and opinion. The leaders are not identified; we can inform them only by making information available to everybody.

The five requirements listed in this chapter suggest what our society is entitled to demand of its press. We can now proceed to examine the tools, the structure, and the performance of the press to see how it is meeting these demands.

Let us summarize these demands in another way.

The character of the service required of the press by people differs from the service previously demanded, first, in this—that it is essential to the operation of the economy and to the government of the Republic. Second, it is a service of a greatly increased responsibilities both as to the quantity and as to the quality of the information required. in terms of quantity, the information about themselves and about their world made available to the people must be as extensive as the range of their interests and concerns as citizens of a self-governing, industrialized community in the closely integrated modern world.

In terms of quality, the information provided must be provided in such a form, and with so scrupulous a regard for the wholeness of the truth and the fairness of its presentation, that the people may make for themselves, by the exercise of reason and of conscience, the fundamental decisions necessary to the direction of their government and of their lives.

References

1. The example of Station WNYC, controlled by New York City, suggests what government may do in domestic communications if it regards private service as inadequate.
2. By the use of this analogy the Commission does not intend to suggest that the agencies of communication should be subject to the legal obligations of common carriers, such as compulsory reception of all applicants for space, the regulation of rates, etc.
3. A striking indication of the continuous need to renew the basic values of our society is given in the recent poll of public opinion by the National Opinion Research Center at Denver, in which one out of every three persons polled did not think the newspapers should be allowed to criticize the American form of government, even in peacetime. Only 57 per cent thought that the Socialist party should be allowed, in peacetime, to publish newspapers in the United States. Another poll revealed that less than a fourth of those questioned had a "reasonably accurate idea" of what the Bill of Rights is. Here is widespread ignorance with regard to the value most cherished by the press—its own freedom—which seems only dimly understood by many of its consumers.

6

"News": An Interpretative Analysis

Issues of international news reporting have become increasingly politicized throughout recent years. The campaign for a New World Information Order (NWIO) has moved the debate over international systems of communication to center stage in many international organizations. Some nonaligned nations, such as Kenya and Zimbabwe, have charged that Western correspondents are overtly biased in their coverage and have therefore closed their borders to selected reporters.[1] Groups of nonaligned states, such as the members of ASEAN (the Association of Southeast Asian Nations), have agreed that a ban on particular Western correspondents in one nation will mean a ban in all (Righter, 1978: 214). Because OECD nations enjoy vast advantages in informational resources, nonaligned nations now tend to politicize international debates while adopting obstructionist stances. Taken together, these and other closely related traumas in the international body politic amount to a current "crisis in international news" (Richstad and Anderson, 1981).

The crisis in international news has many sources. Debates over an NWIO have addressed a plethora of complicated issues. Yet there is consistently one central point of contention: what is "news"? Much of the scholarly and diplomatic debate about an NWIO revolves around this seemingly simple question. Proponents and opponents of the NWIO start with two distinctly different definitions of what "news" is and what it should stand for in an international context. As a result, the two sides take different positions on what sort of "news values" journalists should uphold, and on the proper political role for mass media at the national and international levels. A thorough discussion of these two conceptions of news—news as a commodity and news as a social resource—will reveal the historical development, economic basis and political implications of each definition.

NEWS IN THE WEST OR NEWS AS A COMMODITY

The most concise description of news in a Western context is that news here is treated as a commodity. Western media provide international news in the form of "a merchandise rather than a service" and news stories "are selected for their impact, exoticism, ability to entertain" (Righter, 1978: 41). News items are collected in bits and distributed in markets according to their utility and consumer tastes. The history of international news reporting shows that news has taken this particular form largely due to market forces in advanced capitalist industrial societies. Furthermore, the contents of international news have also been largely determined by these same market imperatives. News as a commodity was developed in the late nineteenth century, primarily in Great Britain and the United States, and was firmly established by the year 1990.[2] Historically, it is a conception of news that has served particular economic interests and catered to specific culture tastes.

If asked to define "news," most Westerners would probably reply that it is factual, up-to-the-minute information regarding recent occurrences. A news report tells what has happened as well as when, where, why and how. A well-written news story on international affairs should also be brief, to the point, and clear about how the foreign event relates to the reader's own life. Not all cultures agree that this constitutes "good" news reporting, but these are all characteristics of news as a commodity.

The earliest uses of "news" referred to something novel or

previously unencountered. After 1500, common usage employed "news" much as it is used today: to refer to "new occurrences as a subject of report or talk" (*Oxford English Dictionary*, vol. VII, 1970: 119). Systematic international news gathering did not arise until late in the eighteenth century when newspaper editors began collecting foreign newspapers and then reprinted their local reports as foreign news (Desmond, 1980: 37). At this time, however, foreign reporting was nominal and foreign correspondents did not yet exist. International news did not approach anything like its current scope or volume, nor did the first international news agencies appear, until the age of high imperialism, the middle and late nineteenth century.

Capitalism, as Anthony Smith argues, has always been an "information system" as well as a system of finance and production (1980: 73). The development of international capitalism incorporated more and more of the world's unexploited areas into the global market. Corporations, transportation and stock markets became "inextricably combined" into an integrated system. "At the heart of it there has to be information, for the central concept of capitalism is the market and, in a global system .... markets [depend on] prices and values [which] are assessed through the distribution of regular reliable information". With the expansion of western colonialism came the creation of a global communication network based on the technology of undersea telegraph cables (perfected in the middle of the nineteenth century). In Smith's terms, the worldwide information network quickly became "a fundamental support" for the development of international capitalism.

London became the news center of the world because it was already the center of international trade, finance and commodity pricing (Desmond, 1980: 62). Of course, gathering news from around the world required substantial financial resources. Support for the early international press came almost entirely from industrialists, bankers and financiers who sought to promote their own success. Because no single newspaper could afford the cost of telegraph cables, foreign correspondents and independent stringers around the globe, independent news agencies which could defray these costs through client subscriptions became necessary. The first international telegraph lines that made news agencies financially necessary also provided the hardware and saleable goods to make them economically viable (Desmond, 1980: 132).

By 1855, three international news agencies existed: Wolff in Germany, Havas (precursor to the Agency France Presse [AFP]) in France and Reuters in London. Of these, only Reuters remains: and it is Reuters which has had by far the greatest impact on the development of international news reporting as we know it today.

Julius Reuter established his first news agency in Aachen, France, in 1849, but only two years later moved his operations to London. Originally, Reuter supplied commercial news to bankers, investors and merchants, while Havas and Wolff carried other sorts of news as well. Reuter was shrewd enough to put his offices in the London financial district and quickly concluded a deal with the London Stock Exchange to provide stock market quotations from the financial centers on the continent. In return, Reuter received privileged access to information from the London Exchange, Reuter's first customers were exclusively bankers, stock brokers, traders, merchants and business firms (Desmond, 1980: 146).

In order to increase his clientele, however, Reuter realized that he had to carry noncommercial news as well. To attract small newspapers to his service, Reuter established a Special Service in 1890 to carry sensational journalism. Since 1880, sensationalism had been rising in popularity among newspaper editors in the United States and in England as a means to create a greater appeal among the growing urban masses. To attract a wider readership, "they departed from patterns of substantial news and information and from considerations of accuracy and truth present stories of crimes and scandals, disasters and accidents of special violence, riots and disturbances .... the more sensational the better" (Desmond, 1980: 333). Reuter created his Special Service in response to competition from the sensationalist Dalziel agency which was owned by the London *Times* (the *Times* refused Reuter's service and competed vigorously with it). In the early years of international news reporting, competition was vicious. Those agencies which did not follow popular trends such as that of sensationalism soon went out of business. Even after the Reuters agency later dropped the Special Service, it was obliged to integrate some of the sensationalist style into its regular service (Desmond, 1980: 345).

Within twenty years of opening his London agency, Reuter came to dominate international news gathering. In most cases, Reuters took the lead, setting the tone and form of foreign reporting. Other international agencies were forced to adopt most of Reuters' techniques and tried to establish themselves in regions not monopolized by Reuters (*e.g.*, central Europe and Latin America). Following Reuters' example, agencies supplied two broad types of foreign news to two types of customers. Trading communities were supplied with "instant, exact and copious commercial and political information" which had direct importance for their overseas holdings. The other market consisted of "a large number of smaller newspapers whose readers wanted romantic headlines, big stories and not too much substance" (Smith, 1980: 77).

In 1857, Reuter signed an exclusive contract to supply foreign news to the United States through the New York Associated Press (NYAP, which, after several reorganizations, became the Associated Press in 1900). In turn, NYAP supplied the foreign news published in over a score of major American cities in the East and Mideast. Accordingly, the conventions and substance of Reuters international reports came to be accepted in the United States as the standard for interstate news. There was, however, one important element of journalistic style which originated largely in the United States, later to be carried across the Atlantic through the agreement between Reuters and NYAP. This was the notion that "objectivity" is essential to news writing.

This element of impartiality, like other characteristics of news as a commodity, developed in the mid-to late-nineteenth century, and also received its impetus from the dictates of the marketplace. Before the American Civil War, news reporting was characterized by "florid description" and "subjective comment." Correspondents often mixed their own views, judgments and personal feelings with the facts of the report. This highly stylized form of journalism was popular, but with the advent of telegraphs and the demands for quick reports on the war, it became too costly. In order to shorten the story (to save on telegraph costs, which were charged by the word), a new style of news writing was developed for war correspondents. This was the summary lead/ body style which also familiar today.

In the story's lead journalists were instructed to state the "five Ws" (who, what, when, where, why). Then in the body, each of these aspects of the story could be elaborated. Opinions, judgments and personal reactions to the war were to be confined to the last few paragraphs. If the story ran too long, editors could start at the bottom and cut out paragraphs as they moved up toward the lead. Editors came to prefer the lead/body format because it seemed to produce more economy and clarity in news stories. This style, begun in the United States in the 1860s, came to "set a pattern for the press of other countries" (Desmond, 1980: 217). Thus it became the one major American contribution to news as a commodity. Just as other elements of news form and content were disseminated in this nation due to contracts between news agencies, so this style was disseminated through the NYAP, via Reuters, to the rest of the World.

By 1900, news on international affairs was presented in a particular format, and it dealt with particular substantive matters. It was primarily news of either a commercial or a sensational nature. It was preferred in the summary lead/body format. The five Ws were to be stated at the outset of each story and all subjective comment was relegated to the story's conclusion (if not cut out altogether). News of the day, especially international news, possessed all three of the fundamental characteristics which Marx attributed to commodities. It developed within the historical context of industrialized, capitalist society. It contained a use value (*e.g.*, information for economic gain, or to cater to an interest in sensationalism). Finally, it was a result of human labour, produced for the use of others, and exchanged within a capitalist market system (Marx: 1-7).

Such was the nature of international news at the turn of the century. By 1910, the "Big Four" of contemporary international news (AFP, Associated Press [AP], Reuters and United Press International [UPI]) existed either in their current form or as the immediate predecessor to their current form (Havas became AFP after World War II and the United Press Association [UPA], established in 1907, became UPI in 1958). Including the Wolff agency, there were five international news agencies in the early twentieth century; two American, one British, one French and one German. Each of these agencies, due to customer demand, felt compelled to write their stories from a national perspective.

American agencies wrote foreign reports with a tie to American interests, and so forth. Added to the stylistic requirements of the lead/body format was a new sensitivity to local values back home. Foreign assignments were to be "treated like a local assignment. The diversity [being] so great .... making order of it for the reader almost require-[d] that it be explained in the relatively 'local' framework of a set of cultural and intellectual perceptions" (Righters, 1978: 59). According to Righter, national slant is still exhibited in Western reporting today however many foreign journalists an agency hires, and however much material may even be a rewrite of the national press or news agency output of the host country."

One recent study of the style handbooks utilized by major news organization shows that journalists are systematically trained to employ this fashion of news writing. These handbooks stress that "to be simple and precise is at the same time to identify facts that are significant to an individual's social life." Alexander quotes from a typical style book, which admonishes its users to remember that "[e]very word must be understood by the ordinary man, every sentence must be clear at a glance, and every story must say something about people. There must never be a doubt about its relevance to our daily life" (Alexander, 1981: 41).

Not only did the major agencies separate their reports according to national perspective, but they also divided their world beats along the lines of colonial boundaries and imperial interests. As early as 1870, the so-called Ring Combination (Havas, Reuters and Wolff) had divided the world into regions with each member of the cartel having exclusive rights to collect and sell interstate news in particular areas. Reuters had the rights to all of the British Empire, Egypt and the Middle East, and most of Asia. The French agency (Havas) was given rights to the French Empire as well as Latin American news (largely by default). The German agency was confined primarily to central Europe. With the advent of the American agencies, cartel members found themselves competing of news sources and clients in the areas of American hegemony (*e.g.*, Latin American and the southern Pacific). This competition was set aside briefly as agreements brought AP and UPA into the cartel, but a resurgence of rivalries brought about the Ring's demise in 1934 (Smith, 1980: 81-82).

It was during the era of the international news cartel that most of the structural arguments in interstate communication were established, structures which critics argue persist to this day. The paths of news flow went from the colonial periphery to the industrialized center, with little or no "horizontal" communication among non-Western regions. Reuters was the most vigorous in establishing the first technological links, and in gaining control of the hardware necessary to news flows. Reuters dominated the Ring Combination due to the fact that the British Empire had a virtual monopoly over undersea telegraph cables (Desmond, 1980: 163). Because Britannia ruled the waves, Reuters was able to rule the news hardware under the waves. Reuters sank its first privately owned cable in 1866; and by 1880, additional cables enabled it to open bureaus in Australia, China, India and Japan.

Control of, or privileged access to, the hardware necessary for international news flow has always provided a great advantage to any agency able to acquire it. The drive to maximize profits and increase efficiency has created a long-term trend in the international news business toward increasing concentration and monopolization. Today there are four giants of international news and each is a multinational corporation (MNC): AFP, AP, Reuters, and UPI. As these transactional news agencies (TNNAs), move into regions around the world, they bring more than just reporters armed with pad and pencil. They also import a whole series of complex communication technologies over which they retain control and from which substantial problems develop for the political economies of developing nations. A postwar campaign by American TNNAs to break the British stranglehold on control of these technologies produced the first arguments favouring a "free flow" of news and information between nations (Schiller, 1976: 26-29; Smith, 1980: 44). This brings us to a final aspect of news as a commodity: the relationship between modes of news reporting and political ideologies.

News as a Commodity and Political Ideologies

Numerous studies by sociologists and communication theorists have tried to establish whether mass media work to maintain the status quo, or promote social and political change. Results from these studies run the gamut from claiming that media (news media in particular) are conservative political forces, to claiming that they are the means for radical change. However, there is strong agreement from both camps that " news suggests a general outlook on the world, an ideology, a frame of interpretation" (Katz and Szecsko, 1981: 7).

Following the lead of Reuters, international news agencies historically have catered to the needs and testes of two consumer groups. Political and economic elites are provided with news that affects their vested interests. The general public is provided with news that satisfies desires for the unusual and sensational. Golding has argued that the "historical process" which led to "the development of news as a service to elite groups" has created a situation in which "the basic goals and values which surround journalism refer to the needs and interests" of elites (1981: 79). Because news media need a broader audience than just elites to say in business, Golding goes on to point out that reporting must draw on common social values an assumptions in order to reach a mass audience. The history of news agency clientele supports Golding's thesis. This is not, however, an argument which crudely asserts that the news media are nothing more than a tool for elite domination. Golding is at pains to point this out:

> Analyses which see news a necessarily a product of powerful groups in society, designed to provide a view of the world consonant with the interests of these groups, simplify the situation too far to be helpful. The occupational routines and beliefs of journalists do not allow a simple conduit between the ruling ideas of the powerful and their distribution via the airwaves.

The important point is that these "occupational routines" (elaborated below) preclude the development of views which might question the legitimacy of elite interest and/or the prevailing consensus.

Recall that the summary lead/body format was originally designed to remove such subjective elements as ideology from news stories. However, another recent study has shown that the criteria of good lead writing depend not only on the five Ws, but also on how well the lead makes a strong normative and moral point (Alexander, 1981). "The lead is a device for summing up the 'significance' of the data-event by relating it, implicitly, to what people would have expected to happen in similar situations or to more general value judgments that would normally be applicable". A style that was originally meant to remove normative and ideological aspects from news stories seems to have become the primary vehicle for retaining these features.

Studies of the organizational structure of large news agencies have revealed an additional source of ideological bias. While many journalists would like to believe that the news is just "out there" waiting to be actively pursued, Golding has revealed how the standard operating procedures (SOPs) of news agencies produce reports which are largely "passive, routine, limited, selective." The selection of events to cover is far from random or merely contingent on the course of world affairs. SOP for any news agency is to reduce uncertainty by "plotting events in advance and determining which are to become news". The use of the standard news diary (a listing of routine news items) predetermines to a large extent what is defined as "news." Heavy reliance even by the TNNAs on "a few defined institutional sources, most notably government," also means that the contents of the news are highly "bureaucratized" and "routinized" (see below) according to institutional norms. These practices are the "working rules" of news media which come to be defended as "news values" by strident opponents of the NWIO such as Leonard Sussman (1981). These working rules, or SOPs, are derived from the two classic determinants of story gathering: "perceptions of the audience" and "availability of material." Therefore, news is not pursued wherever necessary an regardless of its interest. Furthermore, Golding argues, it is only because these SOPs are employed over time that they become "imbued with the lustre of good practice." This is a "classic case of making a virtue of necessity". What were originally commercial necessities become "ethical imperatives" (Schiller, 1976: 29). Because the SOPs produce only a partial view of the world (due to preselection and predetermination of the newsworthy), and because news media exist first and foremost to provide service to elites, SOPs invariably produce an ideology (partial view) largely consistent with that of the national elite's (Golding, 1981: 79-81).

Mass media audiences also receive a partial (even partisan) view of the world due to the bureaucratized nature of news gathering and reporting. A bureaucratized media is one in which legitimized institutions are primarily responsible for defining the content of news reports. It is also a form of media organization that facilitates governmental management of the news. News media rely heavily upon information that is centralized by bureaucracies and facts that are generated by bureaucracies. Rather than pursuing facts objectively and impartially wherever they are available, news is gathered primarily through "[b]ureaucratized and routinized interactions between and among workers in legitimated institutions" (Tuchman, 1981: 88).

Studies of bureaucratized media (Altheide and Johnson, 1980; Bennett, 1983; Tuchman, 1981) reveal that in order to meet deadlines (and according to SOPs) news organizations from the small-town newspapers, to the national networks, to the TNNAs rely upon institutions to tell them things as varied as the amount of financial losses from a fire; the extent of government's stability and popularity; estimates of anti-governmental support, as well as their aims and methods; the impact of inflation (in dollar rather than human terms); the noise level produced by a supersonic transport (from the Federal Aviation Administration rather than from the people living in the flight path). These "facts" are assumed to be "essentially correct and disinterested." Facts from other sources, therefore, are "soft" and "non-objective." This "reliance on centralized sources may blind reporters to occurrences" or to alternate interpretations of a given occurrence. Because the TNNAs themselves are large bureaucracies, they can use their institutional weight to gain privileged access to governmental sources (Desmond, 1980: 312), which inevitably increases their reliance on these official sources. Finally, we find that pre-bureaucratized groups or groups not legitimated by the extant political order (*e.g.*, guerrilla and anti-governmental organizations in Central America) are largely frozen out, given no access to the most important news outlets. The official line them becomes the only voice which is heard. Bennett (1983: 55) and Tuchman (1981: 89) point out that marginal groups are then forced to seek media coverage through the creation of radical or violent events.

Media news coverage presents a partial view of the world and upholds the prevalent political ideology by catering to the interests and needs of certain groups; through the format of lead writing and administrative SOP; and due to its bureaucratic nature. But one can also say a great deal more about specific political purposes for which news as a commodity has been employed. In its earliest forms, international news was full of "imperial imagery" and was used to rally support for colonial wars and imperial conquests (Smith, 1980: 77). In the early twentieth century, the major international agencies became even more closely dependent upon, and associated with, their national governments. Reuters' managing director was even made head of British war propaganda in World War I—taking much of the agency's material directly from the War Cabinet—while he remained as head of the agency (*ibid.*: 80).

The implications of news as a commodity must also be drawn out for the international political context. Early postwar theories of development by Lerner, de Sola Pool, Pye and others held that urbanization and increased literacy would produce modernization in the Third World. Increased literacy would stimulate media use and create a more productive workforce. A free press and enhanced economic output would then produce democratic politics and modern development in those nations. We now know that these theories were overlay optimistic. Indeed, reliance upon Western styles of news and imported technology may have brought increased cultural and economic dependence to many Less Developed Countries (LDCs), rather than providing them with more independence and autonomy. Disillusionment with Western-style development has made the LDCs skeptical of the informational theories on which many were based.

As Western economic models were introduced and Western TNNAs expanded their operations in the LDCs, those nations became increasingly reliant on foreign technologies and MNCs. TNNAs themselves are dependent on the current international arrangements which safeguard the interest of multinationals (*e.g.*, protections against nationalization and the right of compensation). As multinationals, the TNNAs are economically dependent on these safeguards and on their ability to transfer costs and revenues across national borders. A standard TNNA response to charges that they exploit LDCs is that bureaus in developing nations consistently operate at a loss; therefore, they could not stay in business without economic protections. Support for news as a commodity and for the agencies which provide it must necessarily be support for an international *status quo* that protects multinationals, allowing them a free hand to pursue their interests in LDCs as they see fit.

A demand for a free reign to Western MNCs is consistent with the insistence by NWIO opponents for a free flow of international news. This position transposes to the international arena arguments favouring free speech which were originally developed by liberal theorists for a national setting. Although this move raises all sorts of theoretical problems regarding "levels of analysis" and the suitability of political arguments created in a national context to international relations, to deal with these issues here would take us too far afield. Clearly , there can be no doubt the most arguments in favour of a free flow are based on political values held near and dear to liberalism.

One reason that liberal arguments seem to shift so effortlessly from a national to an international setting is that the moral basis of current international relations is essentially "the international analogue of nineteenth-century liberalism" (Beitz, 1979: 66). Beitz has shown quite convincingly that the fundamental values of the nation-state system—national sovereignty and nonintervention into the internal affairs of another state—are the international equivalents of certain classic liberal values for individuals—that each person is an autonomous source of ends, and each individual is morally free to arrange his or her own personal affairs (self regarding actions). Of course, even in liberal society (and certainly in international relations) such values are often violated in practice. But the fact remains that a commitment to the current international *status quo* is also a commitment to certain liberal values (and this by no means excludes the socialist nations).

To summarize, the general implications of news as a commodity for international relations are as follows. To promote or protect news in the Western form of a commodity requires that one defend certain characteristically liberal values as well as certain features of the international economic *status quo*. News as a commodity requires the protection of MNCs and the defence of liberal values which are the moral basis of the nation-state system. It should also be clear by now why those nations which have been disillusioned by the failures of liberal development theory, those which desire international reforms to curb the power of multinationals, and those which have deep reservations about certain liberal values would also be suspicious of diplomats and journalists who defend news as a commodity. These are the nations that are campaigning for the NWIO, and these are the nations which believe that the political commitments underlying news values of Western journalism are contrary to the best interests of the LDCs. This brings us to the second conception of news, a notion offered by the proponents of the NWIO: news as a social good.

NEWS IN THE DEVELOPING NATIONS OR NEWS AS A SOCIAL GOOD

In contrast to news as a commodity—a concept that developed in the age of nineteenth-century colonialism—news as a social good developed during the twentieth-century campaign for decolonization. This was (and is) a time during which former colonies tried to modernize quickly through promoting rapid development. LDCs tried to broaden and improve their industries, educational institutions and the general social welfare all at the same time—and each as quickly as possible. During this period of so-called "late-late" development, others have tried to accomplish in a few short decades that which took Western nations centuries to establish. Such an undertaking required large-scale projects of social engineering and more centralized planning.

Under these conditions, developing nations began to consider the news media and its products as social goods. All national assets (including information) came to be seen as resources held in common, and under absolute sovereign control of the state. Oil reserves and news items were viewed as essentially equivalent in this important respect. Information was to be employed as a tool for rapid development, just as other national resources such as labour and mineral deposits. In fact, news and information regarding all national assets was itself a resource which allowed these other goods and services to be more efficiently utilized.

Many Third World leaders now take the position that communication must be controlled and directed by the state. News should concentrate on reports regarding nationwide projects. Such reports are at the heart of the style of developmental journalism. Developmental journalism centers on long-range works of modernization and its reports are directed at informing the population. It displays a particular concern for reaching the poorest and most underdeveloped areas. In this respect, developmental journalism serves as a substitute means for educating the public (due to lack of schools) about the current national and global situation.

When reporting on international events, journalists of the developmental school go to greater lengths than their Western counterparts in including both the historical background and the possible long-range implications of the isolated data-event. Again this is an educative as well as a purely informative approach. In Western societies, these other aspects of a story are usually gotten from non-media sources (such as educational institutions) or are confined to the "op-ed" page. Due to a lack of alternate means, developmental journalists seek to educate as they inform their readers.

In a national context, developmental journalism is exemplified by the *Famille et Development* project of Francophone Africa. This service covers many nations and provides information on health and family planning while 'rigorously eschewing all other political messages" (Smith, 1980: 149). These are undertaking that attempt to bring communities with low literacy rate into the public discussion regarding development while, at the same time, providing them with useful information and promoting self-education. This is *not* journalism that merely serves as political propaganda to indoctrinate the public to the official government line, contrary to claims by Righter (1978: 18) and others.

Due to a lack of financial resources, a decentralized media structure is not currently possible in most LDCs. In most cases, it is only the central government that has the funds necessary to keep a news agency operating. Therefore, news agencies in the Third World must be either heavily subsidized or state-owned. News coming into the nation is usually "filtered" through the government before it reaches the newspapers or broadcast media, as the state itself is the subscriber to foreign wire services (Righer, 1981: 61). Surprisingly enough, this does not prevent the media in many LDCs from adopting standards of critical journalism, despite such governmental controls (Smith, 1980: 150). News going out of these nations, especially that which goes to the developmental news services such as the Inter-Press Service and the Nonaligned News Pool, usually comes directly from the national ministry of information.

The technology and expertise needed to operate Third World news agencies come almost exclusively from the Western TNNAs and telecommunication industries. Furthermore, as another legacy of the colonial era, the majority of LDC agencies were originally established by the French and British, modeled on their own news media (Katz and Wedell, 1977). These conditions have contributed to the economic dependence of the South on the North and imported technologies have created problems for attempts at internal modernization.

The Ideology of News as a Social Good

The political ideology that supports news as a commodity is subtly concealed but is there nonetheless. The political ideology of news as a social good, on the other hand, is consciously overt. It is an anti-imperialist ideology and a product of the campaign by developing nations against what they see as a neocolonial international order. Political independence was achieved by these nations over the past twenty to thirty years, but they believe that their national sovereignty and autonomy remain severely compromised by arrangements in international economics and technology. According to Smith.

> It did not occur to many people until the last decade or so that information lay at the root of sovereignty and that the movement for independence would have to continue beyond the political stage into economic and informational struggles of equal intensity to those which had led to the first stages of the post-colonial era. (1980: 58).

LDCs now charge that it is necessary to break the structures and patterns of news flows which remain essentially neocolonial and "vertical" communication, with little "horizontal" communication taking place between the LDCs themselves. Third World leaders have also expressed their desires to employ national communication industries to increase national unity and to promote a shared sense of national identity (Katz and Wedell, 1977: 26-27). Most of these leaders currently think that Western-style news and information services contribute to social divisions (Smith, 1980: 156).

Perhaps the most central claim advanced by Third World critics in the midst of the NWIO debate is that current patterns of international news flows contribute to the displacement of traditional, indigenous cultures in LDCs by Western values and modes of thought (Galtung, 1979: 165-166; Masmoudi, 1981: 80-81; Schiller, 1976: 8-20). Anthony Smith quotes Juan Somavia,[3] head of the Latin American Institute for Transnational Studies (ILET), on this point, charging that the current international news system is "a vehicle for transmitting values and lifestyles to Third World countries which stimulates the type of consumption and the type of society necessary to the transnational expansion of capital" (1980: 101-102).

We have already seen how support for the Western free press and advocacy of news as a commodity are necessarily pro-*status quo*. To support news in the form of a social good (and those elements of the NWIO that address this matter), on the other hand, is to support many of the contemporary attempts at global reform. The NWIO serves as an integral part of a larger effort to restructure international relations. The NWIO is seen by its proponents as a necessary concomitant to the New International Economic Order (MacBride Commission, 1981: 46, 53). Those who advocate news as a social good, therefore, are necessarily reformists, oftentimes even revolutionaries, in the international context.

The aim of the NWIO on the conceptual level is to replace the Western notion of news as a commodity with that of news as a social good. In discussing Somovia's work for ILET, Righter quotes him as charging that news from TNNAs destroys "authentic cultural values" and subjugates Third World interests to those of the developed nations through "political penetration" of the former by the latter's news agencies. This is based on news as a commodity, news that "responds to the laws of the market," and news for which "the criteria used in selection are always contrary to the interests of sovereign independence." Somovia's "antidote" for these problems (according to Righter) is to replace news as a commodity with "information as a social good, in the service of development" (1978: 107-108).

Contrary to Righter's own claims, however, developmental journalism and its notion of news as a social good differs significantly from Leninist journalism, which merely repeats the official line and seeks to build support for the ruling elites. **There** are numerous examples of government-owned or subsidized press institutions in the Third World (*e.g.*, in India, Kenya, Tanzania) which seek to advance the style of developmental journalism while, at the same time, employing "the same faculty of critical examination, the same kind of investigative instinct as libertarian journalism" (Smith, 1980: 172; see also 148-150). In effect, this would require that we add a fifth category, that of developmental journalism, to the classic essay by Siebert (1956) on the "four theories of the press"—a new classification that does not fall neatly into any of the old categories. For too long, following Siebert's analysis, the Western view has been that any press not allowed the freedoms enjoyed in this part of the world must necessarily be a propagandistic press. This view represents a gross oversimplification. Under a commitment to developmental news standards, governmental control and critical evaluations of national policy are not mutually exclusive (see Table 6.1). Advocates of the developmental style would argue that critical standards are essential to their task. Such a skeptical posture facilitates evaluations of governmental performance—checking to see if gains achieved through policies of development live up to official promises (thus protecting the interests of the masses—see Aggarwala, 1979). Therefore, the choice is not merely one of either a free press or a Leninist media. There is also a middle

Table 6.1

A Comparison of Three Press Institutions

Variable	*Unstandardized Co-efficient*	*Standardized Co-efficients*	*t-Ratio*
MI	3321.0	.42	1.18
PF	128908.0	.69	2.05
GNP	-11.0	-.37	1.02

Dependent Variable = LUX   Intercept = 155,406

R^2 = .48   adjusted R^2 = .17   N = 9   s.e. = 187, 188

LUX = US dollars spent on selected imported luxury items (source : United Nations, 1982)

Other Sources: see Tables 4.1 and 4.2

road, the developmental press, that seeks to combine elements of the other two. This is the road the LDCs have mapped out for themselves.

On the other hand, it certainly is true that many supporters of the NWIO employ an anti-American rhetoric much like that of our Soviet critics. However, this fact is due more to the popularity in the Third World of neo-marxian economic analyses of the structuralist and *dependencia* schools than to a desire on the part of Third World journalist and editors to emulate TASS (the Soviet news service). The unpopularity of TASS in the Third World media is evident in their general reluctance to reprint its reports, even though they are provided free of charge (Smith, 1980: 70).

Like news as a commodity, news as a social good leaves much to be desired. The media practices based on either conception of news allow for several areas of improvement. One can study the deficiencies of each by contrasting both to a third model on which to base news media organizations. This is the model of the "democratized media."

CRITICAL THEORY AND DEMOCRATIZED MEDIA

The democratized media refers to those media reforms based on critical theories of communication. Critical communication theory is among the intellectual heirs to the Frankfurt school of political theory. Under Jurgen Habermas at the Max Planck Institut, the specific focus of many critical theorists has been that of social communication. This group is unified by its primary concern for the political nature of speech and other forms of communication. The phrase "democratized media" is one employed by proponents of the NWIO as well as by the critical theorists; however, these two groups use it to refer to different contexts. Mustapha Masmoudi (former Tunisian Minister of Information) has used the term to identify those parts of the NWIO aimed at international reform, primarily an increase in horizontal flows of information. The democratized media would promote more news and information exchanges between Third World nations. It would create "machinery for co-operation and mutual assistance between developing countries, such as [the] Press Agency Pool of the Nonaligned Countries" (1981: 91).

NWIO advocates and critical theorists share a common concern in media restructuring. Both groups would decentralize and demonopolize media firms. Again, Masmoudi's interest is in international restructuring: "ensuring equal and equitable use of all communication media, including satellites" (1981: 91). Critical theorists have directed their energies much more toward reforms of the national media in advanced industrial societies. They would break up the national monopolies of media capital owners. They would transfer media control from the private owners (*e.g.*, networks) to media producers (*e.g.*, artists, editors, reporters, writers). They also argue in favour of the "political activation of the masses for communicative emancipation" (Lanigan and Strobl, 1981: 146). This last point would mean bringing pre-bureaucratic, nonbureaucratic and nonlegitimated social groups into the process of informational exchange.

An examination of the democratized media of the NWIO in practice must include a recognition of the fact that they are more bureaucratized than the Western media. Media practices of the NWIO may be a platform for international change, but they can also be used to impede political reforms within developing nations. Media in these nations can be subjected to heavier governmental controls than Western media, as news flowing in and out of the Third World is, in most cases, directly controlled by the central government. This is what Western opponents of the NWIO condemn the most. They argue that there is only one choice: between a free, open Western-style press and a tightly controlled Soviet-style government press (see Sussman, 1981). Such crude oversimplifications only obscure the real issues and contribute to the international climate of antagonism over news flows. Developmental journalism cannot be simply equated with Leninist journalism.

On the other hand, the Western free press, based on the notion of news as a commodity, is also badly in need of improvement. The democratized media of critical theory was developed to promote media reform in advanced industrialized states. The ideological content of Western news is obscured, and even denied to exist. The bulk of critical theory research in communication has been directed at debunking these claims (Lanigan and Strobl, 1981: 144). Western media is over-reliant upon "official," "legitimate" institutions that define what the news is. This bureaucratized media can allow for governmental controls on the news that—while they are less visible—rival the effectiveness of more overt tactics used by nonaligned governments. Nonbureaucratic groups get little or no media coverage and therefore have no opportunity to express their positions. To get coverage, they turn to violence or civil disobedience. Even these more extreme tactics yield only nominal coverage, usually sensationalist reports (the best treatment to date of these issues is Bennett's [1983] discussion of what he calls the "normalized media").

Furthermore, foreign correspondents from the West are not sufficiently trained for international reporting. They carry little knowledge of the relevant historical background with them when they rush off to cover invasions in the Caribbean or elections in Buenos Aires. Fear that reporters will lose their "perspective" (ethnocentrism?) has created the SOP of rotating foreign correspondents from one capital city to another, rarely leaving them in one place for more than three years at a time (Desmond, 1980: 312). Even training foreign nationals to report for TNNAs leaves many of these problems unresolved (Smith, 1980: 72). Because the reports reaching the West are often short-sighted, incomplete, and disjointed, the West works in a "policy vacuum" or suffers from a "policy void" (Spero, 1982). This misinformation reaches the media consumers in the West (congressmen, party leaders, voters) and becomes the basis of faulty judgments on foreign policy.

Finally, as each conception of news has its own peculiar faults, and as each is linked to particular developmental policies in the Third World, misconceptions about the mass media necessarily lead to political and economic failures in LDCs. Two approaches to using media in service of development have characterized prior literature on the subject. Each school of thought on communication for development in the Third World also has its own preferred definition of the term "news" as well.

TWO THEORIES OF COMMUNICATION AND DEVELOPMENT

The question of how modern communication can best serve the

needs of developing nations has sparked both a policy debate and a theoretical debate. The *policy* debate has revolved around the negotiations within the United Nations Educational, Scientific, and Cultural Organisation (UNESCO) on a new information order. This dialogue addresses such areas as developmental policies in the Third World; foreign policies of the West which affect the Third World; standards of international justice and equity; and topics in international law (*e.g.*, the right to communicate). The *theoretical* debate is being fought out in academic circles and professional journals. It raises such issues as the following: What types of information best serve the ends of modernization in LDCs? What means of distributing such information in the Third World are the most efficient? Is the structure of international communication neocolonial? Many of the theoretical issues became politically salient due only to the nature of the NWIO policy debate. The remainder of this study will put the policy debates within the context of the following two theories of development.

The Lerner Thesis

Early postwar development theory—strongly influenced by Daniel Lerner's seminal work *The Passing of Traditional Society*—was based, in part, on certain propositions about how communication operates in a modern, industrialized society. Urban growth necessitates increased specialization, differentiation and division of labour. Specialized expertise becomes necessary to operate modern industries, businesses and schools. A modern or modernizing industrial nation also must rely on particular types of rationality (*e.g.*, ends-means calculations) and particular forms of specialized information (see Frey, 1973: 377-379). According to Lerner's thesis, what is needed primarily are the "bare facts" and the latest, undated information that will allow for effective rational decisions. Raw data is provided to utilitarian decision-makers to enable them to make the best choice of means to ends.

There is also a unique mechanism that has proved (according to this thesis) to yield the best production of this raw data. That is the free market. Employing arguments not significantly different from those of J.S. Mill and Thomas Jefferson (see Wills, 1979: 316-317), Western theorists of development see a free market of news and ideas as the best aid to political and economic development in all nations (see also Merrill, 1981). The free flow of news and information serves as a "market machinery for testing ideas." This position reflects liberal beliefs that "an enlightened citizenry is a political necessity'" and that a "free play of ideas will lead to a citizenry equipped to choose the best possible men and policies" (Wills, 1979: 316).

There were two particular attractions within the Lerner thesis that made it seem useful and especially relevant to Third World nations. First of all it strove to unite micro- and macro-levels of development theory. At the macro-level Lerner and others could discuss the interrelationships among urbanization, education (literacy), communication and national development. At the micro-level, they argued to have found a process that takes individuals from a traditional to a modern worldview. This modern worldview was reflected by increased powers of empathy (Lerner, 1964: 49-54) and/or the "cognitive flexibility" that allows one to accept change and overcome the "trauma level" which comes with rapid change due to modernization (Frey, 1973: 404).

The second attraction of this thesis for development strategies in the Third World was its recognition of the unique political context of many such nations. LDCs are commonly divided by ethnic differences. Lerner and others argued that certain kinds of communication can help to increase levels of political participation, thereby promoting a sense of national (as opposed to subnational) identification, a belief in the legitimacy of the central government and trust and consensus among ethnic groups. Mass media would be used to promote feelings of trust and to help overcome the tendency of ethnic groups to "refuse to accept the electoral victory of another ethnic coalition because they suspect it intentions." Mass media are also necessary in these states to promote the political co-operation required for establishing national systems of defence, taxation and welfare. Mass media help to build the consensus necessary to create a single nation from "previously isolated or unco-ordinated elements of the traditional society" (Frey, 1973: 381-382).

There are two key elements for the successful operation of the process which the Lerner thesis describes. One is information of a particular kind. The other is a particular mechanism for disseminating that information. The information required shares all the characteristics of news as a commodity discussed earlier. It is information which has its contents determined by the demands of the market place. It is concerned more with raw facts than with interpretations of those facts. The key mechanisms for disseminating this information are Western forms of mass media. Lerner (1964), Huntington (1968) and Deutsch (1961) have all made Western mass media the primary tool in their theories of social mobilization. According to Lerner, increased urbanization leads to increased literacy. But these trends create political and economic development through the intervening process of media use (and only by way of media use, according to McCrone and Cnudde, 1967). It is through media use that empathy and cognitive flexibility are developed. It is mass media that "provide a window to a larger and more stimulating world" (Frey, 1973: 404). Media use is said to stimulate economic development by creating a more productive workforce and by increasing individual initiative. It is media use which, according to Lerner, also induces increased political development (*i.e.*, participation such as voting).

Development planning which is based on the Lerner thesis, and which therefore looks to Western mass media as one key to modernization, tends to rely heavily upon Western communication hardware. Films, radio and television programming, and, most importantly, the latest in high-tech hardware are seen as the quickest way for "backward" LDCs to leap into the modern communication age (Davison, 1965: 139). The latest in Western technology (*e.g.*, the direct broadcast satellite [DBS]) is recommended by Lerner and his followers to LDCs wishing to modernize. Unfortunately such recommendations are usually made with little or no evaluation of their advisability given the severe logistical and resource problems of most LDCs.[4]

One would expect the Lerner thesis, given its reliance on information as a commodity and its stress on Western technologies, to offer plans for Third World development along the lines of the Western model. After all, in a free market of ideas the best ideas are supposed to win out. The past has proved to many in the West that the product of this process of "intellectual Darwinism" (Wills, 1979: 317) are the ideas and ways of Western societies. These are the models that "rational" Third World nations must emulate, if they want to modernize. According to this logic, if

Western nations are the most highly developed states, then Western means of development must be best.

Yet many problems of both a practical and theoretical nature have arisen during attempts to apply the Lerner thesis to an understanding of development in the Third World. These problems are best understood in light of a second theory of communication and development, a theory that stands in direct contrast to the Lerner thesis. This is structural theory.

The Structural Thesis

Theories of development that have come out of the structuralist and *dependencia* schools are, in large part, a product of or a reaction to the failing of early postwar attempts at development. The continued hardships and poverty of Third World nations has led these critics to see dependency as the primary source of current Third World problems. Above all else, dependency by LDCs on Western goods. Western-controlled markets, Western tastes and Western cultural is the condition which allegedly "explains" the continuing dilemmas faced by Third World nations seeking modernization.

Structuralists like Galtung and Schiller have argued that reliance by LDCs on Western mass media and Western sources of information are prime—even paradigmatic—examples of this state of dependency. These authors want to see the Third World break out of this condition of dependency by relying more upon its own resources. However, they also argue that such a feat is not possible within the context of the current system of international communication. Hence their support for radically new orders of international relations.

The structuralists offer what is essentially a Marcusean critique of the Western arguments favouring a free flow of international news and information. Like Marx and Herbert Marcuse, they would charge that bourgeois liberties create a state of freedom in which the powerful are free to dominate the weak. The free flow is seen as in ideological mask that allows the Big Four (AFP, AP, Reuters, UPI) to dominate the market in international news. LDCs are required to rely heavily upon the Big Four for news, thereby allegedly increasing their dependency on the West.

To break out of this pernicious cycle, structuralists argue that each LDC needs more control over the kinds of news and information it receives. Each nation must be allowed more control to decide for itself what its people need to know. They agree with Lerner and others that political and economic development must be pursued through communication policies designed to educate the population and promote a sense of national identification. However, structuralists see an equal need for Third World nations to rely more on indigenous resources and low-tech communication hardware. Schiller sees mimeographs as more in tune with the needs and resources of LDCs than is a communication satellite (1976: 60-67). Instead of recommending the importation of costly and advanced foreign technologies, those who believe that "relevance is beautiful" prefer use of traditional communication within LDCs as being more practical and efficient. The chief of communication for the United Nations International Children's Fund (UNICEF), Revi Tuluhungwa, is fond of one example in which employment of traditional modes of spreading information increased the effectiveness of a health education programme more than five times over.[5]

Like Lerner and his followers, the structuralists also want to employ communication policies to increase political consensus in LDCs but the latter group believes that such a task requires governmental controls on media rather than a free market of ideas. Guidelines that reduce that portion of news reports which may serve to divide ethnic groups and instead concentrate on news that concern progress and successes in national development are necessary (according to this account). Media controls are also said to be necessary for the protection of indigenous cultures. Structuralists argue that a free market in news promotes the demonstration effect, thereby undermining such cultures.

Structural theories of development eschew news and information as commodities in favour of information in the form of a social good. Such theories recommend techniques of developmental journalism to create a political consensus and ensure cultural autonomy. The general aim of structural theory is to create development in a form which is unique to the Third World. They would take from the western model only that which is necessary and useful. By integrating these Western traits into more traditional cultural modes, they hope to stimulate development which is more relevant to each LDC's unique heritage and pre-modern ways of life.

Two Sets of Testable Hypothesis

Each theory of communication and development has produced a set of testable hypothesis. Partially because the Lerner thesis was articulated and expanded long before the structural thesis, the implications of the former have been researched to a much greater extent than those of the latter. If the Lerner thesis is correct, certain relationships will hold true between the processes of development (*e.g.*, urbanization, communication) in Third World states. Furthermore, if this thesis is valid, one would also expect certain trends to hold among groups of LDCs. On the basis of the Lerner thesis, one would expect to find that developing nations with free markets in news and information also tend to be those nations which are more politically and economically developed.

On the other hand, if the structural thesis is more valid, those nations that regulate closely the inflows of foreign news and information will also tend to be the nations which are most successful at maintaining their political stability and developing a strong sense of national identification. These same nations would also tend to be those that are least dependent on the West both economically and culturally. If nations with a highly regulated media were found to be those nations with greater political stability and less dependence, this fact would tend to support the structuralist's argument. It would also tend to refute parts of the free flow arguments. Conversely, if nations with free markets in news and information were also found to be more advanced politically and economically, this fact would tend to support the Lerner thesis (free flow arguments) and tend to deny the validity of at least part of the structural thesis.

The first set of hypotheses—those of the Lerner thesis—have been investigated by Alker, Frey, Lerner, McCrone and Cnudde, Ruggles, Schramm and Winham, (see Frey, 1973 for an overview). The results of these studies have been conflicting and inconclusive. Lerner's theoretical link between literacy and political development has been supported by one study (Alker, 1966) and questioned by another (McCrone and Cnudde, 1967)

The same is true of the link postulated by Lerner between literacy and mass media use (Frey, 1973: 416).

At another level, the basic assumptions of the theory have been called into question. Its bias toward a unilinear, mechanistic view of history and development has been severely criticized. A theory that postulates "progress" from traditional to transitional to modern "stages" of development seems much more tenuous today, in light of numerous failures and setbacks, than it must have been twenty or twenty-five years ago. The change in values at the micro-level that is supposed to come about through urbanization has also been put into doubt by studies of Latin America (see Martz, 1971). In that region one finds examples of nations in which increases in the indicators of Lerner's model (*e.g.*, media use) are not associated with the political development predicted by the model. The Latin American experience also stands as a reminder that, by no means, do economic and political development always go hand in hand, as is postulated by the Lerner thesis.

The second set of theoretical claims—those of the structural thesis—remain virtually untested. The untested nature of structuralism is probably due in large part to the overtly ideological nature of this theory. Schiller and others seem to assume that their arguments are correct and feel little need to demonstrate their validity through empirical testing. Western conservatives, on the other hand, seem to assume the invalidity of this theory due to its ideological underpinnings. A critical examination reveals that neither theory has been proved conclusively, and the structural thesis is as much in need of testing as was its predecessor. Structuralism may be better able to explain development in the Third World than was the Lerner thesis, or it may be badly flawed and in need of refinement and overhaul, as was the case with the Lerner thesis. Such is the task of the remainder of this study.

Testing the structural thesis will also serve to test parts of the Lerner thesis, at least indirectly. Through several series of tests, quantitative analyses will allow for numerous opportunities to confirm or refute structural claims. If nothing is found after all these various tests are run, then there is more than *prima facie* evidence to indicate that structural arguments won't hold water. This in turn would tend to support those parts of the Lerner thesis (discussed above) on the points at which these two directly contradict each other.

References

1. Kenya recently threatened to expel as many as 100 foreign (mostly Western) correspondents after charging American and Scandinavian presses with conducting smear campaigns. This is especially disturbing, given the fact that more Western correspondents are based in Nairobi than in any other place in sub-Saharan Africa (*New York Times*, 16 September, 1987). It is also an indication that previously moderate LDCs, like Kenya, which have provided press freedom in the past are falling in behind the more radical policies preferred by Zimbabwe and others.
2. Historical arguments rely on three principal sources: Desmond's three-volume history of international news: Smith's *Geopolitics of Information*; and Righter's *Whose News?*
3. Somavia, a member of the MacBride Commission from Chile, is one of the leading theorists of news as a social good. His work is reviewed in Righter, pp. 107-109, and in Smith. pp. 101-103.
4. According to Bella Mody, who did the governmental study of the social impact of a DBS project in India, the question of whether it made sense to use such a sophisticated technology in a nation as poor as India was never raised. Mody made these comments at a 1984 colloquium on communication and Third World development at the University of Iowa.
5. At the same colloquium, Tuluhungwa said that an African health programme went from 15 per cent to 85 per cent effectiveness simply by turning to the traditional means of communication (that already existed in the area) in order to inform the public of the project.

7

Information Sources and Communication Ethics

News Agencies

For reporting the latest news from around the world newspapers, magazines, radio and TV have three options: correspondents of their own, which apart from the public broadcasting corporations only a few high-circulation daily and weekly newspapers and magazines can afford, press agencies and news agencies. Most medium-sized and small newspapers are completely dependent on agencies, which maintain a network of staff covering the globe.

The Allensbach public opinion research institute conducted a content analysis of a representative sample of newspapers and found that smaller-circulation publications were less likely to carry out independent revisions of political reports they obtain from agencies than were newspapers with a wider circulation. Papers with a circulation of under 50,000 copies publish 35 per cent of agency reports unedited, papers with a circulation of between 50,000 and 200,000 fourteen per cent, and papers with a circulation of over 200,000 eight per cent.

The agencies collect and disseminate news. The lifespan of a report is short and can be schematically described as follows.

The staff member of an agency, the correspondent, after participating in an event, for example a Press conference, prepares a report. He passes this on to the agency's nearest office. DEUTSCHE PRESSE-AGENTUR (DPA), for example, has offices in Bonn and all federal state capitals, as well as other "places of significance from a news point of view." From there, the report goes to the central editorial office, in DPA's case to Hamburg, where, as has already happened in the regional office, it may be re-edited, in other words, shortened, reworded or amplified. If it is significant enough, it is then passed on to customers, *i.e.*, to newspapers, magazines and radio and TV stations, as well as to press and information offices and the press offices of associations which subscribe to the agency's services.

With the advent of electronic media, in the past few years news transmission has fundamentally changed, at news agencies as elsewhere. The correspondent in a DPA state office works at a computer terminal via which he can send the report he has just composed to the central editorial office in Hamburg in fractions of a second. There it is called up onto a computer screen by an editor and, if he sees fit, is passed on to customers, for example newspapers, which for their part work with computerised word processing systems. The editor of the newspaper which has subscribed to DPA services can for his part call the report up on to his screen and alter it. Of course, he can also use it unabridged and unchanged.

Some people argue that the great advantage of this technical development is that newspapers can be more up-to-date. Critics object that how quickly a piece of news gets into the paper is not so important; it is far more important for it to have been thoroughly checked for accuracy. They say the technical ability to transmit reports like lightning from the place where the event originally occurred via the chain of correspondent—regional office—central editorial office—customer (newspaper, radio or TV station), encourages cursoriness.

The most important source of information for mass media in the Federal Republic of Germany is DEUTSCHE PRESSE-AGENTUR (DPA), which emerged in 1949 from the three news agencies of the Western occupying powers (DENA in the US Zone, DPD in the British zone and SUEDENA in the French zone).

It is owned by publishers and broadcasting institutions, who elect a supervisory board which decides on the management and editor-in-chief. In order to avoid the risk of a biased expression of interests:

— no shareholder may own more than 1.5 per cent of the ordinary capital,
— among shareholders several political schools of thought and philosophies of life are represented,
— the articles of association expressly bar the state from acquiring shares in the company's capital.

Hence, for example it would hardly be possible for a single big business enterprise to buy up DPA—unless it could find a large number of companies to act as "front men" who, though nominally holding their share of ordinary capital, would in reality surrender it to the big company. Nothing of this kind has happened to date. Since many small shareholders are dependent on them, the big publishing groups control the agency. This is evidenced by the composition of the supervisory board. As yet there is no scientific proof as to whether this has resulted in the production of reports in favour of the big Press combines.

Every day over 200,000 words reach DPA's head office from a whole variety of sources. The agency relays only a third of them via the DPA basic service, which almost all German national daily papers and broadcasting institutions receive.

DPA cannot, in the long term, afford to indulge in one-sided reporting to the advantage or disadvantage of a particular party, for several reasons:

— its subscribers are adherents of a variety of political lines, so that, for example, if the SPD were obviously disadvantaged, newspapers close to the party would threaten to cancel their subscriptions.
— other agencies also run German-language news services in the Federal Republic: ALLGEMEINE DEUTSCHE NACHRICHTENAGENTUR (ADN), DEUTSCHER DEPESCHEN-DIENST (DDP) the US agency ASSOCIATED PRESS (AP), the British REUTERS and France's AGENCE FRANCE PRESSE (AFP).

Thus any party political imbalance on the part of DPA would be quickly recognised by the big newspapers and broadcasting stations, who subscribe to all the main services, and lead to protests.

So the articles of association, subscribers and competitors ensure that DEUTSCHE PRESSE-AGENTUR does not get tried up with one political party. The reason it is so important for these three checks to function is that around 20 per cent of daily newspapers receive political news of supra-regional significance exclusively through DPA. The monopoly position which DPA holds *vis-a-vis* these papers could become politically dangerous it, under the guise of being "objective and above party politics," the agency were to supply to this part of the German Press reports which were not worthy of such a rating.

DPA mainly runs up against competition in the new German states. Merger negotiations with ALLGEMEINE DEUTSCHE NACHRICHTENAGENTUR (ADN) broke down in the summer of 1990, primarily over the question of how many employees would be taken over. DPA has since built up its own regional services in Brandenburg. Mecklenburg-Western Pomerania, Saxony, Saxony-Anhalt and Thuringia. In 1992, the Treuhand-anstalt sold ADN to Bolko Hoffmann (Effectenspiegel AG, Dusseldorf), who is also the majority shareholder in DEUTSCHER DEPESCHEN-DIENST.

Before the border between East and West Germany was opened, ADN was the official mouthpiece of the SED regime. The close links between agency and official party found expression, for example, in the fact that ADN Director-General Gunter Potschke was a member of the Central Committee of the SED. The agency received its instructions from the Politbureau member responsible for the media, Joachim Herrmann, whom ADN Editor-in-Chief Matthias Wirzberger later judged as follows: "With the aid of hand-picked hirelings and dictatorial means Herrmann .... railroaded through his and his masters' ideas on how the GDR media, including ADN, were to report domestic problems or international events." Herrmann had assumed for himself the right to take "high-handed" decisions about the contents, wording and timing of ADN reports.

Apart from the above-mentioned large domestic and foreign news agencies, many other press agencies operate in the Federal

Republic, most of which specialise in particular subjects. Some examples: EVANGELISCHER PRESSEDIENST (EPD) and KATHOLISCHE NACHRICHTENAGENTUR (KNA) mainly issue church news. VEREINIGTE WIRTSCHAFTSDIENSTE (VWD), owned jointly by DPA, ten leading organisations of German industrialists and thirty Press publishers, supplies reports on business events.

Over 900 Press and information services (around 250 of them free of charge) published by parties, associations, institutions and private individuals appear daily, weekly or monthly. Many are marked "confidential" or "only for the personal information of the recipient" even though they more or less never contain confidential material.

Many magazines (such as DER SPIEGEL, STERN, DIE ZEIT) use news agency and press service reports—which for the majority of publications form the framework of their supraregional reporting—only for initial orientation. These papers often deploy a large staff of journalists charged with obtaining additional information on the spot in conversations with official, and above all unofficial, sources.

Press Offices

State and private press offices, for their part, are one of the most fruitful sources of information for the agencies, and partly also for the other services and for domestic and foreign correspondents. It is among the duties of the PRESSE- UND INFORMATIONSAMT DER BUNDESREGIERUNG (FEDERAL GOVERNMENT PRESS AND INFORMATION OFFICE)

- — to keep the federal government informed on the output of domestic and foreign news services
- — and to keep public opinion-forming organs abreast of the policies of the federal government.

Thus it is simultaneously the "voice and ears" of the cabinet: it carries news from inside out and from outside in.

At the head of the Press and Information Office is the federal government spokesman, who is responsible directly to the Chancellor. In his dual role of taking the part of the government with the Press and of the Press with the government, he is in constant danger of making himself unpopular with both.

In Bonn, as a rule on Mondays, Wednesdays and Fridays, he and individual Ministry spokesmen attend the Federal Press Conference, an assembly of correspondents accredited in Bonn. A journalist once aptly described the difficult position of government spokesmen at these conferences in this way: *"Bonn bureaucrats would prefer to have a deaf and dumb person in this job, but the public wants to be, and must be, informed...If he says too much he has the bureaucracy to contend with, and if he says too little, the public are justifiably dissatisfied."*

Apart from direct talks with the head of government, the most significant way for the government spokesman to obtain information is to attend cabinet meetings. In addition, the press officers of the various ministries send the Federal Press Office reports about their work, position statements, statistical and graphical material for further processing.

The Federal Press Office conveys its news to the mass media both orally and, most importantly, in writing via its publications

— MITTEILUNGEN AN DIE PRESSE (INFORMATION TO THE PRESS)
— and BULLETIN DES PRESSE-UND INFORMATIONSAMTES DER BUNDESREGIERUNG (BULLETIN OF THE FEDERAL GOVERNMENT PRESS AND INFORMATION OFFICE), which primarily publishes statements by the President, the Chancellor and the government on current issues or on matters of policy.

In the hectic pace of everyday life, the government spokesman frequently has no time to obtain information and views from the departments responsible before making a statement. To be topical, as a rule he will issue a statement very quickly, thus time and again having to accept the risk of later having to amplify or to withdraw his words.

— If he has too much of " a mind of his own" he will run the risk of journalists no longer regarding him as the voice of government.
— On the other hand, if he wants to be exclusively "his master's voice" and thus hesitates too often before making a statement, his pronouncements lose their

topicality and journalists may ceased paying much attention to them.

It is the head of government's special privilege to appoint the person he wants as government spokesman. However, he looks upon him not so much as a spokesman for the government as his own personal spokesman. This leads to conflicts, as this author knows from his period as spokesman for the Senate in Berlin (1979 to 1981).

— If, as expected of him, the spokesman highlights the achievements of the head of government by stressing that the governing mayor said, influenced, achieved or decided this or that, he runs the risk of journalists dismissing him as a "court reporter." The consequence can be that even when the head of government has argued and succeeded in getting a decision adopted, the Press ignores it—despite express references by the spokesman to the merits of his boss—and uses the standard formula "The Senate has decided that..."
— In a multi-party cabinet the coalition partner normally also blames the spokesman for a tendency to pay particular attention to the head of government. Yet he will keep on doing this because, in the final analysis, he owes his appointment to the head of government and can only be dismissed by him, at any time, without any reason being given. This special relationship of dependency demands special services from the spokesman in cultivating the image of his boss.

The most time-consuming job for heads of press and information offices is to co-ordinate public relations work, in other words, to clarify which ministry says what, and when. They all vie with each other to announce good news and shrink from disseminating bad news. Two examples: when toxic waste was discovered in Berlin in 1979, several Senate departments spent a considerable time wrangling over who was responsible for dealing with the Press—none of them was prepared to assume this responsibility. At the other end of the scale, in the same year the senate chancellery and the department of trade and industry spent weeks arguing over who was to break to the public the good news that a large international company was planning to move to Berlin—the governing mayor, the senator for trade and industry, or both.

Every government will be concerned to present its work to the public in a good light. In this respect every press office and every government spokesman—whether in Bonn, Berlin, Hamburg or elsewhere—defends the policies of its or his principal. They often only provide information about things which have gone wrong if asked to do so.

Critics maintain that from time to time—above all before elections—the parliamentary majority parties are given preference over the opposition to an inadmissible extent, because with the aid of public funds, the Federal Press Office:

— represents the political views of the government;
— and thus simultaneously conducts publicity for the majority parties.

In its verdict of 2 March 1977 the Federal Constitutional Court declared the public relations work of government and legislative bodies to be essential. The court said it should serve to maintain the citizens' fundamental consensus with the system of government established by Basic Law. However, the general public should always be on its guard against overt or coverts publicity on behalf of individual political parties. The Karlsruhe judges laid down particularly strict standards for the pre-election period, beginning from the day when the President announces the election date. During this period, reports on the government's work, achievements and successes are inadmissible, as is the use of official government pamphlets by political parties.

Critics consider this verdict problematic for three reasons.

1. It ignores the fact that in the Federal Republic of Germany citizens are permanently being called to participate in elections, and that therefore the public relations work of state organs, which the court considers essential, has almost constantly to be subject to restrictions.
2. Where information ceases and publicity begins will always remain a contentious question.
3. No government will be able to succeed in keeping its

information material out of election campaigns, as the court desires.

State Election Publicity Unconstitutional

1. Under the constitution, state organs are prohibited in their official function in respect of elections from identifying with political parties or election candidates, form using public funds to support or oppose them and in particular, from influencing the electorate's decision by publicity.
2. It is likewise inadmissible for state organs to intervene in this type of public relations work on behalf of one party or another in the election of a representative body. The public relations work of the government ceases where election publicity begins.

[From the guiding principles of the verdict of the Federal Constitutional Court dated 2 March 1977]

Journalists and their Profession

In Germany around 60,000 full-time journalists work for newspapers and magazines, radio and television, and public and private sector press offices. Some are employed as editorial staff, whilst others work freelance. Of these :

— over 25,000 are organised in the Deutscher Journalisten-Verband (DJV), and
— less than 20,000 are members of IG Medien.

The attempt to establish a single trade union for everyone working in the media failed in 1984 after years of discussions:

— a majority of DJV members thought it better for jurnalists' particular interests to be represented by a union of their own in which typesetters, printers and clerical staff had no part. They did not want to be exposed to the risk of having to share responsibility for statements made by an executive or a delegates' conference on general political issues.

— the Deutsche Journalisten-Union (DJU) in the printing and paper industry trade union and the Rundfunk-Fernseh-Film-Union (RFFU) in the arts industry union criticised this standpoint, considering it to be "an elitist concern with status." Given the concentration of capital on the employers' side, they thought priority should be given to solidarity with all those employed in a position of dependency in the Press and broadcasting industries. In 1989 these two unions merged to form IG Medien—Druck und Papier, Publizistik und Kunst.

In recent years the organisations concerned have increasingly come to realise that the image of the born journalist with his free-flowing pen is a deceptive one. In addition to knowledge itself, the journalist who is supposed to relay, and comment on information primarily needs the ability to acquire knowledge. Nowadays this is best achieved by a university course tailored to the needs of the journalist's profession.

According to a representative study by the Institute fur Journalistik und Kommunikationsforschung in Hanover, 35 per cent of journalists in West Germany and over 70 per cent in East Germany (as a percentage of those who were resident in the GDR before 1989) had a university education.

For a long time the universities prepared very few of them for real-life journalism. In order to overcome this crucial and much-criticised deficiency, the universities of Bamberg, Bochum, Dortmund, Eichstadt, Giessen Hamburg, Hanover, Leipzig, Mainz, Munich and Stuttgart-Hohenheim among others developed courses to prepare students for a profession in journalism. Numerous practical exercises and placements with newspapers and broadcasting stations are designed to forge close links between theory and practice from the very outset.

Still now, as a rule anyone wishing to become a journalist does a two-year practical training—for a graduate this can sometimes be a shorter period—in an editorial office. In 1990, after a long battle, the DJV and IG Medien managed to negotiate a collective training contract providing for training in several editorial areas, training courses inside and outside the company, and training by a member of the editorial team entrusted with looking after juniors.

Training institutes for journalists include the Deutsche Journalisten-schule in Munich and the Berliner Journalistenschule, the Henri-Nan-nen-Schule in Hamburg and the Holtzbrinck-Schule fur Wirtschafts-journalisten in Dusseldorf, plus the journalistenschule Axel Springer in Hamburg and Berlin, the Hochschule fur Femsehen und Film in Munich, the Deutsche Film- und Fernsehakademie in Berlin and the Schule/Institut fur Publizistik in Cologne.

Institutes of further education include for example the Akademie fur Publizistik in Hamburg, the Akademie der bayerischen Presse, the Deutsches Institut fur publizistiche Bildungsarbeit in Hagen and the Evangelische Medienakademie in Frankfurt. The Freie Universitat Berlin offers a special course for journalists to engage in further training.

Ways into Journalism

The magazine SAGE UND SCHREIBE (No. 4/1993) identified four main ways of getting into journalism:

"— from Abitur (school-leaving certificate) via freelance work and practical work placements to a two-year training placement called in German a Volontariat (around 15 per cent at present , trend declin-ing):

— from Abitur via a school of journalism or various training and educational courses to employment in an editorial office (currently around 10 per cent):

— from Abitur via a university degree of some kind to an often shortened training placement (currently around 50 per cent, trend increasing):

— from Abitur via a university course in journalism, writing or media sciences to a career as a journalist (currently between 15 and 20 per cent, trend open)."

A survey by the magazine showed that:

"Most editors-in-chief prefer a university degree in a specialised subject. Top of the list are subjects such as law, biology or business management. In second place are the humanities, topped by German, history and psychology. Degree courses in journalism and media sciences are bottom of the list. Here the editors-in-chief were unanimously of the opinion that these degree courses were no substitute for a training placement: at best it could be shortened to 18 months—as it could in the case of many other academics with practical experience. At the same time the editors-in-chief are very well able to distinguish between a degree course in journalistic sciences, which they see as overburdened with theory, and the few university courses in journalism which have integrated extensive practical work placements or even practical training placements. This is particularly evident in their evaluation of the Dortmund degree courses: because the students coming from there with diplomas in journalism have completed not only a practical work placement but also a 12-month practical training period as part of their degree course, they are accepted as journalists. So far the Dortmund model is unique, but soon this will no longer be the case: the University of Leipzig is also developing a degree course with an integrated practical training period. To sum up: anyone wanting to study journalistic and media sciences at university has no advantage over those who have completed classic degree courses. It is better to take media sciences as a subsidiary subject: in that way, at least no time is wasted."

Before the political changes in the GDR two out of three people working in the media there started their careers with a degree course at the Faculty of Journalism (from 1969 a department) at the Karl Marx University in Leipzig. As a rule, this cadre training facility, also known as the "red monastery," only accepted students who had already distinguished themselves at school through "social activities" in the spirit of East Germany's ruling SED. In Leipzig, knowledge of Marxism-Leninism counted for more than a specialist qualification. They tried to achieve practical relevance in different ways at different times. Jurgen Grubitzsch writes with hindsight of three and a half decades of training journalists in Leipzig as "a persistent search for optimum training forms and contents for a type of journalism which was an instrument in the service of the system, the results of which must be evaluated in a very finely differentiated way." [J. Grubitzsch: Traditionen, Altlasten und Neuansatze der Leipziger Journalistenausbildung (Traditions, Historic Burdens and New Approaches to the Training of Journalists in Leipzig), in: RUNDFUNK UND FERNSEHEN, No. 3/1990, p. 402].

Some examples of journalists' pay, according to the collective pay agreement of 1 May 1993 for journalists on daily newspapers in West Germany and West Berlin, the terms of which are valid with a 20 per cent deduction from 1.12.1993 in East Germany as well:

— trainees in the first year of training, according to age, between DM2,320 and DM2,573 per month;
— journalists in their first and second year as professionals DM4,376 per month;
— journalists in a special post with independent newspapers, with at least one journalist under them, according to experience between DM7,212 and DM8,133 per month.

Collective agreements also apply to magazine journalists, news agencies and broadcasting (public and private sectors). Generally, the highest salaries—far above collectively agreed levels—are paid for top posts with large-circulation newspapers and magazines and the private broadcasting companies.

Colleagues who are not employed by organs of the Press or broadcasting institutions are called free journalists—misleadingly, for they are the least free of all: they are mainly dependent on their principals, and in contrast to employees, have no employment protection rights, sick pay entitlement or company pensions. However, the "collective agreement for employee-like free journalists"—which applies to everyone with a monthly income of over DM750 from journalism, who is dependent on this income, and has during the last six months on average received at least one third of his or her earnings from a single publisher-guarantees minimum fees for written and pictorial contributions.

Whether one is talking about working hours, income or prestige—local journalists are always at the bottom of the pile. Presumably this explains why publishers continue to experience a shortage of them. In other areas, in contrast, the demand for jobs far exceeds the supply. Journalists with specialist knowledge have the best prospects. On the other hand, the more one concentrates on a single subject, the more one restricts one's flexibility.

Private television and radio have created new employment opportunities. As a result of a postal survey of 65 TV and 176 radio companies, the Institut der Deutschen Wirtschaft (IW) in Cologne found that in 1993 there were 5,410 journalists employed by private broadcasting companies (1,600 in television, 3,810 in radio).

In 1990/91 many people lost their jobs in the heavily overstaffed newspaper and magazine offices in the GDR. Those with highly dubious political pasts also had to go. Quite a few journalists' jobs also went at radio headquarters in Nalepastrasse in Berlin and television headquarters at Berlin-Adlershof, since Article 36 of the Unification Treaty provided for the closing down of these institutions or their transfer into federal structures by the end of 1991. The result of this was the discontinuation of previous radio and television programmes. New job opportunities were offered by state broadcasting authorities and private radio and television companies in the new federal states of East Germany.

In recent years, the practical work of editorial offices has changed fundamentally.

— For example, the Bonn correspondent of WESTDEUTSCHE ALLGEMEINE ZEITUNG used first to write his copy by hand or typewriter and then to telephone his report to Essen. There it was written out a second time, edited and a fair copy made. After that it finally passed to the typesetting section, where it was copied once more.

— Nowadays the correspondent types his article into a computer from the outset. The central office in Essen can edit the text on a monitor without any paperwork, and send it for setting at the touch of a button.

— DEUTSCHE PRESSE-AGENTUR transmits its news reports directly to automatic typesetting machines via monitors in the newspapers' editorial offices, where they can, but do not need to, be edited

Initially, many journalists regarded with scepticism the inevitable, and no doubt in the long-term also cost-saving, advent of electronic equipment in editorial offices, which since 1990 has taken place in East Germany too. They:

— feared that working at computer screens would overtax them and therefore demanded that working time at the computer be restricted to four hours per day;
— foresaw a risk that publishers might one day for financial reasons pass copy unedited for technical production;
— were worried about having to take on work which by its nature should be carried out by technical staff.

Initially, technical problems and instinctive disinclination made it difficult for publishers to introduce computerised text systems. Everyone has since bidden farewell to lead, which stamped the profession of newspaper journalists and typesetters for over 500 years, and introduced electronic page layout. More than two third of permanently employed newspaper journalists now' work at computer screens.

The editorial offices which shape the content of German newspapers and magazines employ different numbers of staff, depending on the circulation and significance of the publication, ranging:

— from sometimes just a few for a regional paper or specialist journal.
— to extensive staffs spread across several departments in the case of large press undertakings.

FRANKFURTER ALLGEMEINE ZEITUNG employs around 150 male and female journalists in its central office alone, plus over 500 freelancers in Germany and abroad. DER SPIEGEL, for example, has over 200 journalists working in the main editorial office and in its other offices in many towns in Germany and the rest of the world, plus another 100 employees in the documentation department, and STERN magazine has just about 300 journalists, correspondents, photographers, documentation and layout staff, while the daily DIE WELT has over 100 journalists.

The population in West Germany does not entertain a very high opinion of journalists. A survey conducted by the institut fur Demoskopie in Allensbach showed that only 13 per cent of the West German population include journalists among the people they most respect. Doctors (named by 77 %), engineers (60 %), clergymen (47 %), miners (42 %) and judges (39 %) all enjoy much higher regard. Herbert Riehl-Heyse of SUDDEUTSCHE ZEITUNG speaks from experience when in this context he observes: "If a German journalist longs for certain approval from his public, the best thing for him to do is to tell people how the status of his profession, or at least a substantial part of it, has gone to the dogs. Oh well, say the readers and viewers, at least he realise it himself" [H. Riehl-Heyse: Bestellte Wahrheiten (Truths to Order). Kindler Verlag, Munich, 1989, p. 16].

Presumably this low opinion is connected with the fact that

- — journalists often criticise, and therefore seem to be running the country and people down.
- — the working methods and behaviour of a few is seen as typical of all ("the racing reporter"),
- — the benefit which, after all, their work creates for everyone in a democracy, is not as evident as in the case of a doctor or engineer,
- — there is no final examination after the practical training period.

Generalisations are dangerous. Nevertheless, Herbert Riehl-Heyse is not likely to be completely wrong in referring to the dubious nature and credibility of reports written by journalists who accept travel invitations: "I will not go into this aspect in detail, if only because I have unfortunately much too seldom had the pleasure of being invited on those famous trips to the South Seas which colleagues who have been on them for the first time rave about for months afterwards—though they can't decide whether they should enthuse more about the uninterrupted streams of Planter's Punch or about delightful Tahitian girls knocking on the hotel room door—unfortunately, one's neighbour's—in the middle of the night as part of the programme. Though these things are not usually mentioned in their reports, it is quite obvious that they had a good time.... Ever since I found out what usually happens on these Press trips and who usually pays for them and compares them with real life, I prefer to rely on the information of friends before I go on holiday" [H. Riehl-Heyse: Bestellte Wahrheiten (Truths to Order), Kindler Verlag, Munich 1989, p. 82/83].

The journalist's privileged position finds expression on many different planes, for example

— legally through the right to information from official sources and the right of the Press not to have to name information sources in court,
— at social functions through the above-average attention paid to journalists by people in public life,
— in the process of development of opinion and will, through the opportunity to communicate highly personal opinions via the media possibly even to an audience or readership of millions.

The Tables 7.1 & 7.2 shows that most West German journalists find their profession attractive because it is varied. Fortunately, though not quite so markedly as ten years ago, the motive of exposing shortcomings in society and being able to criticise them still plays an overwhelming role for many, especially for East German journalists, as the Table 7.3 demonstrates.

Table 7.1

Attractions of Journalism in Print and Broadcasting Media

(figures in percentages)*

Answers to the question "judging as of today, which of these points do you personally find particularly attractive about your profession?"

	West German Journalists total		*West German Journalists in the print media*		*West German Journalists in the broad-casting media*	
	1980/81	*1992*	*1980/81*	*1992*	*1980/81*	*1992*
1	2		3		4	
opportunity to expose and criticise shortcomings	70	67	75	69	66	65
opportunity to write and formulate	68	75	68	75	70	74

(Contd.)

1	*2*		*3*		*4*	
varied, exciting element of the profession	64	82	62	83	68	83
professional freedom, being able to decide tasks and topics for oneself	64	68	63	70	66	65
meeting interesting people	55	67	59	67	50	69
opportunity to speak up for values and ideas	42	49	46	48	36	51
opportunity to develop interests further	38	63	40	63	35	63
lack of routine	37	45	37	42	36	50
opportunity to communicate my convictions to many others	34	34	38	36	30	31
being one of the first to know what's really going on	32	51	31	50	30	54
opportunity to influence political decision-making	29	30	31	34	28	21
interesting people one works with, colleagues	22	56	21	56	23	55
I enjoy working under pressure	20	36	20	34	20	39
because it's somehow gratifying to see one's name and work in print	17	39	15	37	21	43
good earnings opportunities	13	43	11	45	17	43
journalists' standing	2	10	3	10	1	9
good future prospects	1	24	1	25	2	21

* More than one answer may be given.

[*Source:* Beate Schneider, Klaus Schonbach, Dieter Sturzebecher: *Westdeutsche Journalisten im Vergleich: Jung. professionell und mit SpaB an der Arbeit*, (A comparative study of West German journalists: young, professional, and enthusiastic about their work), in: PUBLIZISTIK, No. 1/1993].

Table 7.2

Attractions of Journalism

(Figures in percentages)*

Answers to the question: "judging as of today, which of these points do you personally find particularly attractive about your profession. Please state in each case whether you find the respective point attractive about your profession or not."

	Journalists in West Germany	*Journalists in East Germany living in the GDR prior to 1989*	*Journalists in East Germany living in the FRG prior to 1989*
1	2	3	4
meeting interesting people	67	97	94
varied/exciting aspect of the work	82	96	98
opportunity to write and formulate	74	94	92
opportunity to expose and criticise shortcomings	67	93	94
professional freedom, being able to decide tasks and topics for oneself	68	85	90
opportunity to develop interests further	63	85	74
being one of the first to know what is really going on	51	83	77
working with interesting people, colleagues	56	82	70
opportunity to speak up for values and ideas	49	81	65
getting about a lot	55	78	83
lack of routine	45	74	70
good earning opportunities	43	73	59
opportunity to communicate my convictions to many others	34	61	39
secure job	31	60	32
opportunity to specialise	31	56	38

(Contd.)

1	2	3	4
you enjoy working under pressure of deadlines	36	54	56
because it is gratifying to see one's name/work in print	39	50	53
good future prospects	24	48	32
opportunity to influence political decisions	30	47	47
journalists' standing	10	42	10

* More than one factor may be named.

[*Source:* Beate Schneider, Klaus Schonbach, Dieter Sturzebecher: *Journalisten im vereinigten Deutschland* (Journalists in united Germany), in PUBLIZISTIK, No. 3/1993].

Journalists' Credibility

In the 1960s and 1980s far more viewers, listeners and readers than today answered "yes" to the question whether television, radio and newspapers provide truthful reports and "always present things as they really are." There are many reasons for this loss of credibility, but the people with an active role in the media, journalists, must also question themselves self-critically about their own contribution to this development. The constitution and special laws give them the right to expose misdemeanours and failings, and journalists are rightly accused of lack of credibility if in judging the behaviour of others they apply a standard which they do not regard as applicable to themselves.

It is horrifying that one third of West German journalists under the age of 35 consider it justifiable "to obtain confidential documents by means of cash payments" (see Table 7.3). Thus, for many of them there is nothing wrong in so-called "cheque book" journalism. One can have no great objection to this way of obtaining information if it serves to bring to light behaviour by public figures which is detrimental to the common good. Naturally, journalists who boast of their disclosure should also publicly admit that this was not the result of their research but that they were aided by circumstances such as a third person's thirst for revenge or the bulging wallet of their company. DER

SPIEGEL, for example, paid 165,000 marks to its informant about "Barschel's dirty tricks," *i.e.*, the machinations of Uwe Barschel, as Prime Minister of Schleswig-Holstein, against his opponent Bjorn Engholm.

Table 7.3

The Legitimacy of Controversial Investigation Methods, Classified by Age Group

(Figures in percentages)*

Answers to the question: "Because it is often difficult to come by important information, journalists often resort to unusual methods. Which of the following methods do you consider justifiable and which would you never approve of? Figures refer to the number who consider a given method to be justifiable.

	Journalists in West Germany				*Journalists in East Germany living in the GDR prior to 1989*				*Journalists in East Germany living in the FRG prior to 1989*		
	Total	*18-34*	*35-44*	*44+*	*Total*	*18-34*	*35-44*	*44+*	*Total*	*18-34*	*34+*
1		2				3				4	
if in their articles journalists refer to sources which they do not name	17	68	76	70	74	80	70	73	79	82	73
as a journalist to use secret government documents	75	75	80	72	65	71	65	53	94	93	95
to work in a firm or organisation in order to gain access to internal information	46	53	56	24	43	57	34	30	54	59	45
to give a false identity	28	37	32	11	27	40	19	14	34	38	28
to use hidden microphones and cameras	22	30	20	13	25	33	20	19	31	35	25
to pretend to have another opinion or attitude in order to gain an informant's trust	39	53	36	21	23	36	18	9	55	65	38

(Contd.)

1		2				3			4		
to obtain confidential documents by paying	28	36	28	17	15	22	10	8	31	40	18
for journalists to publish private papers, such as letters or photos of someone, without their consent	10	11	10	8	4	5	4	4	11	9	15
to put informants under pressure	6	9	4	2	3	5	1	1	13	13	13
to promise informants that you will keep their information secret, and to break the promise	3	4	2	2	1	3	1	0	4	4	3

* more than one factor may be named.

[*Source:* Beate Scheider, Klaus Schonbach, Dieter Sturzebecher: *Journalisten im vereinigten Deutschland* (Journalists in united Germany), in PUBLIZISTIK, No. 3/1993].

The question of credibility was particularly topical when considering whether journalists in the new federal states who had previously worked as journalists in East Germany should continue to be employed.

Whether against their will or out of conviction, one thing is sure: most wrote and broadcast in accordance with SED doctrine. There were niches, for example in church journalism, in local reporting, in the radio news programme, and from time to time there was also some loosening up and television programmes which were supposed to demonstrate liberal attitudes, yet it remained a media system guided and controlled from above. Thus after the political changes in the East Germany the GDR journalists were faced with the question of where they stood with regard to their past.

In contrast to West German journalists, who after 1945 largely suppressed this subject or tried to gloss over their doings during the Nazi system. East German journalists took a critical look at their work in the Ulbricht and Honecker eras. Naturally—like the politicians—many of them now suddenly portrayed themselves as victims rather than perpetrators. Others, on the other hand, expressed themselves along the lines of Henryk Goldiberg in JUNGE WELT:

"We were all collaborators. Each in his own way and with his own motive. And why don't we clear this up too my article was not written by Joachim Herrmann or by a national or party executive, nor by the Central Council of the FDJ. I wrote it myself, with my own fingers and my own head. And don't say: under protest. For under the articles there were names, not protests.... And don't say, friends, we had to. We had to, if we wanted to keep on writing. But did we have to want to keep on writing? We ourselves crossed out things which we knew would be crossed out... I know it is hard to reconcile this with mature self-assurance and our understanding of ourselves as critical journalists, but we should still consider it possible that when the day of reckoning comes as to who and what caused this country to change so drastically, people will not be thinking particularly of us. Or they will, but in a way which we won't much like" [Reprinted in: RUNDFUNK UND FERNSEHEN, No. 3/1990, p. 428].

West German politicians and journalists have sometimes tried to bar journalists and reporters, presenters and commentators who previously worked in the GDR from continued employment in, for example, public broadcasting authorities, condemning them with blanket judgments such as "Reds" and "camp followers". In a controversial questionnaire campaign the head of radio at the "institution" (GDR radio and TV) asked for information about Stasi activities and journalists' functions in parties and mass organisations. For the sake of the credibility of journalists in the new federal states it was surely right:

— to expiate legally relevant guilt,
— to replace Stasi collaborators,
— to keep informers and those who justified all excesses of the SED regime away from desks, microphones and screens.

On the other hand the right which others lay claim to must also apply to journalists: the right to make political mistakes. And those who now pass judgment on the people who were convinced supporters of Stalinist-type socialism should consider when making their assessment how they themselves would have acted and the changes that have since taken place in the content of the East German media.

Journalists and Publishers

In 1951 the newspaper publishers' organisations and the Deutscher Journalisten-Verband came to a collective agreement for full-time and permanently-employed journalists in newspaper publishing houses. According to this "the publisher must in the contract of employment commit the journalist to adhere to guidelines on the fundamental stance of the paper."

The owner's right

— to prescribe the general, political, economic and cultural line of his publication;
— and to bind the journalists to this in their contracts of employment arises from the private-sector economic structure of the Press in the Federal Republic.

Express restrictions of this kind on the statement of opinion are also allowed in the light of Basic Law. Press freedom does not go so far that a journalist who at the start of his employment committed himself contractually to presenting Christian viewpoints may subsequently start presenting atheist views in the newspaper.

Since it is very difficult in individual concrete cases to draw the boundary between determining the line, which the publisher is allowed to do, and prescribing the text, which he is barred from doing, as a rule a journalist is dependent on the goodwill of the owner. In other words: he can only hope that the latter does not meddle too much.

Beginnings of Internal Press Freedom

In order to protect internal Press freedom and journalists' independence better than hitherto, and to prevent anonymous business and other forces from misusing the Press as an instrument, journalists and media policymakers proposed, *inter alia*,

— curtailing the publishers' right of disposal over the means of production and organising the Press on a non-private-capitalist basis in the form of trusts or public bodies like broadcasting authorities,

— giving the journalists' a financial stake in the publishing house,
— expanding journalists' rights and granting them participation in deciding all questions of editorial staff policy and in the case of a fundamental change in the political stance of the newspaper.

In Dusseldorf in 1972 the Press law department of the German Lawyers' Conference resolved among other things: "In order to ensure a free Press and free comprehensive information and opinion-forming, it is advisable legally to regulate the internal order of Press enterprises.... In particular, the minimum legal regulations should provide that it is up to the publisher to determine the fundamental journalistic stance of the newspaper. Within the framework of the fundamental stance of the newspaper, the publisher may, by agreement with editorial staff in the case of newly-emerging questions of fundamental significance going beyond the current events of the day and having an effect on the journalistic line of the newspaper, determine the newspaper's position. All editorial staffing changes may only be undertaken with the consent of the editor after hearing the views of the relevant head of department and with the consent of the editorial staff representatives. The editor is selected by the publisher after briefing and hearing the views of editorial staff representatives. Since the editor needs the particular confidence of the editorial staff, he may neither be appointed nor dismissed if a majority of the editorial staff representatives are against it."

The SPD-FDP federal government wanted to put some of these ideas into effect in the Press Law Framework Bill, but its autumn 1974 draft met with criticism from all sides:

– spokesmen of the journalists' unions found fault because the bill only allowed journalists the right to a hearing on staffing and factual questions and not a right of veto, and because journalists were to have only an entitlement to increased compensation if they left the newspaper because the publisher had disregarded the will of a two-thirds majority of editorial staff representatives in the case of a change in fundamental journalistic stance or appointment of the editor.

– publishers saw their present position of power severely shaken simply by the proposed requirements. Most of them completely rejected the idea of legal regulation of internal Press freedom.

After this negative response the SPD and FDP made no further attempt to fulfil the promise made in their media papers that they would legally regulate internal Press freedom. Since the journalists' organisations were also unable to agree with the publishers' associations on an appropriate collective agreement, the owners continue to be masters of the house.

The hope of many people that with the reorganisation of the Press in East Germany earlier attempts at reform would be taken up again, proved to be an illusion. Only the Brandenburg Press Act, which at an early stage of drafting provided for editorial staff participation, stipulates that editorial charters may be agreed. In the meantime some Press enterprises have voluntarily conceded editorial charters. Some examples of newspapers with agreements of this kind are MANNHEIMER MORGEN, SUDDEUTSCHE ZEITUNG and RHEIN-ZE TUNG (Koblenz).

The editorial charter of STERN magazine stipulated:

— "The publisher will not appoint or dismiss an editor if two thirds of the editorial staff committee vote against it."
— The editorial staff elect the seven members of the editorial staff committee.
— "Personnel changes in the circle of deputy editors, departmental heads and political staff of STERN may not be undertaken against the opposition of two thirds of the committee." That said, in rejecting a proposal the committee may only refer to the political stance of the magazine ("free-democratic" and "progressive-liberal") as laid down in the charter.

At the end of 1977 the Bertelsmann Group, majority shareholders in publishers Gruner + Jahr, protested about a critical STERN article on German capital investment abroad. Thereupon Henri Nannen, the editor, dismissed his left-wing liberal deputy, Manfred Bissinger, who was responsible for the article—without beforehand listening to the views of the editorial staff committee, and in the face of their unanimous opposition.

Since the beginning of 1980, when the publisher's board of directors terminated the charter, there has been no editorial staff committee. The editorial staff demanded that it be reconstituted when the head of the house published the Hitler diaries without consulting them and appointed new editors. Negotiations on an editorial charter for STERN and the other publications of the group collapsed in 1986. The journalists regarded as inadequate the publisher's offer to establish a duty to consult on the appointment of the editor rather than a right of veto.

Many of the arguments put forward by publishers against journalists having a right to participate have been refuted by Wolfgang Hoffmann-Riem and Udo Branahl in their study *Redaktionsstatute in der Bewahrung* (Editorial Charter Put to the Test) [(Materials on Interdisciplinary Media Research 2, Nomos Verlagsgesellschaft, Baden-Baden 1975, 365 pages]. They questioned the managerial staff, editors, works council representatives, departmental heads and journalists of some large regional daily papers and found that:

— editorial committees are by no means fighting units which stir up conflicts. However they are capable of giving encouragement to journalists in disputes.
— participation in editorial decisions does not impair the editorial staff's ability to work nor delay decisions through hours of discussions.
— on the contrary, according to 14 per cent of those questioned, it can as a direct result enhance motivation to perform.

At the end of August 1976 the SPD weekly VORWARTS entered into a collective agreement with the Industriegewerkschaft Druck and Papier, the printing and paper workers' union, which came to an end in 1989 when the paper folded. According to this agreement, the publisher could

— change the newspaper's basic stance only with the agreement of a majority of the editorial committee,
— only appoint or dismiss an editor if this body did not oppose it.

If no agreement could be reached, owner and editorial staff were to form a mediation committee with equal representation from both sides, whose decisions would be binding, and onto which both sides together would elect a neutral member. The composition of these new set-ups left it open as to who should have the final say in case of conflict—the publisher or the editorial staff.

Works council representatives on the committee had equal voting rights. According to the Works Councils Act, works councils in Press enterprises have in principle only limited rights to participate in decisions on the appointment and dismissal of journalists. They may only take into account social reasons and not those relating to the content and make-up of the newspaper or magazine. These provisions are laid down in the paragraph of the Act entitled "Tendenzschutz," which upholds an owner's right to require that editorial staff follow a particular line ($ 118).

The Federal Constitutional Court holds the view that it would not be reconcilable with the basic right to Press freedom for a works council to be allowed to influence the determination or realisation of a newspaper's tendency, for this would be an "outside" influence.

The editorial charters introduced to date do not go as far as the demand which is put forward from time to time for the technical and business field to be strictly separated from the journalistic field. In that case:

— publishers would be no more than dealers in printed paper, and
— journalists would have sole responsibility for the printed word and for editorial staff appointments.

In the owners' view a regulation of this kind is undesirable in that it puts at risk the continued existence of the Press undertaking as a business. On the other hand, it is scarcely credible that journalists would be interested in wilfully or irresponsibly endangering the basis of their own livelihood. Even if they are in possession of such rights, in the long term they cannot keep producing a newspaper which the market rejects. Even so, it might be expected that editorial staff teams could be more inclined to reflect on their public duty than individual publishers, who are concerned with profit maximisation.

In order to loosen up the much-criticised hierarchical structure of the broadcasting bodies and improve the position of the individual programme maker, back in the 1970s many of them were already demanding that they, too, should have editorial charters. In 1973 NORD-DEUTSCHER RUNDFUNK (NDR) was the first broadcasting station in the Federal Republic to be granted such a charter. It has since been followed by most of the others. It guarantees journalists rights to be informed and to a hearing in the case of conflicts. Article 4, for example, states: " If a programme contribution by the journalist responsible, which is intended for broadcasting, is cancelled or altered in a way which distorts its meaning, the person who took the decision must justify it to the editorial committee if the author or journalists putting together the programme so request." This means that in future those responsible can still cancel broadcasts: however, they are now obliged to justify such measures if the people concerned so wish.

The charter also grants programme collaborators rights to information and to a hearing if the programme structure is altered, and in certain personnel matters. However, it does not restrict the decision-making powers of the supervisory bodies or the director-general.

individual programme makers back in the 1970s many of them were already demanding that they should have editorial charters. In 1972 NORDDEUTSCHER RUNDFUNK (NDR) was the first broadcasting station in the Federal Republic to be granted such a charter. It has since been followed by most of the others. It guarantees journalists' rights to be informed and to a hearing in the case of conflict. Article 4, for example, states: "If a programme contribution by the journalist responsible, which is intended for broadcasting, is cancelled or altered in a way which distorts its meaning, the person who took the decision must justify it to the editorial committee or the author or journalists putting together the programme on request." This means that in future those responsible can still cancel broadcasts, however, they are now obliged to justify such measures if the people concerned so wish.

The charter also grants programme collaborators rights to information and to a hearing if the programme structure is altered, and in certain personnel matters. However, it does not restrict the decision-making powers of the supervisory bodies or the director-general.

8

Mass Media and National Unity

Sometimes as I reached a gathering, writes Jawahar Lal Nehru in 'The Discovery of India', "a great roar of welcome would greet me : Bharat Mata Ki Jai—'Victory to Mother India'. I would ask them unexpectedly what they meant by that cry, who was this Bharat Mata, Mother India, whose victory they wanted? My question would assume them and surprise them, and then not knowing exactly what to answer, they would look at each other and at me. I persisted in my questioning. At last a vigorous Jat, wedded to soil from immemorial generations, would say that it was the Dharti, the good earth of India, that they meant. What earth? Their particular village patch, or all the patches in the district or province, or in the whole of India? And so question and answer went on, till they would ask me impatiently to tell them about it. I would endeavour to do so and explain that India was all this that they had thought, but it was much more. The mountains and the rivers of India, and the forests and broad fields which gave us food, were dear to us, but what counted ultimately were the people of India, people like them and me, who were spread out all over this vast land. Bharat Mata, Mother India, I told them, you are in a manner yourselves Bharat Mata, and as this idea slowly soaked into their brains, their eyes would light up as if they had made a great discovery," This was adult education in action leading towards national integration, and the media in use was interpersonal communication.

Social integration is a built-in component of national integration. Our society is hierarchical and stratified, and there is lack of vertical mobility in it. The different classes, particularly the rich and the poor, and the educated and the uneducated are separated by varying degrees of social distances which are tending to widen. The various religious groups are also separated by emotional and psychological distance. I was a student of the Tyandakura Middle English School, in Cuttack district in Orissa, between 1939 and 1942. We used to begin our school activities with a prayer at 10 o'clock sharp in the morning. There used to be two rows of students facing each other and separated by a distance of about 15 feet. One row was meant for the Hindu children and the other for Muslim children. The Hindu children used to sing a song in Oriya, composed by Madhusudan Rao, and its first line was "Akhila Brahmandapati Mo Jeevana Swamy", meaning "Oh Lord, you are the king of the entire universe, as well as my Lord". The opening line of the song coming from the Muslim children used to be "Yahan vi too, Wohan vi too, Zamin Teri, Falak Tera", meaning "you are here, you are there, the land is yours and the heaven is yours." How similar were the themes of the two devotional songs! As a child I was curious to know why two different songs, one in Oriya and the other in Urdu, having almost the same theme, were used by us in offering our prayers to God, particularly when all ot us were students of one and the same school. Why could not we use one song, or better still why could not all of us sing the two songs together? This was the question which was constantly in my mind. One day, when I was in the sixth class, (1949), I went to our Urdu teacher, a learned man, popularly known as "Moulvi Sir", and told him about the question which was uppermost in my mind. He thought for a moment and said that he had no objection to the singing of the Oriya and the Urdu songs for prayer, provided this was all right with our "Pundit Sir", a learned Brahmin, who used to teach us Oriya. Pundit Sir was very strict with us. I gathered enough courage to approach him and when he heard my proposal, which had the endorsement of the Moulvi, he was visibly red with anger and scolded me saying "Vidharmi, get out". I ran away, because I saw that the cane was already in his right hand,

and was perhaps equally or more angry at him. But then, the agony of a defenceless school child had to be suppressed. This was in 1941 and during my subsequent two years at the school, the Oriya song was sung by the Hindu children and the Urdu song by the Muslim children. Today, that school is a high school, but the same songs are used in prayer—the Hindu children singing the Oriya song and the Muslim children the Urdu song. Once in 1958 or so, I had spoken about this episode in the Old Boys Association Meeting of the school making a forceful plea of my childhood proposal which was approved by our "Moulvi Sir" and rejected by our 'Pundit Sir', but it had the same fate. Everybody present at the meeting seemed to enjoy the episode, but none did anything about it. In writing about this today I not only express my utter personal defeat in not being able to win over my own friends, but emphatically say that even after all these years of Independence, we have not paid any respect to our Constitution, which is secular, and we have engineered a milieu which works against a multi-religious society we have. What moral right do we have when we say that all our social ills had their genesis in the colonial system? The problems of social integration are also the problems of national integration.

In an article entitled "India: One and Indivisible", published in The Statesman, in 1981, K.R. Malkani had said: " India displays great ethnic and cultural diversity. Viewing it against the homogeneous—I almost said homogenized—Western States, one may wonder how far this diversity is consistent with national unity. But this is what India always was. And this is what India always will be. It has been—and will be—one, in spite of this diversity. The Indian idea of unity is not uniformity but harmony". There is a harmony in our diversity and there is a thread of unity, which encircles all of us professing different religious, speaking a number of languages and belonging to different States. This is a virtue which is inherent in our situation; its values goes on increasing if the people realise its importance and practise the ideals contained in it.

Ethnic Diversity

National integration is a question of the mind and heart, because one has to realise that he belongs to the great country of ours having cultural and ethnic diversity. Such a realisation can only give rise to a faith that whatever be one's religion or language, he is an Indian first and Indian last. Ours is a democratic society and our Constitution is secular. We cannot afford to have passive, indifferent, ignorant and idle citizens as members of our society. Each one of us must know our neighbourhood, our village, our district, our State and our country in order to be able to identify and appreciate the thread of unity, amidst diversity, which binds all of us. Without this complete awareness national integration is not possible.

Communication media have a key role to play in creating such an awareness in each and everyone of us. As the MacBride Commission put it: "If communication is considered in its broadest sense, not only as the exchange of news and messages but as an individual and collective activity embracing all transmissions and sharing of ideas, facts and data, its main functions in any social system may be identified as the following": Information, Socialisation, Motivation, Debate and Discussion, Education, Cultural Promotion, Entertainment and Integration. Integration, as a function of communication, means "the provision to all persons, groups and nations of access to the variety of messages which they need in order to know and understand each other and to appreciate each other's living conditions, viewpoints and aspirations."

India, a country "with sub-continental dimensions, having multi-lingual and multi-religious societies, is faced with a dual challenge of integrating the various cross-sections of her people and at the same time ensuring the preservation and expression of diversity." Communication has a role to play in this national endeavour, and the modern communication technology comes in handy. As the Working Group on Software for Doordarshan emphatically put it : "Modern communication technology can be tapped for playing an 'integrating role' within the framework of sharing and inter-dependence. There is no technological determinism or inherent technological compulsion for one-sided centralisation or one-sided decentralisation. Integration implies that smaller units are knit together on an equal basis. Thus we avoid a situation when stronger units impinge over the weaker units through centralisation or different units get fragmented and isolated from each other and get involved in a vicious circle of parochialism and stagnation via atomisation." According to the Working Group, the model of communication required for the Indian conditions should be one which is integrative, inter-active and participatory; and such a model is not only made possible, but is facilitated by the "very flexible and dynamic character of modern communication technology." This philosophy of communication should be the basic tenet of our National Communication Policy, which is an urgent need.

The Education Commission (1964-66), in its report 'Education and National Development', observes: "Social and national integration is crucial to the creation of a united country, which is an essential pre-condition for all progress. It has a varied content—economic, social, cultural and political—and its different facets are interconnected. It needs:

— a confidence in the nation's future;
— a continuous rise in the standard of living for the masses and the reduction in unemployment and in the disparities in development between different parts of the country, all of which are essential to promote a sense of equality of opportunity in political, economic and social terms;
— a deep sense of the values of and obligations of citizenship and a growing identification of the people not with sectional loyalties, but with the nation as a whole;
— assurance of a good and impartial administration, equal treatment for every citizen, in fact and not merely in law, based on the integrity of the public services; and
— mutual understanding and respect for the culture, traditions and ways of life of different sections of the nation."

Therefore, it is evident that social and national integration will have to be tackled on several fronts including education and communication. The entire gamut of our national endeavour has to play its role for achieving social and national integration. Removal of social and economic inequalities assumes the topmost priority in this task, because inequality of any kind goes against the very foundations of social and national integration.

Over the past several years, everywhere in the world, the

persuading power of mass media has been over sold. It has been realised, to the mutual advantage of the communicator and media, that the role of mass media is more indirect and contributory. Communication experts are now positive that very seldom is the mass media a powerful and direct stimulus to development. Most individuals get new ideas through inter-personal communication. It is not uncommon to find a regular radio listener ignorant about current affairs. A village women, known to me, who is very fond of listening to radio, was under the impression (perhaps she still is!) that the late Feroze Gandhi was an adopted son of Mahatma Gandhi. There is another woman in the same village, who is very fond of listening to songs and plays broadcast over radio, but when it comes to developmental communication, whether broadcast directly or through songs and dramas, her exposure is practically nil. In any communication situation, the audience is the king. And particularly development communication should be viewed as a process that includes the audience, its needs, planning, production, presentation and feedback. Several media carrying the same message give the maximum effect. I do not want to suggest that communication is not powerful. Rather, I would like to say that it is powerful, but not all-powerful. As the MacBride Commission observes: "It cannot transform the tenor of interpersonal relationships nor the substance of social life. Communication is most effective, when its impact is strengthened by other social factors and the messages conveyed are already reflected in public opinion or in emerging interests. As Aesop said of the tongue, all facility in communication can be used for better or for worse. It is the responsibility of the communication policy-makers and professionals to see that such risks are limited and distortions corrected. But in all societies there are other forces to be reckoned with that cannot be reduced to a state of passivity."

Our own communication situation also presents a paradox. India has developed a broad-scale communication system and has built up potential resources in this field. In spite of having a boom in the print media and the expansions in our national radio and television systems made possible by INSAT, we come across many rural areas in the country which do not have access to the modern mass media. There are innumerable villages in India where a written or printed word is a rare thing to see. This is a common phenomenon in many Third World countries. As Yogesh Atal says: "In terms of communication, the vast continent of Asia presents a highly differentiated profile. It is a continent where jumbo jets have not been able to replace the bullock carts, where electricity has not fully replaced the kerosene lamp, where television is still stationed in the cities, where the empress of poverty continues to occupy its enormous citadel." It is also a fact that in the rural areas of India, as well as in other Third World countries, there is a distinct system of communication which caters to the basic needs of the people. Such a system of communication uses inter-personal and traditional media for information, education and entertainment. These media are decentralised and participatory and the messages conveyed through them are situation specific and culture specific.

The methods and media of communication which can bring in and promote national integration have been in operation in our society since long. According to Humayun Kabir, "Custom and folklore, proverbs and fables, mythology and scriptures have been passed from generation to generation and to some extent made up for the lack of teaching through the written world." Our festivals and fairs have had an educational purpose. "The public readings of Puranas with popular interpretations,", says Sardar Pannikar, "the Harikathas and bhajans, folk art, exhibitions and numerous other institutions, which existed and do exist even today were meant primarily for social education." The contents of national integration in the present context can be woven into these media. Our traditional folk drama forms can be used with advantage for promoting national integration. The play "Dharamshala", produced by the Song and Drama Division of the Ministry of Information and Broadcasting, is an excellent example of treating a difficult theme like national integration in a drama form with romance, suspense and humour.

Through the modern electronic media of communication, it is possible to hear and see one entertainment form in another linguistic area. The viewers in Orissa can see the Kathakali of Kerala and the audience in Karnataka can enjoy the Odisi of Orissa, thanks to the potentialities of TV. Having INSAT, the ever-increasing potentialities of radio and television pose challenges before the software producers for meaningful programmes. In our rich heritage, there are plenty of unidentified cultural resources like poems, stories, songs, festivals and fairs, which when properly utilised, can promote national integration. Radio, television and films will have to explore and utilise these cultural resources.

Modern communication technology has made it possible for audio and video cassettes to be used in a non-broadcast mode of communication having decentralised production facilities. Technological feasibility alone is not enough; it has to be matched with distribution facilities and availability of technical infrastructure and production personnel.

The contents of social and national integration can be easily woven into literacy, functionality and awareness. This means that the need-based curriculum has to include the essential components of national integration. It is during the post-literacy and the continuing education phase that national integration can be promoted through post-literacy and follow-up books, bulletins for neoliterates, rural newspapers, posters, personal and group discussions and other available media. The printed media of communication has enormous possibilities to promote national integration. One could possibly start from the village itself, where people from different communities live together sharing each other's joys and sorrows and maintaining the unity and solidarity of the village.

Sensitive Role

The press in India has an extremely sensitive role to play in promoting national integration. How it has been able to play the role during the past decades is a debatable point; but, its role and responsibility as the Fourth Estate have to be always kept in view by the society in which it operates. Each has to perform the 'watchdog' function in respect of the other.

Both media and channel can also be misused to play a negative role. Once travelling in a DTC bus I saw large stickers fixed inside the bus, which read: "Garb Se Kaho Hum Hindu Hai", meaning, "say with pride that I am a Hindu", and I was surprised, because, I did not expect to be exposed to such a message while travelling in a Government carrier, which was the channel to that message. The stickers must be there in that bus even today. And the bus, belonging to a government organisation plies in the capital city of the country. Even in matters of programming, one finds a rather disproportionate weightage given to one religion in AIR and Doordarshan. In the opinion of the Working Group on Software for Doordarshan, "The political leadership in a democracy has a very great responsibility as the guardian of the Constitution of India and as the elected representative of the people. It can through a dialogue and interaction with the communicator rather than through the fiat of authority contribute immensely to the sensitisation of the communicator to the problems, needs and the aspirations of the people. It can expose the communicator to the grassroots view of life in contrast to the ivory tower studio-centred view of the average communicator who has no opportunities for field work among the people. It can also make the communicator aware of the creative tension involved in the situation when vast expectations and hopes are aroused by the political process among the underprivileged and the deprived and yet those expectations and hopes continue to be thwarted by resistance of dominant interest groups having a privileged position in the inherited social structure. An enlightened political leadership can indicate the new dimensions and possibilities of software planning in a rapidly changing and vastly complex society like India".

It is true that communication induces social change, but it is also equally true that social action can accelerate absorption and retention of messages coming from communication media. Inter-caste and inter-religious marriages on intra-state and inter-state basis have to be encouraged to be the order of the day, because these alone can bring in lasting national integration. Indonesia, a country of thousands of islands, has already set the example in this. "Vinneka Tungallika", the Indonesian motto of unity in diversity, is being practised in the country both in letter and spirit. Respect for each other's language, culture and custom lays the foundation for national integration. Elasticity in food habits, which enables one to like the food of another region encourages national integration. It is also promoted by inter-state tourism.

Tourism in India is sold and promoted through an elaborate strategy of marketing and advertising; and the same selling points could also be utilised in promoting national integration. The defunct inter-University youth Festival should be revived as an urgent necessity. Youth choirs, like the Calcutta youth Choir led by Ruma Guhathakurta, should be organised over the entire length and breadth of the country. When we sing in chorus the folk songs and mass songs in various languages of India, we develop love and affection towards the languages and the people speaking those languages. Chorus singing has magical effect on the participants, and this one can say from one's own personal experience.

The village community in ancient India functioned with an economy of peace and a society based on welfare, only because of the fact that there were many village institutions to protect and accelerate the potential growth of society. These institutions fulfilled the social, economic, educational and cultural needs of the village. The vacuum created by the disintegration and disappearance of some of these institutions is now to be filled up by the existing institutions. The home, the school, the temple, the mosque, the church, the gurudwara, the panchayat, the co-operative and other associate organisations are to contribute directly for the promotion of national integration. We have paid and are paying a heavy price by killing Gandhiji's Nai Talim or Basic Education, which had sound educational and ethical principles aimed at the growth of social and national integration. It is never too late to make a beginning again by educating the child according to the Gandhian principles of Basic Education, because it would be the only long-term and permanent way of inculcating the values of social and national integration in our children. And then it would be a new India in which all of us as a unified whole will consider themselves as Indians first and Indians last.

9

Television and Social Imperatives

In this paper we wish to consider the problem which faces producers and editors of television programmes, just as it faces creative men and women in other mass media, of keeping in touch with popular feeling and locating the boundaries of popular morality. The problem is experienced acutely in an insular country like Britain where so much of the communications industry is located in a particular region and, particularly, within a few square miles of the capital and major cities.

Within society the attitudes adopted will very widely on any single subject. Somewhere short of the extremes, however, will come the limits of what is generally held to be acceptable. We take popular morality to be the sum of the attitudes which lie within the limits. Some of them will be expressed through the Law, some through institutions of one kind or another, and others by custom and the sense of what is done. We do not accept that, at any time, these limits are immutable. Indeed, we believe it to be the guarantee of society's vitality that they should be constantly under challenge, constantly subject to tests in changing circumstances. There are many people who feel that, today, too many things are changing and that we must stand pat upon the old rules of society in order to survive. We believe this to be quite mistaken and likely to produce the opposite result.

Controversial Areas : Sex and Religion

The subjects we want to consider have both national and private aspects. The first is religion, a form of which is built into our national life and which for long provided one of the main motive-forces for much of the population. The second is sex, a subject on which the views of society as a whole have become progressively fragmented and which disturbs many individuals incapable of forming their own attitudes towards what is permissible in the absence of any collective guidance. Drugs and violence which follow, are more modern phenomena, at least in the sense that attitudes towards them have grown more equivocal. Finally, there is authority, the embodiment of our wish for order in society, a wish that sometimes seems ambivalent, particularly among the young.

We think the power attributed to television, often by people who wish television to give 'a lead', is frequently exaggerated. Setting aside the fact that the lead requested is likely to be backwards, I think the belief, that television has only to breathe a word for its entire audience to carry out its bidding instantly, is an illusion. One explanation for the widespread existence of the illusion is our reluctance to accept that anything on which we spend so much time could be relatively unimportant. The politician who wishes to build up a reputation for responsibility has only to murmur that television is the greatest force for good or evil in our lives to evoke a warm response in any audience. We want it to be true. If it is not, then perhaps television should claim less of our attention. Let it be true, however, and we can spice our prolonged enjoyment with the knowledge that it may actually be doing us good. The combination is one that many Britons find hard to resist.

Since the creation of the British Broadcasting Company in 1922, religious programmes have occupied a privileged position in broadcasting. First in radio and later in television, they have been guaranteed substantial periods of air-time. Considerable sums of money have been provided by the broadcasting authorities for their budgets. The BBC and many of the programme companies employ specialist producers, some laymen, but others priests and ministers. A central Religious Advisory

Council watches over both BBC and Independent Television channels, protecting the interests of the established faiths which lie within the 'mainstream' of religious life in this country. However, there is no evidence that the favoured place of religious programmes in British broadcasting has enabled the churches to arrest the decline of interest in formalised religion throughout the national life. Hours of broadcasting devoted to services and to programmes intended to attract the non-churchgoer to religion have not succeeded in making the message of the churches appear more relevant to the public as listeners or viewers than it does to them in any other capacity. It requires no theory of a group of humanistically-motivated men at the heart of British broadcasting to account for the churches' failure. The same tale of failure is there in the deserted pews and the ageing congregations of parish churches and chapels throughout Britain Broadcasting cannot lead anyone where he does not wish to go.

We think it is possible to demonstrate the same point in a different context. It is now, as we write, little more than a fortnight since Enoch Powell, at Birmingham, made the speech which The Times has since called notorious. The speech proved to be the signal for the public demonstrations against coloured immigrants on a scale which took most people by surprise. The dockers marched on Westminster, so did the Smithfield porters, and the correspondence columns filled with letters praising Mr. Powell for daring to speak the truth. The first ugly rush of prejudice, newly licensed, will not quickly be forgotten, even in the more sober mood which has now followed. We had taken pride in our tolerance and that pride has been shaken to its foundations.

For years, the Press, with radio and television, had made the case for toleration. The liberal line was the accepted line and it was widely assumed within the mass media that this view was shared by a large section of the population. Swingeing sentences had put down the trouble in Noting Hill and therefore there was no reason to believe that prejudice elsewhere could not be put down by reason and firm justice. In any case, perhaps London was not well-informed on the way things were moving in the West Riding or in the Midlands where coloured immigrants were massing. Perhaps, too, it is only with hindsight that one can learn the lessons of Suez which was seen in some quarters of the country as a much-merited bout of Wog-bashing.*

While the mass media took the liberal line, it is clear that the tide in the country at large was flowing in the opposite direction. The flow was not perhaps as strong as it has been made out to be, nor is it perhaps as irreversible as some people might believe it to be, but it existed to an extent which was not reflected by the mass media. Hence, the large measure of surprise which greeted some of the happenings in the week after Mr. Powell's speech.

It can, of course, be argued that, without the efforts of the mass media to spread an understanding of the need for toleration, things would be very much worse as indeed might be said of the cause of religion in Britain. The truth is very difficult to determine, however much one may wish the observations to be true and not merely a comfortable illusion. Little evidence in support of either side in the argument can be found in one piece of research among the consumers of the mass media. In early 1967, the BBC put out a six-part television serial called 'Rainbow City'. It was a deliberate attempt to spread enlightenment among the races, in particular to increase white understanding of immigrants' backgrounds and problems. As such, it was made the subject of a special study by the BBC's Audience Research department.

Only tentative conclusions could be reached. The study had to be undertaken without the full period of preparation which it was hoped would precede it. And even those conclusions have to be viewed in the light of the serial's own shortcomings (which were sufficient for the run to be ended after six episodes and not renewed). Nobody would expect six episodes of a serial to change attitudes formed in the viewing audience over long periods. Perhaps the only significant and hopeful conclusion is that viewers showed greater sympathy towards the better-educated coloured characters in the serial and that younger viewers showed greater sympathy towards coloured characters in general than their elders.

The anti-discrimination measures now passing through Parliament (May 1968) may make significant impressions on current patterns of behaviour towards coloured people. Yet, if

* I remember hearing an audience in Bradford in 1966 respond with enthusiasm to an artist whose whole act consisted of jokes against the Pakistanis then moving into the city in large numbers.

the majority of the population wish to thwart these measures, then their effectiveness is likely to be slight. As on other occasions, the purest motives may product the most disagreeable consequences. If official life is committed to non-discrimination as a policy and much of private life at the same time is conducted on a basis of discrimination, it is likely that the broadcaster is in for a difficult time when he tries to decide what his attitude should be. Popular morality and public morality, that is, official morality, are in danger of parting company on this issue.

We have referred earlier to the existence of stronger feelings outside London on questions of race. Not only, however, on this question, but on others, there is a gulf between the view taken in London and that held outside London. It has considerable consequences.

London has managed to dominate communications in this country to the almost total exclusion of all rivals. There was a time, when Labour returned to power in 1964, when it seemed as if power might be passing out of London. The Planning Councils were set up and a brave new devolved world was in prospect. Almost nothing has come of those hopes. The Planning Councils made a few brave noises and were even given encouragement by Whitehall as long as they constituted no real threat to centralised control. But as soon as the Councils made demands for real power, the grip of London tightened once more. In the mass media, of course, it had never really slackened. In one branch, the Beatles tried to run their affairs from Liverpool. In another, the Manchester Guardian tried to preserve its headquarters away from London. All of them ended up in London, which remained the gathering-point for the talent by which the mass-media survive.

Yet the Londoner who works in the mass media lives a very different life from that of the provincial cousin whom he left behind. Outside London, it is usual for men and women to work in the community in which they live their private lives, often returning to their homes for a midday meal. The Londoner, however, travels many miles to work, leaving his home for hours on end. He is often found living his business life at a social level far above anything he can attain in his private life. In these circumstances, it is not always easy for a man to hold the two parts of his life together, reconciling one with the other. Out of the struggle arises confusion over values. Where this uncertainty exists, there may be a tendency to turn to fashion as a guide. Intellectual fashions change as rapidly as fashions in Carnaby Street and often bear the same relation to reality.

It is, therefore, unwise for broadcasters to base their codes of conduct simply upon the values prevailing in London and even less wise to trust as universal the values of the West End. Equally, however, the values of, say, Galashiels or Norwich have no right to be elevated above all others. They need to be known and to hold their place in the general body of knowledge about views and attitudes which forms the starting-point for the broadcaster's judgments. The extent of his knowledge will often be his only justification.

How is it accumulated? The more articulate members of the public will write, although there is something about the conservationist which drives him more quickly to his typewriter than the iconoclast. Newspapers and magazines show the way in which opinion flows. Today, for example, certain sexual relationships are taken for granted in a way that would have been unthinkable even twenty years ago. This is reflected in many different ways. Then, the broadcasting services have a series of advisory councils, onto which they can invite members of the public. It is probably true that people of this kind will not always have the deepest knowledge of how less-fortunate members of the community live. In particular, with many different sources of information and a variety of diversions, they may not understand the dependence of the majority of their fellows on the mass-media. Indeed, one of the hardest parts of the broadcaster's work is to discover the real response of the greatest number of his listeners and viewers. Communication between them is fragmentary at best and he has to rely on occasional signs that a programme has succeeded in evoking more than the usual reaction. 'That Was the Week That Was', in the dying months of the Conservative Government, managed to touch off a response at almost every level in the country. But programmes of equal impact are rare.

At present, with communication imperfectly established, the broadcaster might be compared, inelegantly, with the animal whose grazing is bordered by an electric fence. From time to time, he nudges up against the fence, gets a shock and withdraws a little. Then, by and by, he returns to find that the fence has been shifted. The area into which he was trying to move has now come within reach.

Nowhere has the electric fence been more frequently in use than over questions of sexual morality. It is dismal to reflect how much time has been spent, in and out of Parliament, on debates about sexual problems. The fight between puritans and permissives has gone backwards and forwards, almost always confined to the middle-aged, while the younger generation has gone on evolving its own patterns of conduct, noticeably neither happier nor more miserable than its predecessors.

Television cannot stand apart from any reflection of contemporary attitudes to an important, but not all-important, aspect of human relationships. Indeed, one might say that, with the decline of a belief in super-natural influences on man's behaviour, it was inevitable that there should be a much greater-interest in relationships between individual human beings. Television, whose language is primarily prose, is a most convenient instrument for examining those relationships, of which sexual relationships form part. Television playwrights have not missed their opportunities.

It is true, as some critics have complained, that many playwrights have chosen to concentrate on the unconventional in sexual relationships and that for each modern play which supports the traditional view of marriage there are several which, to put it no other way, do not. It may also be true that this has resulted in television giving an impression that the unconventional is, if not the normal pattern of behaviour, the one that should be admired and aspired to. If this impression has got abroad, it is not by any means all the fault of television. It is propagated equally on the bookstalls, in the theatre, and in the cinema. Of course, television is much more accessible to many people and, for that reason, what it urges might be expected to produce more widespread results. But there really is very little evidence that television can initiate profound social changes of the order that would be needed to provoke a wholesale abandonment of the institution of marriage and everything that marriage implies in behaviour and attitudes.

It is important that, on this question as on others, the broadcaster should maintain a sense of balance. If he knows that particular views cause deep offence to a section of the audience, then he should make certain that those views are not heard so frequently that they amount to an attack on the audience which disapproves of them. People have a right to expect that their deeply-held convictions will be respected and the constant promotion of contrary convictions amounts to a lack of respect. Of course, people can hold, and do hold, the most outrageous views with the deepest sincerity and it may well be necessary to attack them in the public interest. But before an attack can be developed, it is necessary for the broadcaster, who is endorsing the attack by the act of broadcasting it, to be certain that the public interest, and not merely his own private prejudice, is being served. Nowhere is this certainty more necessary than in matters of sexual morality.

There are now almost two hundred hours of television every week in Britain. Much of this is intended for special groups of viewers, such as programmes for schools or for farmers. But that still leaves about one hundred hours a week which is designed for the general viewer. We know that many viewers watch a great deal of television. It becomes possible, therefore, for mere repetition to give an impression of imbalance. There are obvious problems in trying to eliminate repetition between the BBC's networks and that of the ITA. But the dangers of repetition need to be guarded against within the two BBC channels. Magazine-programmes, which make up their contents at a late stage and base much of their appeal on topicality, can often, by dealing with subjects already dealt with or about to be dealt with in other magazine programmes, can give this kind of false emphasis. It is perhaps possible to illustrate the problem in relation to drug addiction.

For many years, drugs received hardly any mention in BBC programmes. Addiction was then a minor problem and the Home Office, when consulted by the BBC on possible references in programmes to drug-taking, favoured silence. Publicity of any sort, it was thought could lend glamour to drugs and encourage some listeners to acquire the drug-taking habit. Much the same attitude prevailed among the Press.

But then drug-taking began to become more fashionable among young people. Clearly, this was not the fault of radio or television, both of which had largely been silent about drugs for years. The propaganda for LSD and other, more sinister, drugs spread across the Atlantic and met a response which, if sometimes stimulated, was real enough to suggest that the propaganda, and the drugs, fulfilled some need not being fulfilled in other ways. The scale of drug-taking increased until it became news. Television could not avoid reporting the news and interesting itself in a contemporary phenomenon. When, however, drug-addiction came to be discussed in, or was considered as a possible subject for several programmes, there was a very real possibility that too much attention was being paid to drugs. There was a danger that no magazine-programme would be complete without its own collection of 'junkies', confessing all anonymously in careful silhouette. And so, within the BBC, a watch had to be kept to avoid exaggerating a problem which remained, relatively at least, a modest one.

It may be asked whether, without publicity, addiction would have risen in Britain. The answer, since addiction had begun to rise before publicity was given, would seem to be 'yes'. But would the rate of growth have been slower if there had been no publicity? This is much more difficult to answer and, indeed, you can choose between replying 'no' to it and 'no' to the further question whether television, by displaying many addicts who were clearly inadequate and even repellent, has actually discouraged some youngsters who might have become addicts but for these unpalatable examples.

In the same way, it can be asked whether television has contributed to the growth of crime, and in particular the spread of crimes of violence, in Britain. There have been examples of criminals who claimed that they had seen the models for their crimes on television. Even if we regard the models as no more than marginally inspirational, ought television to be providing any models for criminal behaviour which may be turned into violent reality at the expense of the public?

To write simply that violence is a part of life and must therefore be reflected programmes is not an entirely satisfactory answer. Much violence occurs in programmes whose main purpose is entertainment. We believe most people would draw a distinction, even in entertainment programmes, between the formalised violence of Westerns and scenes of contemporary violence where the action is between people with whom the audience more readily identifies itself. There have been instances of excessive violence in Westerns, where the camera has lingered too long on the incidents of a fight or a beating-up, but in general Western violence has become almost ritualised and so more than a stage in the progress of the clearly-established hero to eventual triumph. Violence in a contemporary setting presents other difficulties. That there is plenty of violence in our society is true. That it is the normal pattern of behaviour, indulged in by most people, is not true. The implication in some programmes that violence is normal is therefore an affront to our society as well as threat. The threat is magnified when the violence, by its presentation, is almost extolled. But, with these qualifications, violence, has a part to play in television programmes. In the theatre, violence is a legitimate element in the satisfaction of the audience, whether through the blinding of Gloucester, or, at a different level, in the carnage set afoot by Mrs. Christie. Even if we make allowance for the different nature of the television audience, there seems to be general agreement that violence should be allowed its proper place. That it does not offend our present tastes can be shown in many ways, but perhaps one need point only to the queues for 'Bonnie and Clyde'. They show that we are now willing to take possibly more horrific scenes than we were a few years ago. We doubt if television in Britain has produced anything as violent as came out of Hollywood in that film.

There is another kind of violence to which possibly more concern is due. Not long before we wrote this paper, 'Panorama' had broadcast a report on censorship. One contributor at least had drawn attention to the contrast between our attitude towards sexual display and our attitude towards the violence of newsfilm and the current affairs report. While much energy was devoted to deciding whether anyone would be corrupted by the sight of public hair, none seemed to be given to deciding whether nightly scenes of destruction by guns and aircraft would have the same effect. Sometimes these scenes, when they overstep some mark, do bring protests, although there are usually counterbalancing praises for showing the reality of the situation. If we assume that very few adults today can be unaware of the realities of warfare in Vietnam and elsewhere, we must believe that the praise come from people who have other grounds than a mere wish to view the truth. Some believe, no doubt, that television is the wrong medium for such pictures. Others believe that constant exposure to violence second-hand robs us of our capacity for shock and so dulls the violence when it really confronts us. It might also be argued that scenes of violence destroy our ability to judge impartially between conflicting views. Victory could go, in these circumstances, to the one which produced the best display of atrocity-pictures, whether real or faked.

Between these arguments the broadcaster has to pick his way with little to guide him except an accumulation of case law. He will not have a great deal of help from his audience, although people may indicate when he has offended them. They will not, however, be able to speak for anyone else. As a society, we have still to come to terms with violence. For many years, we managed to avoid a decision. We were strong and there were policemen. Now we are much weaker and the policemen are not always there.

In these circumstances, some people argue that television ought not to question authority in the way that it does. For them, the law, the church, Parliament and the Monarchy, the embodiments of our morality, should be above public debate. Any channel which permits a challenge to, say, the ultimate wisdom of the High Court is guilty of a species of treason. It is also treason, according to this argument, to doubt the public-spiritedness of all politicians or the complete unworldliness of all bishops.

In particular, it is wrong to interview politicians in anything more than the most conciliatory terms. It is probably true that some interviews have been timed with less than absolute felicity and that questioners have sometimes pressed for answers which simply could not be given in the circumstances, but this is not a reason for banning all such interviews. Whether in the public interest or not, politicians have increasingly deserted Westminster for the television studios. National debates now have a national platform. The demonstrators in Grosvenor Square had perceived this much. It is fair to wonder whether the difficulty which the American Government had in raising support for its war in Vietnam was not at least partly due to the publicity given by television to opposition-groups. Television did not create an opposition, but it gave it credibility. I doubt whether once opposition had reached a certain level, it could have denied it credibility.

It may seem that the appearance of the Foreign Secretary in 'Panseema', or of the Minister of Agriculture in 'This Week', is remote from questions of sexual behaviour on television or the support given to betting interests by the broadcasting of starting-prices, both the subject of much anxiety to many people. But all of them are aspects of our society, affected by the way we choose to lay down rules for co-existence in a single community. Television is involved with them all.

As a medium, it has many dangers. It puts a premium on personality, often at the expense of ideas. It is usually short of time, so that it puts a further premium on compression, even though compression may involve distortion to a more or less extreme degree. It has to entertain a large audience viewing in the centre of many potential distractions and so it places great value on the dramatic stroke that will command attention. And its audience will inevitably be largely uniformed on almost every subject with which it deals. In these conditions, television must move with caution. It can be our guide only as a mirror can be our guide, teaching us a little more about ourselves. Where we are uncertain, as we are in so many things now, then television will also be uncertain. In a free country, that is all we should hope for.

Question of Social Control

I

When Robert K. Merton was asked for some reflections on innovative organisation and its environment, he described the invitation as both perceptive and sadistic.[1] It was perceptive, he said, because it identified an important focus for inquiry ordinarily lost to sight, and sadistic in its awareness of how little investigation, even on the most latitudinarian view, had taken place into the subject. The same could be said about creativity and control in television. Here is a relationship of fundamental significance in broadcasting organisations, but one that has received little study. Why this should be so is difficult to understand. Television is still a recent institution but it is extremely conspicuous and has attracted much notice and comment in the last decade. At the same time television in Britain seems to have developed a resistance towards sustained social enquiry from outside, while producing few professionals with either the time of the qualifications to attempt to diagnose the medium from within.

The standpoint of this paper, written from experience both as a producer and as an executive, is exploratory. It aims to identify and describe some of the main forces which influence decisions in television. The BBC and Independent Television are sometimes discussed together because, although there are differences between the two systems—and between one programme company and another in Independent Television—the similarities in organisation and creative impulses are close enough to allow a general discussion of creativity and control in television.

II

Television presents special problems to the creative man. Anyone who is concerned to bring about something which did not exist before (this may serve as a preliminary statement of a creative act) finds himself at once faced with a large and complex organisation. If an idea is to reach the screen, the writer, the producer and the programme planner know it is imperative to adhere to lines laid down by the organisation. These lines are not, or should not be, artificial, sterile channels stultifying creativity. In a literal sense they are arteries, for without them no idea can survive. In television uncompleted work, in the form of ideas for programmes or scripts which are not broadcast, is unfulfilled work. True creativity, in television as elsewhere, demands completion. If it is not completed the creative act is frustrated. Nothing has been brought into existence—if that is the word for the flickering images on the television tube—which did not exist before.

This need to work through an organisation does not apply to the older arts. A painter sends his painting to an art gallery for exhibition and, possibly, sale. He does not expect the owner of the gallery to tell him what to paint or to alter his work once he has finished with it. The function of the gallery owner is to select artists and work which he considers worthy of display, either because of what he judges to be the intrinsic merits of the work, or because he believes it will sell or, hopefully, both. His knowledge of the market and his own taste and judgment may enable the gallery owner to help the artist towards a more disciplined form, but such advice is voluntary and not in any way mandatory.

The book publisher goes further. He may be liable for defamation, so he must scrutinise what his authors say. There may be cases of obscenity or copyright problems. Moreover, unlike the painter who himself performs all the proceses from first sketches to completed work, the author depends on a publisher to complete his creative act by employing a printer to print the book. Sentences and paragraphs may have to be altered for typographical reasons. Certain passages may be 'improved' (a dangerous word) by editors in the interests of greater clarity or better style.

Yet the book remains above all else the author's book. In the end it is his responsibility and his achievement. The publisher, with access to the printing press and a system of distribution, plays an important part in putting the book into a form in which it can be read and appreciated by large numbers of people. He is the connecting link between author and public. He will properly take pride in the quality of the book and its presence in his list, but beyond that he would not claim it as *his* book.

As the size of the audience increases so, it would seem, do the problems of control. Commercial considerations become more important. Books are commissioned to exploit what is seen as a particular audience need. A successful formula will be widely copied. How many caricatures of the James Bond stories are on sale today? What subject will the 'news team' writers turn to next? The role of the author is reduced. There are many voices he must listen to.

In newspapers the size of the audience, the complexity of the distributive network, and the presence of alert competitors combine with a new factor, time, to produce an environment which is seldom sympathetic to the creative writer. A newspaper's first job is to publish information. It may have secondary functions, but the organisation is primarily set up in order to gather and disseminate information. To do this it must sell enough advertising space to make up the shortfall between the revenue from circulation and the true cost of producing the paper. Partly because of the time factor, and partly because of the different skills involved, the writer of a newspaper story will often not be present when the paper is being prepared for publication. Editorial decisions have to be made about what information to include, how it should be used, and at what length. In some instances the sub-editor will have contributed almost as much to the story as finally printed as the original author.

Therefore, it is hardly surprising that few television producers or writers, outside news and public affairs programmes, accept newspaper or magazine standards as in any way appropriate to television. The independence and individual integrity traditionally attached to the artist or the author, the film-maker or the playwright, are each seen in their way as more congenial models by creative people working in television.

III

In spite of some similarities it would, however, be misleading to stretch analogies between television and these other activities very far. There are a number of distinctions which set television apart. The most conspicuous of these are technical and organisational.

Television broadcasting is an application of three sets of principles: electronics, optics and electro-acoustics. Many technicians are needed to ensure that the action in a television studio is accurately reproduced, either simultaneously or later by delayed recording, and distributed in sound and vision to millions of homes throughout the country. These are skills which will not be shared, or probably not be understood, by the producer or writer. The requirements of technicians must be taken on trust, and accepted at times as necessary constraints on what can be done.

Both because of the complexity of the technical process and because of conscious governmental decisions on the structure of the broadcasting services in Britain, the units of organisation—the BBC and the ITV programme companies—are large in size. They range from the BBC, with a staff of more than 21,500[2] (for four radio and two television services, plus the external services), to the smaller ITV regional companies with staffs of about 150-200.

The presence of technology and organisation as limiting factors are self-evident. They are known and in general accepted, inside television and outside. But what is much less apparent, and in the long run perhaps more significant, is the crucial relationship which lies at the heart of any system of broadcasting. This is the reconciliation between the need for some sort of public control with the need for creative freedom and independence.

To help carry out its public responsibilities the BBC has Board of Governors charged with interpreting the obligations placed on the BBC by its Charter. Independent Television is controlled by a public authority—the Independent Television Authority (ITA)—which is responsible for selecting and appointing the programme companies and ensuring that the statutory provisions of the Television Act[3] are observed. Additionally, in Independent Television the Boards of Directors of the programme companies have a responsibility for the programmes which are broadcast in their name.

Therefore, in a very real sense, television programmes are the responsibility of the BBC Governors, the members of the ITA and programme company directors. They have the right to decide what is broadcast and what is not broadcast; they can ask for changes to be made in what has been prepared for broadcasting; they can exercise control over programme expenditure.

In practice, however, because of the size and output of the broadcasting organisations and the way in which the governing bodies see their roles, these powers are invariably delegated to executives. Each week the BBC alone broadcasts 150 hours on two television channels, 530 hours of sound radio and 670 hours in the External Services. No Board of Governors, whole time or part time, could hope to control this vast output directly—in the sense of approving all the programmes in advance before they were broadcast. Nor could they be involved in day-to-day policy decisions. The Governors must rely on passing guidance downwards and encouraging those below to refer upwards for advice: a process described by the late Chairman of the BBC, Lord Normanbrook, as 'essentially one of editorial control by retrospective review.'[4]

The members of the ITA, also appointed as representatives of the public, resemble closely in background and interests the BBC Governors. They , too, look at the television screen with the same mixture of pride and apprehension as their BBC colleagues. Only Lord Hill of Luton has actually served on both bodies, but there are many similarities in approach towards their public responsibilities. There is, however, one vital difference between the powers of the ITA and BBC Board of Governors. Because the ITA does not itself produce any programmes, it has one hugely powerful weapon in relation to those who do. It is responsible for licensing the programme companies, and these licences can, as they were in the Summer of 1967, either be extended or granted to a competing applicant. For this reason, if for no other, the ITA is always going to be more influential than the BBC Board of Governors as at present constituted. There is not only the possibility, but now the precedent, that a Company can lose its licence by failing to obtain a renewal for a further contract period. This may not be the result of negligence, or poor management, or measurably low standards of programmes. On June, 11th, 1967 Lord Hill of Luton, then Chairman of the ITA, stated the principles which had guided the Authority in reaching its decisions on the new contracts:

> 'First, and all the time, we have borne in mind the quality of the programme service which Independent Television will offer in the new contract period. We have scrutinised the applications from this point of view because the Authority can have no more important consideration in awarding contracts.
>
> The second principle may be put in the form of an answer to a question. Must the doors of Independent Television remain for ever closed to new applicants, however good they are? If the answer is 'Yes', then those companies already appointed are there for all time. But the Authority's answer must, of course, be 'No'.
>
> It follows that the choice may well be not between a good applicant and a bad applicant, but between a *good* applicant and one which, after full consideration, the Authority believes will be a better one.'[5]

In the case of the BBC this absolute sanction is not within the powers of the Board of Governors. They instruct and cajole: but they cannot put the entire BBC Television Service out of business on the grounds that a promising looking consortium might make a better job of it.

Below the two formal controlling bodies a system of devolved responsibility operates. Both the BBC and ITA are still, for the most part, organised on orthodox bureaucratic lines—that is centralised control by those who do not themselves do the job. But there is a tendency in the broadcasting industry at present away from this traditional method of control in favour of a more decentralised system of craft supervision of production.

This type of supervision depends on a shared set of values, a craft lore that can be elevated into an empirical set of principles. Here it is worth remarking that the emergence of a common outlook, shared by producers and executives alike, has been encouraged by the fact that all senior executives concerned with programme matters in BBC Television up to and including the Managing Director, Television (the founder and producer of 'Monitor'), are themselves ex-producers. Above this level there is only the Director-General of the BBC who started his career in broadcasting as a radio producer. In ITV too a number of former producers now hold senior positions.

The background and professional qualifications of executives working in television are relevant because of the influence they have on the attitudes of mind, and therefore the decisions, of the people who are responsible for exercising control within the broadcasting organisations. By virtue of their jobs, producers and executives will inevitably be tempted to identify themselves with different standards. The writer, the director and producer are concerned with individual programmes (or series of programmes), their content, and the way they are presented to and received by the audience. They are in competition with other producers in the organisation and will strive to obtain the maximum budget and facilities. The controller will judge the programme, the budget and facilities allocated to it, and its potential appeal to the viewers at which it is aimed, from a more disinterested standpoint. In deciding when it should be broadcast he will have in mind such considerations as the programmes coming before and after it in the schedules, and what competition it will face at the same time on any alternative channels. He will know how many children are likely to be watching; he will be conscious of rules on violence,[6] and any other formalised or conventional guides to action. He will be aware that a play which might be quite acceptable in itself, such as a story showing army life or prison officers in a bad light, may be inadvisable if there have been several other programmes with similar themes in the recent past.

The controller, as the man who receives the complaints after a broadcast, will be conscious of the likely reactions of special interest groups within the general audience: departments of government, political parties, religious denominations, educational and charitable bodies, and a multitude of other organised groups. Each of these will be concerned not so much with general considerations of the dramatic values of a play or the information contained in a documentary, as with the effect on their own special interest. While the controller knows he must resist any inclination to anticipate these pressures before they occur, he will undoubtedly be helped in retaining a wider perspective if at some time in his own career he has been committed to the values and standards of a producer.

IV

Almost everyone in television will acknowledge the pre-eminence of the creative programme process. In private some engineers, administrators or salesmen may in their hearts cherish doubts about this, but if they are wise they keep them to themselves. Both the BBC and Independent Television have been set up solely in order to produce programmes and broadcast them to the public. The programmes are paramount. Everything else, as Lord Hill emphasised in his statement on June, 11th, 1967, is secondary.

Even accepting the primacy of the programme element in television there is ample room for conflicts of interest during production. A budget has to be set, studio or film facilities allocated, and a timetable agreed. In this process 'instrumental' executives (technical and administrative) will have the opportunity to assert themselves. They will naturally want to try and establish the most economic use of financial and technical resources. They will want to see that normal procedures are followed, and that proper standards of business and technical competence are maintained. All these factors interact with the single-minded desire of the programme producer to obtain to the fullest extent the facilities he seeks for his own programme. Sometimes clashes of interest have to be referred to a higher level before they can be resolved. In any television organisation conflicts of this sort are argued out on a day to day basis between the users of facilities and the providers of facilities. The resulting state of hytempert tension is not only almost a trademark of television, but is, in its way, beneficial. What more powerful antidote could there be to orthodoxy, complacency and routine : factors which are inimical to the atmosphere in which original creative work can best take place?

The programme maker, therefore, has a privileged, although not unchallenged, role. He is an indispensable part of the essential creative process of television broadcasting. Yet labels like 'creative process' and 'programme maker', so easily used in general conversation, are often surprisingly hard to identify and define in practice. 'Creativity' itself has become a jargon word. It is used too loosely and too frequently, although less in television than in some other media, and in consequence has become suspect.

There are times when the emphasis on creativity is obsessive. A London advertising agency, it is reported, has a 'Creative Living Room' at its offices. This is used by 'concept units'. The man in charge explained:

> "We have taken our best creative people (those who are best in the sense of being creative generalists and who are outstandingly good at solving communications problems with a high degree of intelligence and imagination) and we have put them together in units of three —each unit representing a high compression of talent. The primary task of each of these units is to interpret the information they receive, to isolate the most persuasive communications idea, and to arrive at the most dramatic creative differential These Concept Units are supplemented by people who are described as creative specialists —writers, art directors, typographers and film producers."[7]

This sort of over-extended language, combined with the sometimes unusual appearance of creative people, has given creativity a bad name in the mass media. Too often creative people are thought of as bright and imaginative, but at the same time unreliable and irresponsible. True creativity does not demand long hair, and if it is to be sustained over a period it seldom coincides with eccentric behaviour. The creative man is the man who, in Arthur Koestler's language, can bisociate, who can put together two previously unconnected facts or ideas to form a single new idea.[8] This basic idea must then be embodied in concrete and articulate form, let us say a written programme outline, and must be carried through to completion. Some of these creative skills are qualities of the contemplative mind; others call for practical qualities of action if the original concept is to reach the screen.

Sometimes one man will possess enough of both qualities to succeed on his own. But quite often in television it is creative groups, sparking ideas off one another, reinforcing and stimulating the uncertain and the impulsive, which build up enough impetus to push through the really innovative projects. These groups will normally form around a leader who is the dominant personality. This is not to say that the disciples gathered about him are not making a valuable creative contribution, since they may have exactly the complementary qualities which he lacks. But a group cannot exist without a leader whose authority is willingly accepted by its members.[9]

There are many instances of creative groups in television. They vary greatly in size—at one time almost the whole of the programme staff of Granada Television could be regarded as a creative group sharing very similar standards and ideas—down to the more usual three or four people at the centre of a continuing current affairs programme like *This Week.* Apart from factual programmes, fertile groups have been responsible for some of the most successful of recent situation comedy series such as *Steptoe and Son and Till Death Us Do Part.* In drama the BBC's *Wednesday Play* has been another example. Most notable of all, *The Frost Programme,* although seen by the public entirely in terms of the personality of David Frost, is the product of a talented nucleus of like-minded people who have coalesced into a spirited creative group under the leadership of David Frost.

Groups breed the vitality on which so much good television depends, and, as Stuart Hood has pointed out, it is of the utmost importance in organising a television service of any kind to ensure that conditions are created which allow such grouping to form. This is not always easy since by their nature groups tend to run counter to administrative tidiness, fragmenting the symmetry of the organisation chart. But Mr. Hood is surely right in his conclusion that 'administrators must be taught to be patient of little pockets of creative anarchy.'[10]

The tendency to work in a group runs with the times. Marshall McLuhan has reminded us in his book. *'The Medium is the Massage'*,[11] that the idea of individual authorship in the sense we know it today is relatively new. It was almost unknown before the invention of printing. Medieval scholars were often indifferent to the precise identity of the manuscripts they studied. In turn they rarely signed even what was clearly their own. Finding texts was a tedious and time-consuming task, and when texts were found they were sometimes put together for convenience into a volume of miscellaneous authorship. In this process the original authorship was often lost.

> 'The invention of printing' writes McLuhan 'did away with anonymity, fostering ideas of literary fame and the habit of considering intellectual effort as private property. Mechanical multiples of the same view created a public — a reading public. The rising consumer-audience culture became concerned with labels of authenticity and protests against theft and piracy. The idea of copyright —'the exclusive right to reproduce, publish, and sell the matter and form of a literary or artistic work' was born.'

Let us not get too disturbed about the decline in individual authorship. The causes lie in the nature of the new mass media, although few television programmes or periodicals have been able to rival the *Sunday Times Magazine* which, in recent single theme edition, credited a team of no fewer than eighteen writers, six photographers, and two artists.[12] Nevertheless a display of individual intellectual effort is still required if a member of a creative group is to inspire his colleagues or take fire from the leader of a team. It cannot all be done collectively at think-in's and bull sessions. At some time almost all creative people find it necessary to go off and sweat it out alone. Solitude and thought have run together since long before Wordsworth wrote

'The marble index of a mind for ever
Voyaging through strange seas of thought alone.'[13]

Innovation is the key to creativity in television, and yet, despite the craze for novelty, genuine innovation is hard to find. It is true that each television programme is in its way novel in that unless it is a repeat, it will not have been seen before. But many are made to a formula. A basic situation for a series of one-hour dramas will have been set up; constant characters will have been established who appear in all episodes—a 'bible' containing full biographies of the main fictional characters is given to all writers contributing to long-running popular drama series. The producer and script editor prescribe exactly what is required of the writers. Magazine programmes, quiz programmes, and many other regular features of the television schedules may be variable in content, but they are usually stable in shape. And underneath, as T.C. Worsley has pointed out, there is the everpresent gravitational pull of the stereotype: the fictional idea, character or characterisation based not on an observation of life itself, but on an earlier fictionalised version of life.[14]

New ground is not easy to break in television and the creative men on whom the quality of British television depends are those who are capable of leaving behind them the familiar pastures of derivative television territory. Some are individual writers or directors of single anteworthy programmes; some are script editors or producers who devise a genuinely original series or format; some are on-screen personalities; some are controllers with a powerful personality and a vivid picture of the type of programme they want to see. All are aware that in such a fashion conscious medium as television innovation needs not only invention but also a well developed sense of opportunity if it is to reach the screen.

V

To many of these men the programme is *their* programme. It is their responsibility as artist or writer or producer. They have, in a real sense, created the programme. It would have no existence without them. Therefore the integrity and honesty of the production are in a way personal achievements comparable to those of the author of a book.

Here, then, is the crux. The writer or producer may believe, with good and proper reasons, that he is responsible for his programme, and that once its main lines have been agreed its content is his affair. At the same time the BBC Governors, members of the ITA, directors of a programme company, or executives within the organisation, may regard it as something for which they have formal responsibility and consequently their programme. This is the most common, and profound , source of friction in television. To a certain extent it is inevitable, for neither group can afford to hand over all its responsibility to the other. Each has a different form of responsibility and a different justification for it.

The conflict between creativity and control can only be reconciled, in television as in so many other forms of human activity, by going back to the idea of responsibility itself. If responsibility is considered as something to be divided up and parcelled out, then a compartmentalised and rigid organisation, breeding resentment, will be likely to result. The better way is to look on responsibility in the broadcasting organisation as multiple — a number of people exercising different functions, each with a wide, and overlapping, responsibility.

This concept will be realistic only if each interest is aware of and respects the standards and values of the other. Those with institutionalised, formal responsibilities must be on their guard against barking up an organisation which, althought efficient in a copybook sort of way, may tend to encourage conformity and lead to timidity and mediocrity. They must always put the standard of the programmes first in their thoughts and in their actions. The creative people on their part, must accept that organisation and financial control is necessary part of television. Indeed they are positively desirable in a creative sense, for a well administered programme will be more likely to achieve its aims than one which is frustrated by a failure in planning or production. There will always be tension between the providers of facilities and the users of facilities , since the basis for determining priorities will be different. But where both interests have a reasonable degree of confidence in the aims and methods of the other, the conditions for a truly creative organisation will exist.

References

1. *The Creative Organisation,* edited by G. Steiner, University of Chicago Press, 1965, p. 50.
2. Total BBC staff employed on 31 March, 1967 (excluding performance and those employed on programme contracts) numbered 21, 653 full-time and 1,245 part-time, BBC *Handbook,* 1968, p. 172.
3. The first Television Act establishing Independent Television became law in 1954. It was amended in 1963, and consolidated in 1964. The governing statute today is the Television Act, 1964.
4. *The Functions of the BBC's Governors,* BBC Lunch-time Lectures, Fourth Series —3, BBC Publications, London, 1965, p. 13.
5. *ITV 1968: A guide to Independent Television,* ITA, London, p. 12.
6. Both BBC and ITA have defined codes on violence.
7. *Television Mail,* 14 July, 1967, p. 20.
8. *The Act of Creation,* Hutchinson, London, 1964, pp. 35. *et seq.*
9. Some Characteristics of creative groups are described by Antony Jay in *Management and Machiavelli,* Hodder and Stoughton, London, 1967, pp. 104-110. Mr. Jay was formerly a member of the BBC's 'Tonight' team, in its day one of the most influential creative groups in television.
10. A *Survey of Television,* Heinemann, London, 1967, p. 162.
11. *'The Medium is the Massage,'* Allen Lane, the Penguin Press, London, 1967, p. 122.
12. 21 January, 1968.
13. *The Prelude,* Book III.
14. *Financial Times,* 14 August, 1968.

[illegible] of control over the means are met [illegible] the other, the conditions for a highly creative organisation will exist.

[illegible] BBC Publications [illegible]
[illegible]
[illegible]

[illegible] January 19[illegible]
[illegible]
[illegible] August 196[illegible]

10

Media as Social Determinants

A study could be carried out on the broad aspect examining the impact of media on the general public. Similar studies done by Dr. George Gerbner in the U.S., has proven that T.V., medium is by far violent and induces violent behaviour. This medium affects the general population of the United States in a negative way and that effect can be seen on the way people tend to behave after getting exposed to television. Dr. Gerbner in his report to the Surgeon General of the United States has found out that T.V. generally reaches large population in many ways and the impact is really marvelous. He terms what he calls as 'Light Viewer' and 'Heavy Viewer' of television and that generally is applicable to the large audience it reaches. A light viewer is one who is exposed to television for a lesser period than what he calls as a heavy viewer who watches T.V. more often than so. It is needed to be mentioned that the average American family watches television for 7.5 hours a day that they spend more waking hours in front for television than any other activity put together. T.V. has become this much popular that the effect it has on the audience is tremendous.

T.V. can be compared to a vast land in which a person can trek into indefinitely exploring new vistas but never be able to get away from it. Once a person becomes addicted to T.V.

watching, life long he remains so. This is the major problem with television.

As said earlier, T.V. watching can be classified into two categories. These are light viewing and heavy viewing. How do we arrive at this conclusion? It is basically simple and Dr. Gerbner has classified in his research on T.V. that heavy viewer is one who is likely to believe the world as portrayed by T.V. as being real, rather then the usual world. T.V. conditions the mind of heavy viewer into believing the events that go on the TV screen is to the real world and whatever that goes on in there makes a lot of significance to him. The heavy viewer of T.V. tends to watch it every day and he comes to learn about the world from his T.V. and not from any other source. Thus, he comes to learn and live accordingly and as presented by television. That becomes a major problem for him.

To get away from the T.V. world of reality it becomes essentially to remove him from his T.V. set and ask him to attend to a doctor who would offer a solution to his T.V. addiction. This is the case of a heavy viewer and the solution that is available to him. He becomes a normal person when he learns to reject the T.V. world and turns to normal pattern of work. The person who watches T.V. for too many hours during a day becomes not only a patient who needs treatment, but also has a mediated world of reality. He behave in the way that is shown on T.V. when the real world is not so. With the introduction of cable T.V. in India, this problem becomes more acute then ever before.

The "Surfer"

Light viewer can remain so as he attends to his work and make a decent living, provided, he does not fall for the glamour and glitter as provided by television. He watches T.V. for a few specific hours a day and remains so as a light viewer and restricting his choice to programmes like news, documentaries etc. Thus he leaves out the entertainment as presented by T.V. and shuns away from commercially oriented serials and music and anything of the kind. He becomes an abnormal person when he starts watching serials and other entertainment-oriented programmes. T.V. is like a magic box and it mesmerises the audience completely. To turn away from T.V. it needs a strong will-power and education to cure him of the negative effects of television. Already the ill-effects of T.V. on our generation is enormous and this needs definite attention.

In the absence of clear guidelines, the regulation and restriction to be imposed becomes quite obvious from the point of view of the government. There are a number of measures it can put forth into action in order to save the public from become T.V. addicts. First and foremost, it can reduce the number of serials and entertainment oriented programmes and introduce more of documentaries and education oriented as well as information oriented programmes. By this measures, they can save the audience from becoming a victim of T.V. entertainment. Secondly, it can encourage other media in allowing to offer more entertainment and it can bring about a number of legislations in order to solve these problems. Apart from these, it can reduce the number of hours T.V. programmes and make the audience understand that it was in the moral interest of the nation.

Altering the Public

Government can launch a massive publicity drive to alert the public about the pitfall in T.V. watching and the need to alert them is all the more important in the current context now than over before. It can appoint a public ombudsmen to study the effects of T.V. on the general population and have a report submitted to the President of India, on the U.S. lines every year. By adopting these measures, the government as guardian of morality of the population can uphold the same. Thus the audiences are not becoming addicted to the T.V. programmes, if it has followed the above-mentioned measures. Addiction of any kind does not come into India. Indeed, Government does have a major role to play in upholding our cherished culture and also the public sentiments come into picture. It is needless to say that television can perform its said goals effectively by showing more education-oriented programmes. Although the commercial interest of Doordarshan is, by and large, important, but at the same time, the moral sentiments and approved community standards are to be maintained, at least some thought need to be given to these. It should be noted that they are not sacrificed to commercial interests.

If it is sacrificed, then the government must be able to intervene to set right the situation. The government has a role to play in upholding public interests and public welfare causes. The public health of the country should not be neglected in favour of making a large turnover by way of putting more serials into television. The government must have a control over anything that is shown to public and uphold the virtues of the public by the following these measures:

1. Control over the programmes that are being shown to the public.
2. It should strive to broadcast more T.V. programmes of educational nature.
3. The time allotted for commercially sponsored serials is reduced in terms of time duration.
4. It allows more of small time producers who produce culturally and educationally oriented shows and programmes for broadcast on T.V.
5. Many such rigorous control measures are introduced in the day-to-day working of the medium.

It all this and more are done, then the standards in public sentiments can be upheld this precisely means that the standards do not falter away. Thus the Doordarshan performs its role as educator, entertainer, and informer as effectively as possible.

Virtual Reality vs. Real Reality

We all want to know what is happening some where else, to someone else. One may call it the motivation to be up-to-date with the world affairs or just being nosey. It is a human trait whose roots can be traced back to the prehistoric time. Its origin may be a prehistoric post-hunt or after-dinner get-together when someone lucky enough to have passed through the neighbouring territory entertained and enlightened the fellow tribals with his narration of what he saw and what he did. This account was most likely to be spicy and coloured in order to give a lift to the narrotor's 'social image'. Nevertheless, he was the window to the world for those who had no such opportunity to step out.

Since then, we have come a long way. In this era of satellite communication we have innumerable places and people to know about and a considerably larger number of trained narrators to carry out the task of entertaining and informing. We also have a variety of media systems to choose from. It can be said that we now have not one but several windows to the world.

The question is, are we alert enough to open all these windows? Are we responsible enough to analyse the parts seen from each window and then synthesize the whole?

Today, the trend, it seems, is to depend more and more on audio-visual mass media—especially on Television and to a lesser extent on films—as the most valid and trustworthy sources of information. Nothing surprising about it. 'Seeing is believing is an old belief'. Seeing something creates a longer lasting impression than just hearing something. The accompanying visual image give the words more authenticity. In fact, the capacity to convincingly represent reality in motion was a prime quality which inthralled people when cinematography was first invented in late 19th century. Continuous technical developments gave film-makers greater and greater hope about capturing 'reality' due to convenience in location shooting and on-the-spot recording. Consequently, audiences started putting greater faith in the reality presented on screen. Anything on television or film certainly seemed more real compared to any other medium. The aim of this article is to examine the myth of absolute reality on screen and to question overdependence on television and film as the exclusive sources of information.

Let us fist discuss the factors which affect the presentation of absolute reality on screen.

1. *Influence of the Process of Film-making on Representation of Reality :*

Two movement in the history of cinema were significantly devoted to presentation of reality on screen. The first 'Kine-eye'—was initiated by the Russian film-maker Dziga Vertov (1896-1954) in 1924. Vertov rejected all theatricality and artificiality in favour of an uncompromised actuality. According to Vertov 'films should pass right over the heads of actors and over the roof of the studios, directly into life and truth, multi-dramatic and multi-detective reality'. The second movement, that of 'Cinema-verite' (1960) followed the same principle-camera recording the life as it is;

without any manipulation and uninfluenced by artist's personality.

Unfortunately, the complex process of film-making does not allow this. Robinson (1973) summarises the flaws in the purist ideals of these movements in his record of history of cinema.

"The flaw .... is that camera always lies. As soon as there is any relationship between the subject and the camera there is artifice. As soon as the angle of the camera is selected, as soon as the film and the sound are cut and edited, as soon as one piece of film material is juxtaposed with another, their must be an element of subjective interpretation. The verite becomes the truth of the artist : there is no such thing as absolute truth, revealed only to the cine camera". Thus, any presentation on screen becomes a selective arrangement of elements. This arrangement depends upon what the film-maker judges to be worth showing in limited time available and in what context. That brings us to the second factor affecting reality on screen.

2. *Who is Presenting and Why :*

What we see on the screen depends upon the elements chosen by the film-maker and this selection process is highly influenced by his personality, previous experiences, environment and aesthetic inclinations. In many a case the producer and/or the sponsoring agency also play a crucial role in this decision-making.

The issue of bias and subjectivity appears here. If the film-maker is presenting a conflict he may be, sonorously or unconsciously, more sympathetic to one. If it is an event the treatment may be influenced by the film maker's perception of it whether he considers the event great, trivial, aspiring, disparaging, joyful or grave. If the focus is on an individual, the presentation would reflect the appeal he or she has for the film-maker. Even if none of these occurs, the chances of the presentation being a wee bit spicy or coloured are no less than those with the pre-historic narration.

Reality on screen, therefore, is shaped by several personal, artistic and ideological preferences of the decision makers. The purpose of presentation brings equally great influence and creates much greater scope for debate. Does the film-maker merely want to inform the audience about something or does he want them to take sides? Does he want people to be just aware of the facts or does he want to motivate them for action? In case of films produced for a government or particular political or ideological group, more often than not, there are contradictory claims and blames regarding the purpose. A particular group would confidently call its own film informative or educational and label a similar one of the opposite group as propaganda. On what bases can one differentiate an 'informative film with some persuasive messages' from a 'persuasive film based on information and facts'? What guidelines has the audience to judge whether it is being informed or brain-washed?

One solution to this problem is to be exposed to maximum possible points of view and to maximum possible sources of information, preferably primary sources. This raises yet another issue pertaining to presentation of reality on screen because all sources and all points of view do not have equal opportunity to occupy the screen.

3. Limited Access to Audio-visual Mass-media in the Capacity of Communicator :

Even reality has multiple dimensions and every issue has multiple points of view. One man's victory is another man's defeat and both may have totally opposite yet significant information to give. But only a very limited number and a limited stratum of people get a chance to present reality (as they see it) on screen. People in general have much better access to print media and hence a greater diversity of opinions is expressed through print media.

Films and television programmes, first of all, are very expensive to produce. They require special equipment, technical knowledge and greater investment. Hence, it is either a government agency/department which has the decision making control or it is a small clique of people with concentration of money and power. These handful of people decide what is important for us to see and what is not. It may very well happen (it does happen) that a trivial national event featuring some prominent people wins over a significant local event. The decision regarding what to show on screen also depends upon what can be shown on screen which leads us to the fourth and the last factor influencing reality on screen.

4. What can be Shown :

As with any other medium, television and film too have their limitations and aesthetic conventions. Past experience of film-makers and programme producers has taught them what usually attracts audiences and what bores them and a larger audience is always welcome. Birt (1981) elaborates on this problem with the following example:

> "A well-made report on a famine, or even on one starving family in Appalachian, will be more watchable than a report on the world food problem. A programme on living conditions in Watts or Harlem will be more diverting than a report on housing policy."

The main consequence of this is that Television Journalists prefer story journalism to issue journalism. It is easier to do and it is more fun. As a result there are very few issue-oriented programmes.

"Thus, visual interest forces Television programmes and sometime documentaries to be set in narrow context, relying heavily upon the staple diet of inaugurations, festivals, strikes and natural calamities all visually interesting events without a perspective."

The discussion so far pin-points that reality on screen is subjective depending upon what is selected as worth-showing, who selects, how and why. It is important to note that the objective of the discussion is not to condemn or abolish television and film. As important and highly popular media they are here to stay. They definitely contribute to our awareness of the world. They give us a glimpse and sometime deeper understanding of places and people we may otherwise never be able to see. They entertain us while they inform at relatively low expense and right in our home. They, really, are the windows to the world. But it is equally important to consider other windows. Today, for a large number of people in India, television is becoming an exclusive source of information. Authenticity of screen image is taken for granted. Bronouw (1975) observed a similar trend in America right in sixties and commented:

"Television played a crucial role in shaping public ideas about world events. But few viewers realised that the networks through which the world news came to them, had only thin channels of information concerning many foreign events...."

The issue of television's emphasis on screen-personality rather than on political views and commitment during election campaigns has long been in debate. Though having no support from research, social scientists accuse television of promoting passivity and gullibility in the viewers by inhibiting the desire for actual participation.

Let us not, then, be blind to limitations of television and films. Let us direct our efforts at shaping a new generation of viewers with critical attitude and higher media literacy. Recognising the need to cross-check and supplement the information from diversified sources will help widen our perspective of world affairs. Exposure to alternative media including radio, newspapers, magazines and even publicity or propaganda material would create a balance of competitive influences. Interest in primary sources and personal experiences would depen our understanding an issue. Let us open all the windows and the world may look more clear, more balanced.

Media and Child Psychology

Today's Child is exposed not only to films exclusively designed and produced for children but to many others shown on television. As Wilbur Schramm pointed out, "overnight a new box has appeared around which all leisure is organised". Television has a great impact on life. The child and the adolescent of today are living in a highly complex socio-cultural environment in which many forces, influences and impacts have constant interplay. The spread of the mass media, combined with rapid urbanisation, has been gradually blurring the distances that had earlier existed between rural and urban children. It seems to me that, before long, television will succeed in creating a universal child viewer whose demands for information, entertainment and sociolisation will be very different from what they are today. Here lies the real challenge for cinema and television dedicated to children.

The four decades since independence have seen a virtual media flood, responding to the profound socio-economic and cultural changes that have been taking place in the country with ever-increasing speed and, in turn, influencing the character and direction of important changes in social mores, tastes, attitudes, etc. And the media reflect the stresses and uncertainties faced by society in ample measure.

Taking just one modern medium, television, we observe that there has been an almost exponential growth in the size of the infrastructure, coverage, configuration and audience, especially since 1982, the year of Asiad when the people of India really dared and let their fancy soar high. Doordarshan went colour and a rapidly developed network emerged. Doordarshan's expansion plan could be realised because of substantial developments in indigenous technology.

In a few giant strides via Insat, a very large part of the country was covered. Low purchasing capacity is still a critical factor in access to television, yet over 500 television transmitters take the signal to around 30 million sets, viewed more or less regularly by a polyglot audience of adults and children from 4 to 6 hours everyday.

Although children below 18 constitute 45 per cent of the population, television programmes exclusively made for children do not even cover 3 to 5 per cent of broadcast time. Again, only 5 per cent of the films made in India, the world's largest film producer, are children's films. Children of different ages do see many other television programmes also—family drama, detective fiction, historicals, news and current affairs, comedy etc.

With the steady increase in the number of VCRs and proliferation of video libraries offering a haphazard collection of televised fiction, the average urban home is being invaded by all sorts of alien and destabilishing influences making nonsense of the concept of parental direction or guidance. High voltage video music with all its glitz and sensuality, expressed through provocative body language, is yet another entertainment format which is assaulting the juvenile psyche.

Television, which includes video, has thus come to constitute in the last three decades a most significant element of the complex media environment in which the Indian child lives and grows. A major study conducted in 1986 by Doordarshan at Madras and Delhi established that "television viewing makes up a significant chunk of the leisure time activities of children. Dance, music, science fiction, sports, movies and quiz programmes were cited as the main areas of interest. Advertisements seem to have a marked impact as judged by recalls. Parents were found to be apprehensive that this viewing was affecting the children's studies. Mothers were worried about sex and violence. Interestingly, the Delhi study showed that, contrary to general belief, the child viewers were selective. Again compared to programmes specially prepared for children, feature films with appeal to the sense of fantasy and action were found more attractive. The influence of peer groups was found more significant than that of parents".

Indeed, the contemporary child is a wash with myriad images, not all of them edifying, which constantly inundate him and eventually propel his mental and physical growth along certain lines.

The radio too is a source of multiple information flows as it reports on daily events and happenings and spouts a vast medley of impressions, ideas and beliefs. The 124 radio stations and 29 Vividh Bharati centres constitute a powerful network with an outreach of 90 per cent of the population.

Yet another component of the popular media kaleidoscope is children's literature tabloids, story books, comics and, now, kid-pulp written with an eye on the articulate adolescent, all adding layer upon layer of sensory and intellectual impact on the young.

The film, a far more complete art form having a much longer standing as a means of opening up a world of new experience to the child, now exercises a somewhat limited impact, unless it uses the vehicle of television to overcome the age-old distribution problem. Organised viewing for children is still an urban privilege.

Violence Overdose

Newspapers, magazines and periodicals also contribute to the media environment. It will be useful to study the impact on the child, more so the adolescent youth, of daily reports of violent crime, oppression and unmitigated cruelty, often illustrated by striking pictures. This heavy dose of information is being constantly processed in the child's mind. Some is rejected. Some stays with an indeterminate status and some leaves a mark.

Seen from the child's point of view, each imaginatively presented exposure is a pleasurable experience, and after stimulation eventually spurs the child to discover the multi-faceted world around him with increasing excitement.

How does the child adjust to information impacts? Some film and television entertainment is familiar, soothing to the eye and reassuring and, therefore, ultimately affirmative in character. Some is unfamiliar, weird, bizarre and disturbing and, therefore, ends up by arousing fear and creating confusion. The resolution of conflicts on the basis of projected information, however, equips the child to understand life. Unresolved tension, which merely pummels the senses for momentary thrills, leaves him highly vulnerable to unhappy influences.

The point to underscore is that the modern child can learn to cope with his environment provided his sensibilities are not bruised and his basic values not smothered. Problem-based television viewed along with the parents can encourage the child to understand life without being overwhelmed. But not many parents find the time.

The plight of children in suburban and rural India is worse. Most of the viewing is in groups but there is hardly any opening provided for explanation. The factor of cultural dissonance makes things more complicated. As Packard, author of the *Hidden Persuaders* has shown, consumerist advertising causes the rise of unrealizable aspirations. Researchers here and aboard suggest that "television advertising can influence children and teenagers indirectly through subtle mechanisms" because the "attractive imagery of advertising enhances the perceived attractiveness of the product".

Quantity vs. Quality

While there is no dearth of criticism that television tends to promote increasing passivity and non-participatory conduct in children, who slowly become addicted, there is evidence that cinema and television have great informational and educational value as well. TV is indeed an instrument of expanding the child's consciousness, sharpening his cognitive faculties and empowering him to construct his individual world-view through gradually enhanced comprehension. Why, then, is society so worried about "too much" television? The answer is that it is not "too much" television that tends to make a recluse of robust child or even contribute to the slow breakdown of family life as alleged, but the way the content is programmed. In fact, television can prove to be socially integrative since shared knowledge and experience bring people closer.

Besides, the parents or social scientists who sometimes express apprehensions are really worried about the increasing spate of violence in television entertainment, some of it of a very pernicious variety, which definitely has the potential of affecting the adolescent's social behaviour. Worst in this category are the "horror programmes" which frighten the child, invade his dreams and overwhelm his imagination.

Before we take a final view of this question, let us fist consider whether children really have a preference for watching violence on television. A number of recent studies have shown that under normal circumstances, apart from adventure stories, which often include extra violence, the children usually prefer comedy and light entertainment made for the family. Say Barrie Gunter & Jill McAleer: "Television is not a one-eyed monster lurking impishly in a corner of the living room ..... waiting to exert an evil influence over young members of the household. It is a channel through which a range of entertainment, drama and learning can be experienced and increasingly these days under the control of the viewer".

There is concern about excessive viewing having an adverse effect on studies and sports which are so important for the child. It has been observed, however, that the extent of viewing gradually gets reduced as the child grows into an adolescent and finds outdoor activity more satisfying than indoor pleasure before the box.

Evidence in many countries suggests that if the child or the adolescent could get invalved in interesting social pursuits and creative activities, his preference for unsuitable canned entertainment progressively declines. If parents exercise benign care, the child can be guided to give proper attention to his priorities. The problem arises when children are deprived of parental care, even parental presence, in the house. That pushes the child to addiction out of sheer loneliness.

"Tube Trap"

The situation has, however, recently became somewhat complicated due to the easy availability of video entertainment which is often loaded with senseless and unjustified violence, brutality and assaults on the cherished values of decency. Now, due to the rapid spread of cable T.V. there is a real danger that we may fall into a double trap unless society asserts its will to abjure violence and reject media output which threatens individual integrity and social stability.

Why do children watch television in the first place? Several surveys carried out in Britain and the USA have tried to identify the major reasons responsible for increasing viewing. According to the survey by Bradley Greenberg carried out among children in London, who were aged 9, 12 or 15 years, the main reason for watching television was "to pass time", "as a means of diversion", "to escape drudgery", "to learn about things", "to learn about himself", "for relaxation" and of "companionships" and as "a habit". The US survey produced similar findings. The Indian study referred to earlier also lists similar motivation for televiewing and the range of preferred entertainment.

It is interesting to observe that, by and large, even the adult viewers offer the same reasons for telewatching, since "television offers a fantasy world into which they can escape from everyday problems of humdrum ordinary living". The escapism function of television operates for children as well as adults and is one of the central mechanisms of television's entertainment function. Viewers can become vicariously involved with the "characters and events, and even act out in their minds ways of dealing with their problems".

It is here that we reach a point of departure and ask: "What is the impact of television on social behaviour? How is the child influenced to adopt certain behavioural attitudes?"

There is evidence that for children and impressionable adolescents, television creates a condition in which viewers identify with the characters they find interesting. Wilbur Schramm has described this process of identification thus: "The experience of being able to put oneself so deeply into a television character .... feel oneself to be so like the character, that one can feel the same emotions the character is supposed to be filling or experiencing, is the essence of the impact of television on value formation".

Basic Change

It is recognised that the effects of television slowly bring about some basic behavioural modifications. The more attractively the story is told, the more alluring the central character is, the more instant is the identification with the values of televised reality. Characters on television provide role models whom children may strive to emulate. Even if they do not directly copy their favourite characters, children may acquire certain views, attitudes or behavioural norms projected by television on cinema characters.

At this point, our examination should shift to the content of present day television, and to the phenomenon of standard stereotypes, including gender roles, propagated by televised fiction. In Indian films and television, perhaps unwittingly, some racist, communal and ethnically divisive values are projected. These fix inherited prejudices on young minds. Films for children must keep such stereotypes out and consciously promote harmony.

Fortunately, all social impact is not negative. Some experts have indeed noted the possibility of television being used as an effective agent of countering undesirable stereotypes. In a recent book called *Positive Images*, Jerome Johnston and James Ettema report on an American project in which television was successfully used to improve children's sex roles. Our films and television, however, persist with traditional roles for women.

Basic Values

Advertising is also sometimes guilty of perpetuating certain stereotypes. A safe conclusion is that it is not the medium of television *per se* which has the potential for distortion, but the mindset and the world-view of the creators of television entertainment and, if the point is stretched further, it depends upon the system of basic values enshrined in a country's ethos or socio-political system. A servile and fractured society carrying the deadweight of old prejudices cannot be expected to produce images of equal and truly liberated men and women.

The most powerful threat to young minds comes from an increasing induction of violence. The National Coalition on Television Violence (NCTV) has been agitating for the removal of violence from all popular television programming.

George Gerbner's studies at the Annenberg School of Communication, University of Pennsylvania, have drawn a violence profile of American network television which is truly alarming. That is the stuff pushed through vigorous exports to societies recently introduced to television. It is to the credit of Indian television that it has resisted the temptation to grab this sizzling stuff.

Similarly, James Halloran and Paul Croll of the Mass Communication Research Centre, Leicester, have carefully analysed the content of BBC and ITV during one week in 1971 and felt that violence was not as prevalent here as on American television.

All the same, in nearly 48 per cent of fictional programmes a major character was involved in violence either as aggressor or victim. They found that the most violent type of programme in the fiction category was the cartoon. Barring cartoons, there was little violence in children's programmes.

How does violence change attitudes? Barrie Gunter and Jill McAleer have described the sequence of arousal, disinhibition, imitation and desensitisation in television violence on the basis of selective studies.

Confronted as we in India are with the ambient phenomenon of increasing coarseness in social behaviour and endemic violence in almost all walks of life, we need to pause and assess the impact of violence in films, cartoons and television entertainment on the impressionable minds of children and adolescents. Similarly, increase in teenage crime in our country should draw attention to the most disturbing problem of the child and the adolescent picking up para-social roles, attitudes and values from televised entertainment, which has of late contained a surfeit of violence and has projected a highly aggressive way of life.

Violence and Morbidity

When violence is glamorised, the harmful impact on the imitative behaviour of the young increases manifold. Many social psychologists and media analysts have established beyond reasonable doubt that continuous and unmitigated exposure to violence tends to desensitise the young minds and indirectly to promote among teenagers the culture of revenge and justice outside the judicial and moral order of society, so blatantly advocated in some recent films.

In a recent publication entitled *What T.V. does to our Children: The Effects of T.V. on Malaysian Children*, the Consumers Association of Penang (CAP), Malaysia, has given some very telling examples of the effect of television violence on Malaysian children. It broadly says that television affects Malaysian kids in three ways: (*i*) By imitation of TV characters, (*ii*) through immunisation to violence, and (*iii*) by justifying violence.

CAP Report No. 1 (1983) documents the impact of violence on children who are more vulnerable. Before developing a coding pattern for the study, violence was defined as "the use of physical force or verbal abuse which is psychologically or physically injurious to a person or persons, and the destruction of property and animals, the act being either accidental or intentional".

Then a number of popular programmes such as *Kojak, Streets of San Francisco, Strike Force, Battlestar Galactica, New Adventures of Superman, All New Pop-eye Show* etc., were analysed. The report took cognisance of two categories of violence, namely, physical and psychological violence.

The survey revealed that—On the average, a child watches TV 2-3 hours daily during weekdays and 3-4 hours during weekends. This adds up to about 1,200 hours of T.V. in a year compared to 1,040 hours a year in the classroom.

In the 13 T.V. programmes which CAP surveyed, there were 736 instances of violence within a total of only eight and a half hours of viewing time. The violence included 66 killings, 91 injuries, 94 shootings, 106 shows of weapons, 147 instances of verbal violence, 92 demonstrations of physical strength and 140 other forms of violence like bomb explosions and car chases.

Children's Views

About 68 per cent of the parents reported that their children imitate the T.V. superheroes and 65 per cent said the children requested for toy guns and war games.

Asked what they would do to a crook, 12 out of 50 children said they would shoot him dead. Most of the others would "box him", "beat him", "wallup him", "poke him with a knife", "hang him" or "put him in a case".

Many of the most violent programmes are purveyed by cartoons (like *Popeye)* which, according to psychologists, have a great impact on children, or by police shows. "The cartoon", says the report, "tends to reduce the intensity of danger, pain and suffering and thereby given a false picture of reality. Children are more vulnerable than adults". One has not come across similar work in our country though the urban child is exposed to this violent stuff in print and on the screen (*He Man*).

To be fair, we should also take note of the other point of view, which says that when the child watches aggression in westerns or the like, he more often than not acts out in fantasy his aggressive impulses and is eventually purged of his inherent aggressive tendencies through a sublimation of aggressive feelings. However, the catharsis hypothesis put forth by film-makers is countered by the opinion that if aggression depicted in film and television programmes is without conclusion, or aggression overwhelms the child's capacity to cope with it, the televised violence would always tend to hover in his mind until later he finds a chance to express his pent up feelings in real life.

The author of the imitation theory, Albert Bandura, an eminent communications scientist, has established that exposure to an aggressive film model tends to reduce the child's inhibition against acting in a violent manner. Most television heroes, he notes, have achieved their goals by being aggressive. He has cited many examples of knife fights observed and recorded in San Fancisco in which the protagonist was directly imitating the cut and thrust of a violent hero seen in a television programme the night before. He adds that "successful villainy may outweigh the viewer's value system".

Televised Aggression

Similarly, Berkowitz severely criticises televised aggression because the "sight of aggression on television primes the aggressive drive in the viewer". There have also been instances where television has taught crime techniques to potential juvenile delinquents. The Indian film since the late seventies has been seeped in a culture of violence despite increased sensitivity and a stricter certification code. These films are not only easily available on video but are also telecast.

Increase in crime in actual life, which film producers cite as the reason for showing violence, is no justification for this kind of fatal permissiveness, particularly when the young are often exposed to it.

Fortunately, our television has been trying to save the children by discouraging entertainment using violence as a source of excitement. However, some cartoons popular in the West and imported into India are loaded with aggression and violence. Initially people thought that cartoons were funny and the violence depicted in them was make-beleive and phoney. But now people think differently. It is in response to universal criticism of violent entertainment that the European Broadcasting Union recently undertook a study of the programme content of the BBC and French television. They were relieved to observe that there had been a conscious attempt to reduce the element of violence in programmes for children up to the age of 12 years as well as in programmes for adolescents. There had also been attempts to consciously promote through the media greater social awareness and ethical sense, so that when the adolescent grow into a young person he may try to arrive at a balanced view of life.

Barrie Gunter and Jill McAleer have summed up the debate on the effect of televised violence convincingly. Children's minds and social consciousness, they say, are malleable and immature in many ways. Therefore, young viewers may be susceptible to subtle influences, often unintended, of television which most adults are immune to. Hence, the need for special care.

We have so far taken note of the information flows delivered through televised entertainment or films. But what about the influence of life around the child and the adolescent? Any kind of clash of values of which the child is constantly exposed with ever-growing intensity leads to dissonance, for instance between the visible conduct of parents, who are closest to them at home, and the latter's actual behaviour outside the home. Those children who have acquired a fair amount of sensitivity and power of observation feel greatly distressed when they are confronted with the clash of two images and are left highly confused.

In present-day life, there are far too many chinks in the family scene and most parents appear in poor light. The child's firm base of ideals is eroded. This social phenomenon also contributes to the uncertainty and consequently cynicism which marks a fairly large section of the youth.

Yet another cause of confusion in the values and ethical principles of the child is the contemporary prototype image of the successful man or woman being constantly projected in the media as well as in actual life.

If the child sees the patently dishonest and unscrupulous emerge successful after overcoming the built-in resistances and hurdles of the system, no amount of ethical education through cinema and television will succeed in establishing a proper ethic in a young child's life.

While it will be wrong to imagine that crime will result after every exposure to televised crime or that an act of violence will follow exposure to violence on the small or big screen, to rule out the possibility will be dangerous in the face of strong evidence.

In fact, there is a pressing need to undertake a careful appraisal of the situation in India today. The present transition of perceptions accelerated by media impact as well as by the socio-cultural changes around children must be managed by comprehensive educational and cultural policies.

It is wise to remember that while, thanks to the effort of the Children's Film Society and Doordarshan, a child now gets an opportunity to see good films informed by a humanistic vision on the screen or over television, the continuing exposure to hurtful coarseness and aggression contained in a lot of imported television entertainment in video format is going to increase his aggressiveness. There is a need of a holistic approach which takes cognisance of the phenomenon of the child and the adolescent caught in the vortex of clash of values within the home and outside. With no access to a firm formal anchorage either in personal faith or family tradition or even in societal norms, the child and the adolescent indeed face a cruel predicament.

It is virtually impossibly these days for a child to be completely sequestered in a protective cocoon of homespun ideals. Yet it is absolutely necessary to make a conscious effort to shorten the trauma and to moderate the uncertainty to which the child and the adolescent are exposed in the present turmoil of values. The anti-social content of media products must be barred or countered with pro-social content through programmes which educate and entertain simultaneously.

Finally, we cannot forget that film and television are but a part of the complex network of contemporary information and emotional impacts of a very wide outreach. The programme philosophy for children's television should encompass the whole range of influences moulding the mind of the child and should be forward-looking. The child of today has already put one foot on the critical threshold that leads to the 21st century. The question is : Is he going to enter the new world with a paralysed and frightened mind and atrophied sensitivities, or with an awakened empathy for humankind, which alone can enable him to find a secure place in the society of future?

Rural Children and the "Tube"

It is essential that our policy makers should ensure that the electronic media should not be manipulated by the marketing forces to expand their frontiers in total disregard to the simple living and high thinking ethos that has fortified our society for ages. It is imperative that projection through high profile advertising and glossy programmes on the electronic media is kept within certain parameters so that the younger generations living in the rural areas do not find themselves a totally deprived lot. During the last few years, with the spread of the electronic media network, the scene has undergone a big change. An evaluation of the impact of television on the rural children at this stage will make the new media policy more meaningful to society.

Thanks to the instant transmission of the events in the urban and rural areas as a whole, the shame and pride of every event is equally shared by the people all over the country. Children in rural India are now better informed than their elders. Radio and television have almost eliminated the information gap between the urban and rural children and children in the rural India are now trying to catch up with their brothers and sisters in the urban areas. The visual impact on the impressionistic minds of these children is discemible in the hopes and aspirations as reflected in their day-to-day attitudes towards their environment. Though living in the lap of nature, they are equally aware of the good things of life. Given a choice, they would easily discard the age-old concept of simple living and high thinking and adopt all that is available to the elite in the country.

With the spread of national network of Doordarshan, the television sets have made their appearance in the far-flung villages. Community television sets have been installed by the Government. In fact the middle class farming families are gradually going in for their own sets. Through television the children in the villages are now able to know the latest developments in the country and outside. Slowly the cult of consumerism, till now a bane of the cities, is making its way into the thinking process of the younger generation in the countryside. Whether their parents have the capacity to provide them with the good things of life or not, but the children are certainly now aware of all that is missing from them and all that they should get if they have the means.

The hopes and aspirations are directly linked to what they see on the idiot box. Neat and smart children participating in the Republic Day parade, playing in the spacious playgrounds or children performing in the colourful cultural programmes are repeatedly shown on the television. Every such programme hammers into the minds of the rural children of the gap between what they should have and what they actually have. Every child in the rural India would like to imitate what is seen on the National Network.

Alarming Rate

The expectations of the children in the rural areas are rising at an alarming rate. They would like to have the same facilities which their counterparts in the cities are enjoying. They see on the national network the facilities available like well-maintained schools, open playgrounds, reading rooms, better living standard and modern amenities. Against this, they have to face the schools run in the open, no proper playgrounds and virtual lack of facilities for cultural activities. There is a lot of gap between what they see and what they have. This brings in an inferiority complex which they would not like to suffer.

In the earlier days, the children practically depended on their parents to decide—be it dress or the games to play. But now the children are becoming too vocal. Earlier they did not have access to the life in the urban areas and virtually did not know what was happening outside their own village or the surrounding villages. Parents can no longer keep their children fed with fairy tales and topics of mythological value. The children would like to have concrete results on their living standards. While on the one hand, the cost of living is increasing, the value of their products is no more sufficient to provide a composite life. Hence the parents in the rural areas caught in between two opposite trends—rising costs and increasing demands of their children.

As in the case of the slum dwellers in the cities, the children in the villages do not find things in real life what they see on the television. Catchy advertisement of a child taking a soft drink for instant energy to emerge as a champion, of the latest brand of soap, of children taking soft drink in groups, the latest brands of toothpaste and toys—all these projections tantalise the thinking process among the children. The films screened on the idiot box of film stars making glazy appearance, motorbikes and cars speeding, latest music instruments on display and gala parties with people smiling. All the demonstrations make the children too obvious about their lacklustre life in the village. They would prefer to run away from the village and join the band of merry makers in the cities.

A random talk with a group of children in any village would reveal startling facts. Vast majority of them watch television on the community set or at the neighbours. Almost all of them discuss what they see on the television. All of them would love to possess what they see. Very few children show preference to stay back at the village when they grow up in life. While on the one hand so much of consumerism is projected on the television which has direct bearing on the minds of the children in the very sensitive stage of their life, the economic scenario in the villages is not changing at the matching rate.

The children in the rural areas are showing more interest in the sports activities. In almost every nook and corner of each village children try to convert the open space available into a playground. They play with the improvised bats and sticks made out of the wood available locally. But the children would like to have better organised playgrounds and playing kits as are shown on the national media. The interest of the children is gradually shifting from the traditional rural games like wrestling and kabaddi to the modern games particularly cricket and football.

The children expect the teachers to discard the stick rule and be more friendly with them. They would like the gap between the students and the teachers narrowed down. By choice, they would like to attend classes in the well-lit rooms with all amenities. Their schools should match with the schools available to the children in the cities.

Parent-Child Equation

The children also expect a drastic change in the parent-child equation. In the earlier days the children used to be very scared of their parents and older members of the family. Children do no more like to be browbeaten. The children are not inclined to show mute respect to the parents. They would like to argue on equal footing and if possible carry their point of view. With the breaking up of joint family system, the grip of the elders in the family on the children is gradually disappearing. Children are also not interested to live in large families. In the earlier days each couple use to have large number of children but the family size is now shrinking.

The children in the rural areas would like to have better standard of living. Examples of austere living no more impress them. Given a chance they would expect their parents to provide them well-ventilated house with modern amenities. When they find most of these things missing in their daily life, they tend to become impatient. Pride in poverty is no more taken as a virtue. Parents are finding it difficult to explain the economics of running a family in the rural areas with low income and rising costs.

The village schools are now producing better results and there is greater attendance in the schools. Children would like to complete their studies at the earliest so that they are able to leave the village and get a job in the city. That is the reason of higher pass percentage in the rural schools. It is now common to find the parents engaging tutors to teach their children so that they could perform better in the examination.

Gone are the days when one could find the rows of khadi-clad children with white caps on their heads standing for morning prayers. Children come to schools in proper uniform and the era of caps is over. Given a choice, they would come to the schools in the fancy dresses. The children have no more liking for the village-made shoes. That is the reason why the shoemaking industry in the villages is gradually perishing.

The parents in the village expect their children to share the burden of farm operations before and after the school hours. Perforce the children have to do a bit in the fields. However, they no longer cherish to come to the schools in soiled condition.

The wind of change in the rural India is perceptible. From a bunch of docile kids ever willing to blindly obey their parents, they are now more vocal, inquisitive and independent in thinking. Though they are presently deprived of most of what they see on the television, they have an urge to improve their lot at the earliest opportunity. The time is fast approaching when bulk of the best sportsmen, best civil servants and best technocrats will hail only from the Indian villages—a development healthy for the India moving towards the 21st century.

References

1. Schramm, Wilbur: The Effects of television etc. (1964) quoted in Grant Noble's Children in Front of the small screen.
2. Khurana B.K.; Krishnaswamy, Chitra and Malik, Saroj : Impact of television on children, Doordarshan India (1986).
3. Packard : The hidden persuaders.
4. Yadav, J.S.: Does television advertising harm children? IIMC Mimeographed paper (1987).
5. Barrie Gunter & Jill McAleer : Children and television, the one-eyed monster, Routledge (1990).
6. Greenberg, Bradley : Viewing and listening parameters among British youngsters, in Brown (Ed) : Children and Television. Cellier MacMillan (1961).
7. Schramm, Wilbur & Lyle, J : Television in the lives of Children, Stanford, (1961).
8. Schramm Wilbur : How do children become involved with television characters, Ch. 3 in Grant Noble : Children in front of the small screen : Constable, London (1975).
9. Clayton Routh in National coalition on television violence (NCTV)'s Newsletter, March-April 1984.

10. Gerbner G : Violence in television drama : trends and symbolic functions in television & social behaviour, Washington, DC (1972).
11. BBC : Violence on television : programme content & viewer perceptions, Halloran and Croll, (1972).
12. Indris, SM, President, Consumers' Association of Penang, Malaysia: What television does to our children : The effects of T.V. violence on Malaysian children (1984).
13. Albert Bandura : Vicarious processes in the chapter : The thomy problem of television and violence in children in front of the small screen by Grant Noble, (1975).
14. Berkowitz, Leonard : Some aspects of observed aggression : Journal of personality and social psychology (1965).
o$ 3
15. Halloran & Elliot : Children's programming policies : Study commissioned by European Broadcasting Union, (1969) Chapter 9 of Children in front of the small screen.

11

Mass Media and Existing International Law

A. INTRODUCTION : LEGAL INSTRUMENTS

A number of principles of possible relevance to telecommunications and computer services will be presented here. We have derived these principles from a number of international legal instruments. A brief initial survey enabled us to select certain instruments for more detailed examination for the purpose of extracting relevant principles.

It was not possible to undertake an exhaustive and detailed examination of all the international instruments within the restricted framework of this report. The initial examination of international instruments was primarily aimed at identifying those containing principles of particular relevance to transborder data flows and international computer services, as well as instruments directly regulating telecommunication services.

This methodology undoubtedly limits the report but this is relatively unimportant since the report does not aim to discuss in detail the interpretation of the selected principles, but rather to define them in general terms with a view to their application to telecommunications and computer services.

Nevertheless, we want to stress that the legal instruments discussed are a selection and that others may have been overlooked due to the brevity of the initial survey.

In the first stage of the project a list of all the international instruments selected for initial examination was circulated with an assessment of their possible importance. The final selection was made after receiving comments on this list from a number of bodies, including the ICCP secretariat at OECD.

We will briefly introduce those international legal instruments from which the principles discussed in the section B are extracted. The instruments are briefly identified but are not described in detail. All the instruments selected are multilateral in nature.

1. Existing Transport Treaties

Treaties concerning transport are obviously a possible source of relevant principles. In this area regulation has had time to develop and the principles are therefore well established and have stood the test of practice. The selection made represents both older and more recent instruments concerning transport. A number of principles are common to several treaties. For that reason a limited selection is sufficient.

Treaties in this area have no direct link with telecommunications law and serve only as basic material for the possible extraction of principles which might by analogy be applicable to transborder data flows.

(a) The Convention and Statute on the International Regime of Railways:

This Convention was adopted in Geneva in 1922. The main aim of the Convention is to secure and simplify transportation by rail. It was drawn up in the international situation following World War I and the League of Nations was at that time the sponsor of this type of activity. The intention to establish a railway convention was moreover implied in the Versailles Treaty.

The substantial rules in the Treaty are contained in a regulatory chapter. For our purposes the most relevant rules are those dealing with international railway traffic. They include principles of innocent transit, national treatment, priority for major traffic routes, etc. Other principles deal with matters such as use of carriages belonging to another railway company and relations between railway companies and passengers.

(b) Convention on International Civil Aviation:

This Convention was adopted in Chicago in 1944. This is the most recent of the international instruments concerning transport. It was established following the major technical developments in aviation during World War II.

The Treaty has four main sections. For our purposes the first part which regulates civil aviation is the most relevant. The rules in the treaty aim primarily at increasing safety. They include several principles relating to technical equipment and the standardisation of rules and procedure between countries. The rules on transit flights are also of interest. The Convention is based on accepted principles of transit taken from the railway convention mentioned above and from other previous transport treaties.

(c) The Barcelona Convention and Statute of 1921 on Freedom of Transit:

This Treaty was adopted in Barcelona in 1921. Unlike the two treaties mentioned above this one does not deal with a specific mode of transport. It deals with an important area of concern to all types of transport. Like the railway convention it was drawn up shortly after World War I on the initiative of the League of Nations.

The Convention, as its title indicates, deals only with the freedom of transit. In this important field it establishes most of the principles accepted in international trade, such as the principle of custom-free transit and the most favoured nation principle.

2. Treaties Regulating Telecommunication

These treaties could well contain principles and rules generally and directly applicable to transborder data flows. Since this study is confined to the legal aspects of such data flows we have only included principles apparently applicable to conventional telecommunication networks, without considering their special or noval implications for transborder data flows.

There is not such a wealth of treaties in this area as within the area of transport. There may be several reasons for this, such as the speed of technological development. There are always problems in regulating a developing area and this phenomenon is particularly acute in regard to transborder data flows.

The two treaties selected are perhaps the main ones in this area but are by no means the only ones.

(a) The International Telecommunications Convention:

The most recent text of this Convention was adopted in Torremolinos in 1973. The Convention also forms the basis for the Union but itself establishes important principles of substance. The latter are intended to improve and co-ordinate world-wide telecommunications. Emphasis is placed on technical aspects.

For the purposes of this report the most important principles are to be beyond in Chapter II of this Convention, setting on general rules for telecommunications. Among these one may mention the principle of sufficient technical quality of equipment and those encouraging the establishment of uniform rules and procedures. The Convention contains a large number of extremely detailed rules on technical standardisation. Some principles of interest are also to be found in its Chapter III which deals with radio communication.

(b) Universal Postal Convention:

The most recent text of this Convention results from the treaty adopted in Vienna in 1964 and revised in Rio de Janeiro in 1979. Strictly speaking, the Convention does not regulate transport of data but rather physical objects such as mail. Such objects may either represent information (letters) or contain goods. However, the Convention may be seen as an instrument which could regulate the transport of data.

An important and fundamental set of rules of this Convention addresses freedom of transit, including the rule making the sender the owner (in the strict sense) of mail while it is in transit. This principle has great practical value in regard to mail since the duration of transportation may be considerable. Although telecommunication usually implies a dramatic reduction of time in transit, the principle may still be of importance.

3. Treaties of Possible Value for the Regulation of the Material Aspects of Data Flows

This last category of treaties or international instruments is a rather diversified selection. They all contain possible examples of rules which might apply to the material aspects of data flows. They are however more diversified than those selected in the first two categories of treaties within which it would not have been appropriate to include them.

Four treaties have been selected dealing with quite different areas. In general they have no direct relationship with telecommunication problems. Unlike the treaties mentioned above none of them deal expressly with communications.

(a) Universal Copyright Convention:

This Convention was adopted in Geneva in 1952 and revised in Paris in 1971. The Berne Convention for the Protection of Literary and Artistic Works which includes more detailed rules in this area has been in existence for longer (since 1883). Most countries party to the Berne Convention also adhere to the Universal Convention which is, to some extent, the smaller common denominator in the field of copyright or intellectual property law.

The substantive rules are not separated from the formal ones. An example of an important principle is that of national treatment referred to in Articles II and III.

(b) The Paris Convention on Protection of Industrial Property:

This Convention originated in 1883 but has been revised on a number of occasions.

Important principles in the Convention include the principle of national treatment set out in Article 2. Although there are exceptions to this principle it is nevertheless clearly stated. Article

13 which mainly concerns the creation of an agency for the protection of industrial property also includes elements aimed at the standardisation of rules and procedures. Such standardisation may itself be viewed as a principle.

(c) General Agreement on Tariffs and Trade (GATT):

The Convention dates from 1945. It contains two important principles, namely the most favoured nation principle in Article I and the national treatments principle in Article III. These basic principles are relevant to telecommunications and data flows but are of a more general nature. Article V concerns the principle of free access to transit and show that the agreement also relates to transport.

(d) The OECD Guidelines on the Protection of Privacy and Transborder Flows of Personal Data:

These guidelines were adopted in 1980 by the Council of the OECD. As indicated by the title, the guidelines are not legally binding. In reality, however, they could have a considerable influence if Member countries strive to conform to them.

The guidelines apply directly to personal data flows and include a number of principles of interest in a more general context, notably security measures to prevent loss and unauthorised use of data. Likewise, the principle of openness in relation to development and policies concerning personal data are also established.

B. SURVEY OF EXISTING INTERNATIONAL LAW

1. General Principles

The principles presented below are rather general principles of a substantive nature which apply more to access to international computer services than to transborder data flows themselves. They include the national treatment and most favoured nation principles, the right of the public to use international telecommunications facilities and what might be described as the "transparency" principle.

One of the most important substantive principles is that of *national treatment of foreign interests*. Briefly, this principle implies that discrimination among persons, goods or services on account of their foreign origin is unjustified. Foreigners should be treated in the same way as nationals or residents, and foreign goods and services should receive the same protection and treatment as national goods or services.

The principle appears in a number of the treaties mentioned above, *e.g.*, Article III of GATT which has rules entitled : "National treatment on internal taxation and regulation". Corresponding principles are included in the Universal Copyright Convention and the Paris Convention.

For computer services the principle may have major implications. Firstly, it should be stated that hitherto the principle has not been generally recognised in regard to transborder data flows. An example of this is given in Annex I : under Brazilian law management information services may only be offered by foreign firms if the underlying services are truly international in character.

Reluctance to accept such a principle has several economic or political causes, often associated with general political issues such as national security or national culture. It should be noted that the adoption of the national treatment principle in practice implies acceptance of an international market for computer services where possibilities of promoting the national industry would be severely limited. In this way the principle of national treatment may be seen to be closely related to the principle of the free flow of information.

Information retrieval from foreign data bases is a rapidly growing service. Some countries have pioneered the establishment of on-line data bases to serve as resources for technical and scientific information as well as other needs. This effort has been successful as long as one country accepts depending on data bases located in another country.[1] This concern does not arise in regard to foreign use of national data bank since this is advantageous to the national information retrieval service industry and does not imply adverse effects.

There are several ways of the meeting the challenge of foreign information retrieval services. Prohibition or severe restrictions of the right of nationals to access foreign data banks for information retrieval is perhaps only a theoretical possibility. The practical problems of ensuring that owners of dial-up terminals conformed to such regulation would be rather severe. Also such a restrictive attitude would probably have other negative effects on national industry as well.

An alternative might be the adoption of a telecommunication tariff structure designed to encourage what is seen as desirable use of information retrieval services. A third possibility might be the adoption of technical measures to restrict access to foreign providers of information retrieval services. The most obvious solution would, however, be to encourage growth of national computer services so as to offer an alternative to the services of foreign suppliers. This would seem to be the course open to countries to reduce or eliminate what is seen as the negative effect of relying on foreign information and retrieval services. Moreover, this would be an approach to services that would be consistent with the principle of national treatment.

Some of the above examples show how the principle of national treatment is relevant in regard to information retrieval services. The adoption of this principle would clearly encourage the development of an international market for computer services where national industry would not be privileged. Implementation of GATT nevertheless demonstrates that forms of discrimination are numerous and that it may be difficult to maintain the principle when important national interests are at stake. This is, however, not a valid argument against national treatment to foreigners if the object is to establish a legal environment designed to promote the free flow of data across borders.

In substance, the most favoured nation principle has much in common with the national treatment principle. Briefly stated, if it is extended to cover persons as well as goods it could mean that foreigners benefiting from it would be treated in the same way as citizens or residents of the third state having the most privileged position. The principle is clearly not as far-reaching as the principle of national treatment since the country in question may still introduce protective measures for the benefit of its national computer service industry.

Generally there are exceptions to this principle, especially where countries have close economic, social or other relations with one another. A country outside the group in question may no longer benefit from the privileges extended within the group.

The most favoured nation principle is the basic principle of GATT and appears in its Article I. Detailed rules concerning the principle are found in a number of places in the GATT agreements.

The principle could be of broad and interesting application in relation to international computer services. It might have some of the same advantages and disadvantages as the principle of national treatment. One distinction however, may be pointed out. It would seem easier to accept to the extent that purely national interests of countries would not be considered as an obstacle to its application in the same way as would be the national treatment principle. Referring again to the example of the "restrictive" Brazilian legislation, the privileges award to national providers of information retrieval services would not necessarily conflict with the most favoured nation principle as long as no foreign country was given preference over another. The introduction and application of the principle would therefore seem to give rise to fewer problems.

Furthermore, the principle would also encourage the growth of the international market for computer services. For example, a provider of processing services may offer his customer access to the service through leased lines. If the national telecommunication authority accepts the establishment of a node through which national users may access the leased lines this would, in line with the most favoured nation principle, imply that all providers of processing services could establish similar nodes (subject to certain specifications) so that other providers are in a position to benefit from the same treatment.

The *principle prohibiting dumping* could be seen as complementing the principle of national treatment and the most favoured nation principle. These principles aim to create equal competitive conditions for nationals or residents of different countries. The prohibition of dumping contributes towards this same aim. The principle is included in GATT Article VI but is set out in greater detail in the Anti-dumping Code of 1979 which is part of the extensive GATT regulations. The principle prohibits the sale of exported goods at lower prices in the importing country than in the producing country calculated on a cost-benefit basis. The principle is set out in Article VI:

"Anti-dumping and countervailing duties.

1. The contracting parties recognise that dumping, by which products of one country are introduced into the commerce of another country at less than the normal value of the products, is to be condemned if it causes or threatens material injury to an established industry in the territory of a contracting party or materially retards the establishment of a domestic industry."

GATT sets out conditions for the application of the prohibition principle. This principle could also be applied to services and would have as much importance as for products. However, the practical problems involved in exportation of goods are not present in the exportation of computer services through the telecommunication network. Transport costs and time in transit are not major problems. A provider of computer services may differentiate his prices to achieve optimum market structure. In the international context such developments might have negative consequences and thus an anti-dumping rule might be appropriate, especially to protect small providers of computer services from being forced out of business by international providers able to differentiate prices.

The principle without any doubt raises political problems and may be controversial. The GATT Article demonstrates the sensitivity of the issue.

If the principle is considered desirable, enforcement might need the same degree of detailed implementation as is found in GATT. A typical example of circumvention would be the sale of services through a third country. In the case of GATT this is dealt with in the Anti-dumping Code of 1979, Article 2(3):

"In the case where products are not imported directly from the country of origin but are exported to the country of importation from an intermediate country, the price at which the products are sold from the country of export to the country of import shall normally be compared with the comparable price in the country of export."

A principle of a quite different nature is the principle of *granting the public a right to use the equipment*. This principle appears in Article 18 of the International Telecommunication

Convention entitled "The right of the public to use international telecommunication services".

> "Members recognise the right of the public to correspond by means of the international service of public correspondence. The services, the charges and the safeguards shall be the same for all users in each category of correspondence without any priority or preference."

One may observe that the principle not only includes the right to use the international telecommunication network but also the additional rule that all users in one group shall be given equal treatment. In this respect the principle of public use is related to the two principles discussed above.

It may also be noted that the principle is restricted to granting the public a right to use established services, but that no obligation to establish such services—for instance, computer services offered in other countries—is imposed on national telecommunication authorities.

Article 18 of the International Telecommunication Convention applies directly to computer communication, to the extent that international telecommunication networks are used for such purpose. The principle in Article 18 is however rather general and is not explicit as to its detailed application. There may be problems in applying it to computer services.

The example may be considered of a national scheme of licensing international leased lines. If considerations other than those of a technical nature were taken into account when granting such lines it might be considered that there was a conflict with the principle of equal access of the public to international telecommunication facilities. It may be noted that the Brazilian legislation given above as an example imposes a system of licensing for "international links for teleprocessing systems" which is important mainly in relation to the use to be made of such links. We do not claim that the Brazilian legislation is in any way in conflict with the ITC Article 18 but we give it as an example of the possible limitations of the principle.

As the example may have shown, Article 18 makes necessary more specific additional rules. It could be seen as a possible basis for the principle of the right of the public to use international computer communication.

The classic area in which this principle might be of importance would be that of countries which, for political reasons, want to shelter their citizens from the rest of the world. This situation is not too acute in respect to OECD countries but the principle remains nevertheless of great importance. It will be appreciated that it constitutes a specific application of the principle of the free flow of information.

The principle would not restrict indirect regulation of international communication by, for example, tariff structure. The more blatant forms of censorship might however be easily seen as a violation of the principle.

The principle might also be thought to imply a right to offer a computer service in a given country. If there were persons in a country interested in accessing a computer service offered on the international market the principle might direct that such access should be permitted. Conversely, it might imply that where such interest could be shown to exist, a provider of an international computer service might argue that he should be allowed to offer his service in the country concerned.

It may be mentioned that the principle of granting the public a right to use equipment could also have implications for internal and national communication. It could mean, for example, that if a national authority operated a teledata service of the teledoc type, the public, represented by private organisations, might have a right to use this service for making their own data bases available. The principle would then furnish arguments for the organisation of "a free and electronic press".

The last of the five principles in this section is the general principle of transparency. This principle states that it should be possible to easily obtain information as to the existence and nature of personal data and the main purposes for which they are used.

This principle appears in the OECD guidelines on the protection of privacy and transborder flows of personal data (Part II, Article 12). For the purposes of this report the principle may be considered as covering general communication policies.

Such a principle could easily be no more than a declaration of ideal intentions, were it not to be given any specific content or if not backed up by procedures for the exchange of information and related ideas. The principle does not however require a permanent exchange of information and national interests and policies may easily curtail its scope.

2. Substantive Principles Applicable to Transmission

This section discusses substantive principles directly applicable to transmission or transport. These principles therefore differ from those dealt with above in B.1. The parallel with transborder data flows may consequently seem easier to draw. On the other hand, the principles themselves concern the transportation of goods (*i.e.*, physical objects) rather than the communication of data and the possible usefulness of some of the principles will have to be discussed.

One of the major principles in this context is that of *innocent transit*. This principle applies to transport from one country to another which crosses the territory of one or more countries on the way from sender to addressee. In such cases goods should be allowed to cross the territory concerned without delay.

This is a basic principle of Conventions dealing with transport (*see* above, A.1) and should be seen as one of the most important principles of international trade, and even perhaps as a prerequisite for such trade. It appears in a wide range of treaties (*e.g.*, ICAO, GATT and UPU).

In its Article 1, the Universal Postal Convention (French original) states:

> "Freedom of transit
>
> Freedom of transit, the principle of which is set forth in Article 1 of the Constitution, shall carry with it the obligation for each postal administration to forward always by the quickest routes which it uses for its own items, closed mails and a decouvert letter-post items which are passed to it by another administration."

This Article establishes quite clearly the principle of innocent transit. But it also extends the principle somewhat to include an obligation beyond that of not delaying the transport. The national authority is required to facilitate the transport to make it the most rapid. In this way, we argue, the principle of innocent transit also implies some of the same principle discussed below under section 3 and which relate to the technical quality that national authorities should maintain in their networks.

It should be noted that the principle is qualified by the term "innocent". This suggests that certain transport is not covered by the principle. The treaties refer to exceptions, including the transport of dangerous substances or radioactive materials. One would expect any transport found to conflict with public order (order public) not to qualify as "innocent" transit (see Article 19 (2) of the International Telecommunication Convention).

The principle, if applied to transborder data flows, would encourage the free flow of information. It could certainly be applicable to transport through telecommunication networks. This type of communication would frequently have to make use of physical lines and equipment within the territory of third states when establishing links between a service bureau in one country and users in other countries. The principle might therefore be important for all types of service relying for international telecommunication.

A problem might arise in regard to the communication of data not considered as "innocent". Two examples may be given of this.

First, let us assume that the communication includes making a copyrighted text available form the service bureau to the user. The activity of the bureau would constitute an infringement of copyright in the transit country if the communication had terminated there. Even if the telecommunication authority was aware of the nature of the communication the latter should nevertheless be deemed to be in "innocent" transit.

Secondly, let us assume that the communication includes personal data in such a form that it represents a violation of the data protection legislation of the transit country. If the data refers to citizens or residents of the transit country, and the telecommunication authority is aware of this, it is likely that this may be seen as a threat of public order.

Both examples do, however, bring out the differences between transborder data flows and the transport of goods : the nature of data flowing through the network of the transit country is not generally known to the telecommunication authorities; it is not declared at the border by bills of lading or transport documents. If this practice is upheld (*see* the principle of secrecy of correspondence) the principle of innocent transit in fact cannot be qualified one way or another.

It will be noted that the principle does not directly apply to telecommunication using satellite links, even though this sort of link is implicated, since the satellite is deemed to be outside the territory or jurisdiction of any national state. The principle might however be extended by analogy to apply to the satellite segment so as to derive a principle of free and unhindered transit through outer space (*cf.* the Outer Space Treaty).

A principle subordinate to the principle of innocent transit is the principle of *custom-free transit*. This is also a principle of international trade and is designed to avoid multiple customs duties for a given cargo. At a theoretical level it has been discussed weather this principle is in fact no more than the result of a particular application of the principle of innocent transit or whether it is actually a principle in its own right. For our purposes it is unnecessary to take a stand on this point. But while the principle of innocent transit emphasizes the physical integrity of the goods the question of customs duties is not directly resolved.

The principle of custom-free transit is stated, for example, in Article 24 of the International Civil Aviation Organisation Treaty:

"Customs Duty

(*a*) Aircraft on a flight to, from or across the territory of another contracting state shall be admitted temporarily free of duty, subject to the customs regulation of the State."

This principle may be felt to be less importance in respect to transborder data flows due to the fact that such traffic is generally free of duty or levy. Indeed, this is true not only for data in transit but even for data "imported" from a country—no duty is paid for the service or the data received through the telecommunication network. However, there is basically a practical reason for this : it is difficult to trace such imports. Future developments, where a major part of transborder data flows are channelled through network operated by telecommunication authorities, or where international leased lines are subject to licensing and control by such authorities, could change all this. Since the question of whether and how to tax computer services is in a state of flux, it might be useful to see the principle as a possible preventive measure to direct national policies in a desired direction.

There may also be differences in customs duties where data is imported on physical material such as magnetic tape. The latter is taxed, for example, under item 92.12 of the Norwegian Customs Tariff. The duty is calculated according to the weight of the physical material rather then the value of the information and is therefore more an indirect tax on data. The situation is rather similar in most countries.

A third principle which might apply to transborder data flows is the principle of *free landing*. This derives from civil aviation and that, to our knowledge, is its only area of application. To some extent, it is a particular application of the principle of innocent transit.

The principle authorises brief and necessary stops on the territory of another country when an aircraft passes over that territory. Transit stops for longer periods are not directly related to the principle of innocent transit, but are obviously of great importance for efficient and safe civil aviation services.

Article 5 of the ICAO states the principle:

"Right of non-scheduled flight

Each contracting state agrees that all aircraft of the other contracting states, ... shall have the right, ... to make flights into or in a transit non-stop across its territory and to make stops for non-traffic purposes without the necessity of obtaining prior permission...."

The principle might have some application to transborder flows, which may be routed across a number of territories en route to their destination. Although the concept of "landing" is difficult to apply to transborder data flows, in practice, it would be conceivable for a communication malfunction to cause the data to be temporarily stored on the territory of a transit country. This country would then not be allowed to temper with the data.

A possible example would be the temporary storage of a personal register on the territory of a state whose data protection legislation made such a register, even of a temporary nature, subject to a licence or similar provision. The principle of free landing would suggest that such temporary storage of the register would be possible without prior authorisation.

The principle of free landing has perhaps been launched as

a slogan for another principle of relevance to transborder data flows: the right for a provider of a service to "land " that service on the territory of any other country. This would for instance be important for information retrieval or data processing services. In our terminology the question of being allowed to market a service in a given country is part of the right of the public to use equipment discussed above in section B.1.

In regard to conventional mail it is important to be able to determine at any time who has the right to dispose of the letter or—from a more practical standpoint—goods in transit. The principle has thus been established that *the title remains with the sender*. The question of deciding who owns mail in transit is crucial if, for example, the goods in transit are of some value and one of the parties becomes or is proved to be insolvent. For the mail service it would be rather cumbersome if this were to be determined by the contract between the parties. This principle is therefore extremely convenient.

The principle defines who is authorised to dispose of goods in transit. Obviously, it does not determine who is the owner of the goods, nor the risks borne or liability incurred by the parties: these matters will depend on the national law applicable to the transaction and on the contract between the parties. Indeed, such problems are decided in quite different ways for different legal systems and the principle discussed here has only indirect relevance to the question of determining ownership.

Article 5 of the UPU defines the principle clearly:

> "Article 5. *Ownership of postal items*
>
> A postal item shall remain the property of the sender until it is delivered to the rightful owner, except when the item has been seized in pursuance of the legislation of the country of destination."

The principle that the title remains with the sender might be applied to transborder data flows, determining which of the parties has the right to dispose of data in transit. Computerised data might easily be extremely valuable, *i.e.*, a computer programme or a message in an EFT system. The time in transit is generally very brief and this will severely reduce the practical importance of this principle as applied to telecommunication.

Another aspect should however be mentioned. An EFT service will frequently imply that a certain form of processing is taking place in the course of transit. For example, the message may be an order to credit a certain account. Such messages are collected and stored until the time—when all such messages are used to update the system and new messages are sent out to creditors giving notification of the transaction. Until notification actually reaches the creditor, the sender may wish to alter the original order. The above principle would make such alteration possible and systems should be designed to enable fresh orders to be given at the latest possible stage.[2]

The last principle identified is that of *secrecy of correspondence.* This principle is considered as a fundamental human right. It appears in Article 12 of the Universal Declaration of Human Rights.

> "No one shall be subjected to arbitrary interference with his privacy ..... home or correspondence ...."

The principle is also mentioned in Article 8 of the European Human Rights Convention:

> "Everyone has the right to respect for his private and family life, his home and his correspondence."

The Convention of the International Telecommunication Union mentions the principle in its Article 22 which provides that the members of the organisation agree to take all necessary measures, compatible with the telecommunications system used, to ensure the secrecy of international correspondence. This principle has led to the installation of technical security systems to ensure secrecy. The OECD guidelines also contain a "security safeguard principle" which provides:

> "Personal data should be protected by reasonable security against such risks as loss or unauthorised access, destruction, use, modification or disclosure of data."

Obviously, transborder flows of non-personal data could also benefit from the same principle. The principle would imply that the parties to the communication, the sender and the addressee, should take appropriate precautions to protect the data from unauthorised access. In certain cases this may involve encryption. However, the principle also concerns the telecommunication authorities who would have to provide facilities for the necessary network security, especially to protect data from unauthorised access. In this way we feel that the principle is related to that of the technical quality of the communication discussed below under Section 3.

It will be noted that this principle as drafted in the OECD guidelines (Part II, 11) is designed to give protection against unauthorised access. It might be thought desirable to expand the principle of secrecy of correspondence into a principle defining what access is deemed unauthorised. This might, for example, mean that telecommunication authorities would not be permitted to copy data transmitted through the network, unscramble coded transmissions, etc., unless they had some special reason for so doing. This might include the assessment that the communicated data was a threat to public order or national security in application of normal court procedures for licensing wire tapping.

Where the principle to be extended in this way it might ease some of the concern in regard to future developments of tariffs in telecommunication networks. It might, for example, mean that telecommunication authorities operating a package-switched network could interpret the address and other communication-relevant data, but that the package had to arrive "unopened" at its destination in the same way as a sealed envelope. It might also mean that encrypted data would only be permitted subject to the above qualification and that telecommunication authorities could only demand access to keys in the cases mentioned above.

The principle of secrecy of correspondence is based on arguments closely related to those concerning data protection. The principle may be thought quite clear but extended in the above sense could be of considerable importance to transborder data flows.

3. Principles Relating to the Harmonization of the Technical Aspects of International Data Networks

The harmonization of the technical aspects of computer communication involves several principles which partly overlap. We shall not distinguish in detail between these related principles but will merely set out their basic characteristics.

The first step towards general, international regulation in a particular field is quite often the regulation of technical aspects. This is a convenient approach since policy issues are not so predominant in relation to technical matters as they are in more substantive areas.

The position in regard to transborder data flows is the same as in other fields. Principles governing the technical aspects of computer communication already exist, *e.g.*, in the form of standard communication protocols. Moreover, outside the scope of existing treaties such as the International Telecommunication Convention, technical aspects might be appropriate for international regulation at a quite early stage of development.

The first type of technical principle is that relating to *standards.* Standards obviously have advantages in facilitating transborder data flows by reducing costs and increasing efficiency.

Standards may also have drawbacks and can, for example, increase vulnerability. An external enemy could more easily interfere with a standardised communication network than with a mixture of different equipment. This argument could well be used to oppose standardisation.

Standards may be imposed or encouraged by different strategies. The latter may of course also be combined as deemed appropriate within a given regulatory regime.

(*a*) A treaty or international instrument may of course *intervene directly to impose standards* and define their content in detail. This approach would certainly give the regulatory authority (*e.g.*, an international organisation) more control over the standards. On the other hand, there are obvious disadvantages in having detailed regulation in a given area. Control may be impractical due to the scope of the regulations and may also lead to a lack of flexibility inappropriate in a field of rapidly developing technology, as is the case with transborder data flows.

(*b*) To overcome the disadvantages of direct regulation another approach might be followed. One possibility would be to introduce by a convention a number of terms based, for example, on those used to regulate international trade (*e.g.*, "FOB", "CIF", "CF", etc.). For a given transaction a type of regulation might be selected from among the range of possible standard terms. This would be appropriate to resolve problems of liability arising in connection with transborder data flows. The use of standard terms to trigger off contractual clauses specified in the international legal instrument would be a quite flexible solution, which could more easily accommodate new technological developments and the individual requirements of the parties concerned.

(*c*) The most extreme strategy is to fix technical standards. International legal instruments generally refrain from establishing standards directly. They prefer to adopt or refer to standards developed by outside organisations or agencies, standards which in themselves might have no particular authority. This solution might be appropriate in an area where there was a need for a number of quite detailed rules but where there was a lack of technical expertise for their formulation. It is also used in cases where there is no appropriate organisation to develop such rules.

Leaving this brief discussion of alternative strategies, a number of possible standardisation principles may be mentioned. The first might be a *general principle of standardisation* which would state that standards are desirable and should be developed. For telecommunication this is to be found in Article 4.1. (c) of the International Telecommunication Convention which states that the aim of the International Telecommunication Union is "to harmonise the efforts of nations" within this area.

This general principle may be split into two (or more) sub-principles which are discussed below: the principle of standard rules and administrative procedures, and the principle of technical standards.

Although the general principle of standardisation may be an important political issue, principles which are more specific will normally be necessary to give effect to it.

The first of the more specific principles, that of *standard rules and administrative procedures*, directs the parties, so far as possible, towards uniform rules and administrative procedures so as to reduce diversification and thereby facilitate international exchanges, international trade and contacts. As an example, one may mention the Convention on International Civil Aviation which in its Article 37 under the title "Adoption of International Norms and Practice", first paragraph, states that:

> ".... each of the contracting parties agrees to co-operate to obtain the highest possible uniformity of the rules, norms, practice and organisations relating to aircraft, personnel, air

traffic routes and ground organisation in all questions where such uniformity will facilitate and promote aviation."

In our opinion, this principle should certainly also be considered in relation to transborder data flows. It may be thought that the efforts of OECD and the Council of Europe, as well as other international organisations, are aimed at a degree of uniformity of treatment for personal data flows.

Of course, the principle may have drawbacks for individual countries which might have to introduce new legislation, change established organisational patterns, etc., in order to comply with it. Data protection is a good example of this. Data protection authorities have been set up although this has not been a simple matter for certain countries. There is of course also the problem of identifying which roles and administrative procedures to standardise.

An area where standardisation would be desirable and perhaps a necessary prerequisite for routines of the required efficiency would be that of electronic fund transfers. Procedures of authentification in international trade cannot be developed without being recognised in different countries, either by acceptance in an international instrument or by incorporation in the contract between the parties. The latter approach may have drawbacks (*e.g.*, for those not party to the contract) and the first suggestion may therefore be more advisable.

Mention may also be made of a principle of *standard equipment*. Equipment necessary for communication should be standardised in order to facilitate transborder data flows. The utility of such a principle should need little explanation in relation to computer services, an area which is haunted by problems created by lack of compatibility.

This principle would in general govern computer communication. Article 28 of the ICAO and Articles 9 to 13 of the Railway Convention offer examples of such a principle.

The principle of standard equipment is, of course, closely related to the principle on standard rules and administrative procedures. There may, however, be distinct problems of application of this principle. Standardisation of technical equipment is undoubtedly desirable, but the question of cost and national interests may obstruct the process. For less developed countries it may be too expensive to upgrade technical equipment to standards adopted by more advanced countries, but for standardisation to make sense it must be based on norms established by the most advanced countries. Standardisation may also imply production of rather expensive equipment.

The problems of introducing technical standards as mentioned above may be eased by the establishment of a *classification scheme* for communication networks. This has the advantage of avoiding direct economic consequences for participating countries. The classification scheme would facilitate the documentation of the technical specifications for the network of a given country, and the classification would range from less developed to the most advanced technology.

Possibly, such a scheme would encourage development towards compliance with the most favourable classifications, especially where this involves the ability of the national service industry to compete on the international market. A classification scheme may perhaps have the same advantages as more direct standardisation, but without some of the drawbacks.

The principle of *technical quality* is related to that of standard equipment. This principle is implied, for example, in Article 23(1) of the International Telecommunication Convention and in Article 6(2) of the Railway Convention.

Some of the same observations as those made above would also apply to this principles. It is easy to appreciate the advantages of high technical quality in the network, of high speed, absence of disturbance, etc. obviously, this is also a matter of costs, and it might be difficult to reach international agreement on something which has direct consequences for national budgets. The principle of standardised or classified equipment implies guarantees of minimum technical quality, *i.e.*, the quality to which the equipment performs.

4. Conclusion—Free Flow of Information

A number of principles have been discussed above, varying greatly in content and possible relevance to transborder data flows. Some of the missing areas will be referred to below in Chapter IV which may be seen as an extended conclusion to this Chapter.

Although this conclusion may be seen as negative, it will however perhaps be appreciated how the principles extracted from other areas might be pieced together to attain the ideal of the "free flow of information".

The ideal of the free flow of information has often been presented as one of the poles in the transborder data flow debate. The ideal suggests that it would be desirable to encourage a situation where there were no legal, technical or economic barriers to transnational data flows. The elimination of economic barriers may mean the abolition of taxation, duties and other charges bearing on international communications at higher rates than on national communications.

It should be noted that so long as this issue polarises the debate, a distinction cannot be made between those who want to push the realisation of this ideal to its extreme and those who wish to accept some limitations. It could be made between those advocating the ideal as an argument for fewer limitations than at present (or using it as an argument against *increasing* restrictions) and those in favour of maintaining or stepping up current restrictions.

The idea of the free flow of information lends itself to relative rather than absolute arguments.

This is perhaps the point made by one of the foremost experts in Europe on transborder data flows, Jan Freese, when he stresses that it "is unlikely that there has ever been a free flow of information, either within countries or internationally". This has made him rephrase the slogan, "to make the ideal not free flow of information but *free and balanced* flow of information".[3]

Another prominent expert, Peter Robinson, has made an attempt to specify what Freese means by "balance" in a number of respects. In relation to flows of data and information between a subsidiary company in one country and the parent company in another, Robinson[4] has suggested the following explanation of "free flow":

> "....the right to transfer, or have access to, essential data and information in a manner that recognises the obligations and responsibilities of the corporations to the government and to the citizens of both countries concerned."

Using the discussion above we might try to piece together an alternative understanding of the ideal, relying on the principles identified in international instruments in force.

These might include:

(*i*) The *principle of national treatment* which would guarantee the equal treatment of foreign and national providers of computer services or, if this is thought to give too little room for national policy, the *most favoured nation principle* which would acts as a guarantee against unjustified discrimination among foreign providers.

(*ii*) The principle of *granting the public the right to use equipment* which would ensure that nationals of one country could use computer services offered by providers in another country.

(*iii*) The *principle of innocent transit* which would guarantee the speedy transmission of data from one country to another across the territory of a third country and which should be combined with the principle of *custom free transit*, making this flow exempt from duty or tax in the third country, and strengthened by the principle of *free landing* making intermediary storage possible without being caught by regulations governing data or data collection within that territory.

(*iv*) The principle of *secrecy of correspondence* which would prohibit telecommunication authorities from routinely sampling or supervising the type of data transmitted, the content of the transmission, etc.

(*v*) In addition, one might want to introduce *technical standards* facilitating international communication and reducing problems of incompatibility in telecommunications equipment, computer hardware or software.

This outline of five main categories of principles taken from other fields could provide a general framework for the "free flow of information" in regard to transborder data flows. Since this framework is based on principles, taken from legal instruments in force, it is possible that a regime based on them might be acceptable to OECD Member countries. This is undoubtedly one of the advantages of trying to design an new regime from existing elements of current international law.

In this paper we shall not however take this outline beyond the limits mentioned above. Nonetheless, it will be noted that the outline applies to transmission of data. To regulate the international market for computer services it would be necessary to adopt a much broader approach. In the following section we shall attempt to define a number of additional legal problems relevant to the aims of this report.

ASSESSMENT AND IMPLICATIONS

Introduction

It follows from the conclusion of the previous section that principles extracted from legal instruments in force offer no more than a partial legal framework for transborder data flows. Basically, while transmission of data seems to be adequately covered, principles applicable to the international market are not so easily found.

This report does not intend to assess the implications of the emerging international market for computer services in political terms. It deals merely with current legal issues and, to the extent that it is decided to allow or encourage the development of this market, it is necessary to identify areas appropriate for international co-operation.

Five problem areas seem to be of interest (but do not cover the entire field) for the development of an international legal framework for transborder data flows. Although we suggest rules to be adopted either by states or by private actors, this does not mean that the problems considered are to be dealt with in a single legal instrument or by a single international organisation.

The five problem areas mentioned are as follows:

- — Liability and security.
- — Recognition of rights to data.
- — Taxes and duties.
- — Authentification.
- — Choice of applicable law.

Liability and Security

The liability of the provider of a computer service is in principle regulated by the contract between the provider and the user. This contract may be quite rudimentary, consisting merely of the opening of an account by the user.

If the contract is adequate it will define the liability of the parties. If it is rudimentary, liability will by implication be governed by the rules of the legal system governing the contract. Since such contracts are by nature international it may involve two national systems of conflict of laws which may be at variance with each other.

If the contract has an international element, problems of liability are inseparable from that of the proper law of the contract. For this reason an examination of liability problems involves problems connected with the conflict rules determining the proper law of the conflict which will be examined below in section F.

Data security is a concept with differing implications. It generally indicates physical or organisational measures to protect data against unauthorised access or destruction due to human error, fire or other cause. Data security may also be used in a slightly broader meaning, indicating *the financial predictability* of the operation.

In this sense, the financial predictability , which may mean impossibility of obtaining insurance against telecommunication malfunction, will depend on more general considerations where at least three aspects are relevant : the volume of international trade in computer services, the risk of financial loss due to a deficiency in the service provided, and the possibility of two national legal systems having different rules to resolve the question of liability.

Three types of reason may explain a deficiency in computer services. Firstly, the data communicated may for some reason be incorrect, incomplete or otherwise erroneous. Secondly, the service may malfunction: long-term breakdown, programmes not available or malfunctioning, etc. Thirdly, the communication may malfunction or data may be lost, for example, in transit.

These deficiencies may mean a financial loss for the user. The loss may be direct : paying for a service one does not get (the user pays for access to a non-operational computer system) and/ or indirect : erroneous advice given to a customer of the user or incorrect figures for a project. The legal rules governing liability in these three cases naturally differ considerably, even within a given national system.

Losses incurred may be substantial. The provider may be willing to accept liability for direct losses. However, since it is difficult to assess indirect losses and express them in terms of a financial risk, the provider cannot make a financial assessment so as to cover his risk by an increase in the price of his services. From this legitimate need for predictability flows a need to include in the contract terms allocating risks and liability between the provider and the user.

Also, the provider of services will hardly in the contract accept liability for possible malfunctions during transit since he has no possibility of influencing the type of equipment, the route through the network, etc., which are matters for the telecommunication authorities. The responsibilities of such authorities will have been defined by statute and other legal instrument. To our knowledge, most telecommunication authorities have reduced this liability to minimum cover for direct loss (the price of a telegram is refunded if it is lost in transit) (*cf.* also Article 21 of the International Telecommunication Convention).

In this respect there is a contrast with conventional law. In the case of complex transport operations, liability lies with the first carrier. The first carrier may use sub-contractors who may in their turn sub-contract. But liability will be channelled to the first carrier. If the addressee receives goods in an unsatisfactory condition he may hold the first carrier liable. The first carrier may then proceed against one of the sub-contractors. This channelling of liability thus makes for relatively straightforward relations between the two parties, not-withstanding the fact that a number of other parities are involved in the transaction. The system of channelling liability to the first carrier is justified by the fact that such carrier usually had some possibility of choice. This freedom of choice justifies the fact that he is liable if the use he makes of such freedom results in a loss to the addressee.

The situation is completely different in the field of international computer services : the provider has no freedom of choice in using national telecommunication facilities and he cannot negotiate contracts with the authority or company operating these facilities. There may be nuances to this blunt statement since national telecommunications structures vary, but we think that it is nevertheless generally true.

The provision of computer services involves a financial risk which may be regulated in the contract between provider and user.` Where liability problems are mentioned, telecommunication malfunction is not dealt with expressly but is implicitly understood. The need for more explicit resolution of this problem may increase as the market for international computer services develops.

It might be possible to draft general clauses establishing the liability of providers of computer services. These clauses could offer two or three alternatives, since liability problems arise in different ways depending on the type of service. The warranty offered by a provider of information retrieval services might be rather different from that offered by a provider of management information services. In the first case the warranty should include, for example, the principle that the data are what they are declared to be (if a legal data base specifies the most recent update the provider would be liable if statutory amendments prior to that date were not included and the user suffered financial loss by relying on the data supplied). In the second case a warranty covering functional aspects (*e.g.*, updating response) may be of greater importance.

Such clauses could be included in the contract between provider and user. They might be given code-terms similar to those used in international trade. However, the problem of the law applicable to the contract would remain.

The financial risk resulting from a telecommunication malfunction would however still not be covered. So far as we know, no regular insurance policy is available . Today, the risk is borne by the user who is unable to cover himself by insurance. Whether this is seen as a problem or not depends very much upon the actual risk of such malfunction occurring without notification.

In the case of a closed user group sharing, for example, a management information service the users could by contract distribute among themselves the risk of malfunction both in the telecommunication system and in the service itself. We understand that the SWIFT network is based on such an arrangement. This would not work as smoothly in the case of services provided to open groups. The provider would have to charge the users more to cover the shared risk and the extra charge should be seen by users as an advantage rather then an extra expense. Such a solution would give assessment of the risk a market value giving the provider offering such warranty a competitive edge.

The need, by contract or otherwise, to regulate the risk of financial loss due to some deficiency in the service must correspond to the actual *risk* of malfunction. Increased technical reliability may reduce the need for legal protection. This argument could be used by telecommunication authorities: the services they provide, combined with routine communication protocols, are such that undetected malfunctions in transit are rather unlikely.

The level of security offered by a computer service provider is an important factor for the user. On the international market standards defining the level of security obtained by a provider of computer services might sometimes be thought desirable. The standard could then be included in the contract between the parties and used as an element in competition.

Security standards have already been proposed for international computer services based on standards used for ships.[5] Data protection may also require a certain level of security. The Danish Data Surveillance Authority has established two standards for firm processing personal data, depending on the type of processing undertaken.

Recognition of Rights to Data

When considering relations between a provider of computer services and his customer it should not be forgotten that the provider may himself have obtained access to the data by means of a contract with a third party. The contractual relationship between the provider of data and the provider of services may specify limitations to the use to which the data are put. Similarly, the law may impose restrictions on the use of data.

An example of the contractual limitations would be the licence given to a provider of information retrieval services in regard to copyrighted material. The copyright owner may have made the licences subject to territorial limitations. If the provider offers his service internationally the copyrighted material may be retrieved by a client in a jurisdiction where another licensee has the exclusive right to provide copies. The use will then probably constitute a copyright infringement and the user will be liable *vis-a-vis* the exclusive licensee.

This example may be illustrated by the "Coditel" decision of the European Court of Justice in Luxembourg of 18th March 1980.[6]

Another example of statutory limitation is found in the law on data protection. Where data includes personal data, national legislation may make transborder flows subject to licence or other provisions.

Such limitations may also effect services where the *personal* element of the data is not predominant : for example, in the case of bibliographies containing both personal data along with non-sensitive information on books by the authors. The Swedish legal information retrieval services thus possess personal data on judges, lawyers, etc., and a licence for transborder data export would have to be obtained before foreign users could access Swedish case law.

In addition to these two sources of limitations (copyright and data protection) others may also exist. In contracts there is in principle no limit to restrictions accepted by the provider of services. The user will have no possibility of determining whether his use of the service constitutes an infringement of restrictions accepted by or imposed on the provider. In some circumstances (perhaps most) the penalty would be borne by the provider. If, for example, the provider exports personal data without proper licence, national data protection authorities may take action against him, but it would be difficult for them to punish the user who will usually be outside their jurisdiction. The "Coditel" case is nevertheless one example where the penalty was imposed on the user. If a user accesses a foreign information retrieval service and copies a piece of a literary work, which constitutes an infringement of the exclusive licence granted to a person in his own country, the licensee will probably take action against the user rather than the provider since, in the latter case, it would be difficult for him to bring action against a party in another jurisdiction.

In this report, the examples have been taken from the field of information retrieval services. This problem, however, applies to a wide range of services. The example might have been more dramatic in the case of licences for computer programmes than in the case of the reproduction of a copyrighted work.

Where, for example, a user in one country accesses a provider of processing services in another country, using a programme offered by the provider, can it be said that there has been an infringement of the exclusive licence to the programme granted to a provider in the user's own country?

An appropriate provision in the contact might perhaps be a warranty from the provider to the user that the service provided does not constitute an infringement within the user's jurisdiction. If the user is sued he may then take action against the provider under this clause in the contract.

In fact, even where the contract is rudimentary in nature, it would be possible to interpret it to mean that the provider is aware of the law in the user's jurisdiction. In practice, the provider is the only person able to control this risk.

This principle is rather similar to that of the *polluter pays principle.* It is not identical since there is no "pollution". It is not the nature of the data but rather the legal context which will determine whether or not their use represents an infringement.

The problems may be rather more complex than those mentioned. A Norwegian example may be cited. A Norwegian social researcher was found guilty of espionage because he had published his findings on the implications of NATO defence installations. The findings were the result of piecing together information retrieved from official publications. A number of the crucial documents were restricted in Norway as containing matter affecting national security. The same documents could be obtained on-line from United States providers of information retrieval services in accordance with the Freedom of Information Act.

Taxes and Duties

Computer services are also subject to taxes and duties. The most important is perhaps value added tax. Services are generally exempt from value added tax but it appears that computer services are usually not included in the exemption. The VAT system nevertheless varies from country to country and may have an impact on the international market for computer services.

An example may be taken from the Norwegian context. In

Norway, services are generally exempt from VAT, but an exception is made in respect of a number of important categories of services, including computer services ("data processing"). In Norway, a provider of such a service must add 20 per cent VAT to his customer's bill. The financial impact of this addition depends on whether or not the customer can deduct VAT which he pays from VAT which he receives. In some cases the entire amount is borne by the customer. If the customer switches to a foreign provider of computer services no tax is calculated on the imported service. This contracts with the rules for the import of goods which may be exported without VAT whereas they are imported with VAT. If the foreign provider of services has a lower VAT he may have a competitive edge and the additional cost of international telecommunication paid by the Norwegian customer is thereby reduced.

This rather simple example shows how taxes and duties on computer services may affect the structure of the international market for telecommunication services. Examples could be given of other countries which would show that existing legal rules would require VAT to be paid by both the provider and the user, so amounting to a kind of double taxation. In the United Kingdom, the Teledoc service provided by Prestel has been exempted from tax by the Customs and Excise Department in line with the treatment for news wire services, even though Prestel data banks contain only a small proportion of news. This is in contrast to the position as regards traditional information retrieval services.[7]

It will be noted that this is not taxation or duty on transactional data flows as such. It is rather the services or activities causing the data flows which are subject to taxation. However, since the service is provided from one country to users in another, two legal systems will be involved. It would seem that today computer services are treated differently by authorities of different countries and that these differences may result in anomalies and unexpected impacts on the international market for computer services. As mentioned in Annex I, it is sometimes difficult to distinguish between processing services and the production of goods in the form of reproduced listings, etc.

It is clear that differing systems of taxation may in themselves by enough to create problems for transborder data flows. Solutions to this problem are difficult to find, since not enough is known about how VAT and similar taxes are applied to national and international computer services. Additional unformation would be necessary in this respect.

Authentification

In the course of trade it is often necessary to have some practical guarantee of the authenticity of a piece of information. This is generally resolved by having a document signed by the party making the statement and perhaps having it witnessed by other persons or officials. Such procedure guarantees the authenticity of the document and hence also of the information it contains. Legal rules have backed-up this factual security by giving special force to documents made in accordance with specific procedures, *e.g.*, negotiable instruments, wills, transport documents.

In these cased the document may be said to have three distinct functions—it is a *carrier of information*, it serves as *evidence* of this information and it represents the legal *rights* expressed by the document (this latter function is perhaps associated only with negotiable instruments).[8]

Where the information contained in such documents is in the form of data transmitted by or between computers problems will arise. This is especially true for electronic funds transfer services where the problem of authentification of the signature arises.

Since a computerised set of data may be tampered with without leaving physical evidence (paper documents have been around for sufficient time for the risks to be known) the change of medium represents an unknown change in the risk which may the parties involved reluctant to rely upon EFT services.

However, more formal reasons may also be found, since legislation is frequently worded in such a way that legal consequences do not follow in the absence of a physical document. A bill of lading is physical document and the legal functions of such a document will not be attached to a print-out from an EFT service even though the information may be identical.

The nature of the concept of "information" discussed in section E where it was pointed out that information in the strict sense is rarely made subject to legal rules which will apply to the physical object carrying the information, is at the root of the difficulties. When computer systems separate the two things, conventional regulations will have problems in coping with the change.

The major difficulties experienced by the common law countries in the field of evidence may also be seen as a consequence of this basic feature of computer services. The main obstacle to the admissibility of computer output as evidence would seem to be the traditional hearsay rule.[9]

A signature is viewed as a traditional method of securing authenticity. It may be disputed whether signature really is very reliable, since a false signature is difficult to detect except by those perfectly familiar with the signature of the writer. Even comparison is none too effective. In spite of this, signature is recognised as a convenient form of authentification and the forging of another's signature is a crime.

When replacing the physical document with a massage for transmission through the telecommunication network it is obviously necessary to find new methods of authentification. This may be achieved by conventional cryptography, but this would imply a limited user group (as in the SWIFT network) and a high degree of data security to avoid unauthorised access to the code.

It has been maintained that to be cost effective EFT services must be based on a sound authentification method. An ideal method is not currently available.

In their survey of authentification methods, Greguras and Sykes found a combination of a plastic card with a personal identification number and signature analysis to be the only two viable possibilities. Fingerprint analysis, hand geometry and voice analysis were found less appropriate for authentification in EFT services.[10]

The problem of authentification requires a whole range of very specific legal questions to be addressed. It does not seem possible to resolve all the problems in the same way or with the same document.

However, some international solution has to be found since in international trade paper documents cannot be replaced by computerised messages unless the change is recognised by national legal systems. To some degree, the parties to a contract may remedy this absence of official recognition by expressly including in the contract some authentification provision, *e.g.*, by cryptography, but it would seem that a more general solution should be sought.

Some schemes have found practical applications.[11] An ambitious scheme was suggested by the United States Cargo Data Interchange System (CARDIS) but has not yet been realised.

It seems necessary to look for an authentification method as easy to use as a signature on physical documents. It will be difficult to find such a method appropriate for general use. However, a method which looks very promising and would be suitable for use by "professionals" is the one-way trapdoor function.

These functions are thought adequate for public key cryptosystems. Such functions have twin codes, A and B. Messages coded by A can only be decoded by B. Since there is no feasible way of working out A from B, B can be published. If a message can be decoded by B then it is proved that it originated from the party able to code it by A and, consequently, the authenticity of the message is established. Such functions are described in a number of papers and their application to EFT services has already been proposed.[12] It is reported that these functions have been incorporated in a chip. This would probably greatly facilitate their use and protection.

Choice of Applicable Law

In regard to a number of the issues discussed above it has been suggested that the contract between the provider of computer services and the user or customer should include a provision on the law applicable. Standard clauses could be designed, for example, by an international organisation, and incorporated in a contract *in extenso*. As contracts are often rather rudimentary, however, it might be easier to formulate several types of clauses in order to facilitate their use in contracts.

In this way one might rely on contract to resolve the substantive legal issues involved in transborder data flows. By making the contractual relationship more visible the parties would be encouraged more conscientiously to seek higher quality of computer services and the key role of the latter in competition on the international market would thus come to be recognised.

It would, however, still fall some way short of complete international harmonization. In court proceedings the court's decision will depend on the private international law of its jurisdiction (*lex fori*) as regards interpretation of the contract. The conflict rules used to determine the proper law of the contract (where the contract is silent on this point) may vary from country to country, although it seems that a consensus is emerging that the proper law of the contract is that of the legal system with which the transaction has the closest and most substantial connection. In the case of a number of computer services the location of the computer bureau of the provider of the service might constitute such connection, making the law of that country the proper law of the contract. However, the principle cited implies an assessment which may vary from case to case, and from court to court, so that the contracts of one provider could in fact be subject to a number of different national legal systems.

Stricter rules in regard to the choice of law are imposed by the 1951 Hague Convention. These rules, however, only apply to the international sale of goods and will consequently not directly apply to trade in computer services.

Although contracts may include clauses defined in international legal instruments and recommended for use, case law and interpretation may fragment the initial unity into a number of national variations. To avoid this happening three slightly different strategies seem to be indicated.

Firstly, the private international law of most countries recognises the freedom of the parties to choose the law applicable to their contract. Where standard clauses deal with the applicable law or where this is otherwise expressly dealt with, such choice will be generally respected by national private international law. In our opinion, such clauses might be extended to cover arbitration, which perhaps could be used to channel all disputes on standard clauses to one jurisdiction and one arbitration board.

Such a strategy would go a long way to correct possible fragmentation of the initial international unity. There are, however, also limitations to this strategy. The clause dealing with the applicable law would have to be interpreted in the context of the *lex fori* and naturally this might restrict its application. For example, some national legal systems do not recognise the validity of the clause dealing with the choice of a law applicable to the contract if the contract has no real connection with that country. For purposes of harmonization the law of country A may be chosen as the proper law of the contract by means of a standard clause, although the contractual relationship is between a provider of computer services in country B and a user in country C. The law of the *lex fori* may recognise in need for such a clause and hence accept it but this problem should be dealt with in international legal instruments dealing with standard clauses. Similarly, rules of the *lex fori* may be applied in order to prevent nationals escaping from restrictive national regulations through choice of law clauses.

Although choice of the clause on applicable law will leave part of the problem unsolved, this should not be exaggerated. In international trade such clauses are frequently used and seem to function satisfactorily.

One problem *not* solved by a choice of a clause relating to applicable law would be that of the creation of the obligation. The applicable law of the contract will not govern the very real question of whether contractual obligations have in fact been entered into. Here again national laws vary; the English doctrine of "consideration" is somewhat different to the doctrines of continental Europe.

Since explicit choice of applicable law clauses do not resolve all problems, it might be felt desirable to adopt an international legal instrument providing explicit solutions. Such instrument might also include standard contract clauses applicable by express agreement of the parties. In addition, the instrument might address the conflict of laws, determining what would be the proper law of the contract. A special arbitration board could even be proposed to decide disputes concerning standard contract clauses.

This international legal instrument would then have to be adopted by countries to the extent that it involved amendment of the private international law rules of such countries, which would usually require an instrument of ratification incorporating the treaty into the national legal system (*e.g.*, by Act of Parliament). Obviously, such a strategy would mean a higher degree of international co-ordination. Although the impact would be considerable, the risks of national diversification would not be totally eliminated since the rules of the treaty, embodied in national legal systems, would then be interpreted by national courts. It would not be appropriate to set up a special supernational court to handle such matters.

Consequently, we think that even an international convention would not secure complete international unity in the application of standard clauses incorporated in contracts for computer services. If the risk of national diversification is accepted as difficult to eliminate, we think the drawbacks of an international convention would be greater than its advantages. The drafting and negotiating of a convention is a long-term project and might be inappropriate in a rapidly developing field in which national policies are perhaps not sufficiently well defined.

If we discard the idea of a full-fledged convention in this way we might then return to the idea of some sort of recommendation setting out standard contract clauses on liability, rights to data, etc. These clauses could also be brought into play by express agreement between the parties. If providers of services found them useful they would include them in their contracts.

The third possibility would be to set up an international organisation to follow practice based on the standard clauses. This organisation could amend clauses or examine new ones if the need arose. It could combine clauses into standard contracts which could be adopted by agreement between the parties; the INFRETI clause might enable standard clauses to be brought into play concerning liability for information retrieval services by giving a warranty in regard to the right to use the data accessed and specifying a certain level of data security.

This scheme is rather similar to a scheme suggested by Bing in 1980, where the international organisation is compared to a classification society. In this paper it is pointed out that national authorities may actually require that foreign providers of computer services conform to certain standards set out in sets of standard contractual terms. This would authorise the use of the standard clauses without incorporating them in any international agreement of a formally binding nature.

This third possibility could be realised in a rather informal way; it could be sufficiently flexible to follow technical and international developments. Conflicts of laws would be resolved by standard contract clauses, which would mean a degree of uncertainty. Some measure of co-ordination might, however, be achieved through the activities of the international organisation which would make information available on practice in different countries and would make recommendations for explicit harmonization measures where this was felt necessary.

CONCLUSIONS

In this final section of the report we would like, by way of summing up, to offer some conclusions. Many of the problems discussed in this report have uncertain outlines. The conclusions will therefore take the form of suggestions as to what might be the next step towards a firmer grasp of the issues. It must be kept in mind that these are very tentative suggestions put forward without the benefit of the broader political perspective that might result from discussions between representatives of several countries or, indeed, from the secretariat of an international organisation. The suggestions have the limited purpose of reiterating the possible stages in the approach outlined in the report.

Public Key Encryption Systems

Reference is made above to the problems of authentification and signature. Such problems are specially severe in relation to EFT services. No real solution can be found outside an international context. At the present time public key encryption systems seem to constitute a promising solution to part of the authentification problem. However, it is not clear how appropriate such systems are to the solution of the legal problems. A study might therefore be suggested to examine.

(*a*) the practical application of such public key encryption systems to communication between parties in a legal context (is it, for instance, necessary to maintain the keys as software, or should they be integrated in chips?), and

(*b*) the extent to which such systems actually resolve authentification problems in relation to specific legal transactions.

Taxes and Duties

It has been mentioned above that different national systems of taxation and customs duties (in particular VAT) may create difficulties such as double taxation for providers of international computer services. Before examining the possibility of international harmonization, a better understanding of the situation is necessary. OECD Member countries could be asked to provide information concerning the treatment of computer services under national taxation systems. On the basis of such information consideration could be given to problems appropriate for international action and to the form such action might take.

Free Flow of Information

The examination of existing international instruments has had a positive result, *i.e.*, it gives an outline of a possible specification of the ideal of "the free flow of information". It might be asked whether sufficient basis exists to develop guidelines which, as concerns transborder flows of non-personal data, would specify to what extent such traffic would be unrestricted. Obviously, important policy issues would have to be dealt with at the same time. Whether such action is considered appropriate may to a large extent depend upon whether countries have policies sufficiently explicit to enable them to take a stand on the issues discussed. The outline given as a conclusion to chapter III may however be sufficiently detailed to allow discussion on the advisability of further development.

Standard Contract Clauses and Express Declarations

In the Section above it was maintained that a number of questions could best be solved in the contract between the provider and user of computer services. Before accessing a computer service the user has to enter into more contractual arrangement with the provider. This contract may be rather rudimentary and involve no more than the identification of the user for accounting purposes. When users are comparing offers from different providers of computer services, assessment would be facilitated if contracts could be considered in terms of standards defining the quality of the service.

Issues which might be addressed are those of liability, warranty of the right to use data, physical data security and the choice of applicable law.

A set of standard terms might be examined and included in an international instrument by way of recommendation. For each issue, optional terms might be developed to meet the different needs of providers and users and the different types of service provided. Each standard term might by assigned a code term similar to terms such as "FOB", "CIF", etc. The inclusion of the term in a contract which could be rapidly communicated to the terminal of the user, would bring the standard term into effect and make it an integral part of the contract.

Further development along these lines might be considered by working out standard sets of terms combining the appropriate standard terms for a specific type of service. Such combinations would then be similar to standard form contracts. Each type of contract could also be given a formal code, reference to which would be sufficient to bring the contract into effect. Consideration could also be given to recommending certain standard form contracts for use in relation to certain types of computer services.

Lastly, an international body responsible for the administration of contracts and recommended clauses could be set up. This organisation could keep track of the use of terms and contracts, publish relevant case law and provide a forum for their further development.

This strategy would provide some degree of international harmonization while leaving the parties to contracts free to design their own contractual terms. The recommended terms and standard form contracts would be options, their use perhaps mainly dependant upon their adequacy and usefulness; they would offer a simple way of drawing up contracts and comparing terms in contracts offered by different providers.

References

1. See Gottlieb. A.; Dalfen, C.; Katz, K., "The Transborder Transfer of Information by Communications and Computer Systems : Issues and Approaches to Guiding Principles", in the *American Journal of*

International law, 1974, pp. 246-248; and *Transnational Data Report World Survey*, 1980, No. 2, pp. 9 and 10. Edited by G. Russell Pipe, Amsterdam.

2. Sitre, Ingre, Marie Dons, *Bankgiro. Saerlig om ansvar ogtilbakekall*, Institute for privatretts stensil—series, No. 48, Oslo, 1976, pp. 80-82.
3. Freese, Jan, *International Data Flow*, Student-litteratur, Lund, 1979, p. 17.
4. Robinson, Peter, *Scientific and Technological Information in Transborder Data Flows*, Toronto, 1980.
5. Bing, Jon, "Regulating international computer services : The problem and a possible solution", in *IBI World Conference on Transborder Data Flow Policies*, IBI, Rome, 1980.
6. *Transnational Data Report*, No. 1, published by G. Russell Pipe, Amsterdam, 1981, p. 70.
7. *Transnational Data Report*, No. 6, Vol,. II, published by Russell Pipe, Amsterdam, 1980, p. 4.
8. Henriksen Roger, "Legal Questions of Security", Nordic Legal Committee, Oslo, 1981, p. 2.
9. Tapper, Colin, *op. cit.*, pp. 149-180 and Bender, David, *Computer Law : Evidence and Procedure*, Bender, New York, 1979.
10. Greguaras, Fred M., Sykes, David S., "Authentification in EFT : The Legal Standards and the Operational Reality", in *Computer/Law Journal*, 1980, pp. 67-86.
11. See Gronfors, Kurt, "Transport Documents and Computerization", *Marius*, No. 22, 1977, p. 46.
12. Renschou, Knut, Helge, "Konossementer og EDB", *Marius*, No. 50, Oslo, 1980.

12

Media and Development Communication : Case Studies from Developing Countries

I

Introduction

Easy access to recorded information is important for all those who need such information. This calls for speed, ease, convenience and accuracy in the transmission process. Lopez deals with the collection of relevant information covering two aspects namely, 'intellectual' content and the 'mechanical' means for supplying information, starting with the operational definitions of terms like data, resource, information, information retrieval and mechanisation.

The need for access to recorded knowledge must be satisfied by providing rapidly, conveniently, economically, and with precision that a particular fact, information or data that would be useful—to a particular individual or entity; at a particular time; for a particular problem or interest; and in a form that is useful to him, regardless of—where it was generated; in what form or language; or how it must be located or processed.

It is an accepted fact that planning as a process, relies on vast amounts of data and on a continuing basis as planning does not end after completion or implementation of a plan. Development planning as a process involves a series of steps or stages, and from one stage to another, statistics and data are a vital requirement.

This paper will, therefore, dwell on the collection and availability of relevant information for provincial development on two aspects—the "intellectual" content of work in the development activity and the "mechanical" methods for providing the information for intellectual operation.

Experience in technology, in industry, and in government proves that the availability of knowledge is essential to management. The provincial manager's (the governor and the government entities of the province) job is deeply involved with resource flows. He must direct the efforts of the province's human resource, which utilises fixed-use resources to convert current-use resources into finished goods and services. We have also the money resource as the facilitator of this process of creating utility (*i.e.* the acquisition, utilisation and disposition of resources). This area of resource flows, as well as the nature of the management.

MIS for Development

These considerations demand that the terms relevant to the function and purpose of this paper be defined.

Data refer to an accumulation of facts concerning a category of knowledge. The data resource represents potential utility to the management in making decisions concerning resource flows. Using data to signify a resource seems warranted in that they have potential utility if processed correctly; namely, they can be processed to generate *information*, which is the basis of division making. As data are selected and recorded in the form of inputs to the data processing systems, emphasis is placed on generating specific types of information outputs. The processing may take the form of classifying, sorting, calculating, or summarising the data resource inputs.

Information is thus the most usable form of data in that it relates specifically to a need of the manager, *i.e.*, to a type of decision which must be made. In this respect, it is the output of the data resource system.

Also, *information* is more than records, documents or books. The physical form may vary considerably to include pamphlets, periodicals, newspapers, reports, photographs, films, charts, maps, indexes, letters, memos, circulars, etc. We, therefore, may consider as information any recorded knowledge that may be useful to some decision maker.

Information retrieval is looking through or exploring thoroughly through recorded knowledge in order to find something. The information retrieval system of a public management control system is enormously important, as without an efficient data retrieval system, where data are properly classified and available in a reasonable period of time, no management control system can be effective. It consists mainly of five elements or stages as data input, storage, processing, output, and communication (transmitting data to the user).

Mechanisation involves the organisation of the powers of a complex body, and therefore, implies that a machine is to be considered as more than a single physical device; it is to be considered as a system that consists of interacting parts. These interacting parts may include devices, human beings or procedures. Thus "mechanisation" for the purposes of this paper, may be ascribed to card filling, that requires card manipulation techniques or to an information centre that utilises various mechanical equipment to a large-scale digital computer that has been made part of a sophisticated system of information retrieval.

Iloilo Provincial Development Assistance Project

Iloilo Profile:

One of the 18 priority provinces in the Provincial Development Assistance Programme of the National Economic development Authority (NEDA) and the USAID is Iloilo.

The province of Iloilo is primarily agricultural. Rice is the major agricultural crop, and as such has gained the distinction of being the No. 1 rice-producing province in 1970 and is still one of the top three in the entire country. The province's performance in rice production plus remarkable increases in the production of sugar, mango, coconuts, mango, citrus fruits and root crops have made Iloilo also the Philippines prime agricultural province. Sugarcane is the next most valuable agricultural crop in the province. With the three new sugar centrals which started operations in 1970 (in addition to one already existing), sugarcane production has increased considerably. Another fact is that while the country is deficient in fish and millions of pesos worth of fish products are being imported every year, the province is a top producer of marine and inland (fresh and brackish) fish.

Iloilo has probably the most number of schools and colleges of agriculture and fishery in the country. Because of the abundant educational facilities, Iloilo lead the rest of the Western Visayas region in levels of educational attainment.

Besides, all regional offices for the Western Visayas (Regional VI) of the agencies or departments of the National Government are located in Iloilo.

The Provincial Government of Iloilo and its Information System :

The Provincial Government of Iloilo is essentially the same in structure today as it was prior to the declaration of Martial Law in September, 1972. However, the history of the Provincial Development Council goes back to President Marcos' Executive Order Number 121 creating the Provincial Development Committees for all provinces. In this is provided the legal basis for the organisation of the Provincial Development Council. Shortly after the issuance of the Executive Order, the Office of the Governor received information that the Province had been selected as one of the pilot provinces under the National Economic Council (NEC) Provincial Development Assistance Project (PDAP).

The Executive Order named the Governor, by virtue of his position, the Chairman of the Development Council, who was called upon to establish co-ordination among the different provincial and national government agencies. This established the Governor as the most logical institutional leader, rather than someone either from any one government agency or from the private sector. The Development Staff was created as the "workhorse" of the Council and was placed under the direct control of the Governor, the Chairman of the Council.

An Administrative Order set forth a basic procedure for the preparation, compilation and implementation of a Provincial

Development Programme. The procedure reveals at the same time the data gathering function of the Development Council which falls mainly under the Research and Statistics Unit : Quoting from the Administrative Order :

1. The Research and Statistics Unit will first collect, collate and analyse all significant data from all national, provincial and commercial sources. This information shall be prepared in reports and submitted to the Executive Officer and other elements of the Development Staff.
2. The Executive Officer, in consultation with the Chief of Planning and Programming shall identify the priority areas which require immediate attention. The Executive Officer shall request the Chiefs of Task Forces concerned to draw up projects accordingly. Upon submission of the projects, the Chief Planning and Programming, shall list the projects in order or priority together with estimated costs. The Executive Officer, together with the Chief, Planning and Programming will draft a provincial development project or programme and submit it to the Governor for his consideration. The Governor shall then return the draft programme to the Executive Officer with his comments and/or amendments and direct that these changes be incorporated. The Executive Officer shall then return the amended draft programme to the Chief, Planning and Programming for amendment.
3. The Chief, Planning and Programming shall publish a recommended programme which incorporates the amendments directed by the Governor. He submits the recommended programme to the Executive Officer who then refers the programme to the Provincial Development Council.
4. The Provincial Development Council will consider the recommended programme and return the programme to the Executive Officer together with comments, amendments and/or recommendations.
5. The Executive Officer then amends the recommended

CONCEPT OF OPERATION AND FUNCTIONAL ORGANIZATION FOR PRIME IMPLEMENTATION

SUPERVISING COMMITTEE

Data Research and Collection Group

- Plans and executes data research covering all possible data source agencies.
- Studies functions and System of reporting of source agencies.
- Gathers secondary data through reports, publications, summaries, etc. of source agencies.
- Establishes and maintains harmonious relationships with source agencies.
- Maintains a directory of source agencies.
- Provides continuous up-date of PRIME data.

Data Evaluation and Prime Co-ordinating Group

- Plans and co-ordinates the smooth flow of PRIME data.
- Provides guidance to data researchers and checks their performance.
- Receives and evaluates gathered data concerning relevance to PRIME.
- Provides data processing specifications particularly the output reports.
- Anticipates and studies possible on-line terminal queries for guidance of the on-line programming team.
- Coordinates for the administration support of the PRIME work groups.

Computer Data Processing Group

- Designs data conversion specifications and provides guidance for coding and keypunching.
- Designs computer processing and executes programming.
- Plans and implements the integration of data modules into a common data base in support of on-line operation.
- Produces specified PRIME printouts.
- Specifies on-line operation parameters.
- Provides guidance to terminal operation group.

Presidential on-line Terminal Operation Group

- Operaters the on-line terminal in support of Presidential requirements.
- Feedbacks PRIME Coordinating Group as to the trend of Presidential queries.
- Maintains harmonious relationships with on-line customers and rationalises infeasible requirements.
- Studies on-line concepts and contents of data base.

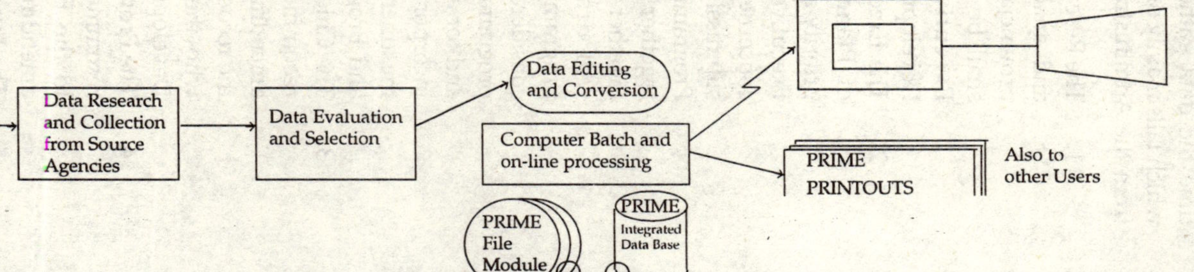

programme along the lines suggested by the Development Council and returns the amended programme to the Governor for his approval.

6. The Governor shall then approve the programme and instruct the Executive Officer to implement it, project by project, as the available funds permit.
7. The Executive Officer shall then prepare directives for signature by the Governor instructing the Chiefs of the Task Forces concerned to implement the projects as soon as possible.

A Barrio and Municipal Development Approach Through an Information System Developed by Local People :

The province of Iloilo undertook in 1972 an economic development planning project for the municipality of Passi. It was a project of a duration of 8 months of study and analysis of the needs and solutions to the various problems of the municipality consisting of the fifty-one barrios. Development data were evolved from actual surveys and field observations and the experience gathered in a series of five barrio assembly meetings held at thirty day intervals in each of the fifty-one barrios. During each of these meetings, notes were taken and data were compiled.

Iloilo 'Masagana 99' Rice Management Information System

Since Iloilo is an agricultural province has since rice has remained its most important springboard for economic development, the province applies a set management procedure which is followed by 43 target provinces for the country's "Masagana 99" programme.

Masagana means beautiful, a beautiful harvest being 100 cavanas per hectares or "99" to use a "catchword". The Masagana 99 national rice programme therefore aims to make the country self sufficient in rice. It is being supervised by a national management committee headed by the National Food and Agricultural Council.

Masagana 99 Objectives :

1. To establish an information network on a nation-wide scope that would provide the Department of Agricultural and Natural resources (DANR) with timely reports on the progress of the Masagana 99 Rice Production Programme.
2. To develop subsequently a continuing information system for other food programmes of the DANR.
3. To provide the nucleus of an expanded system to cover other information requirements of the DANR.

Work Procedure :

With the monitoring of the implementation activities of the Masagana 99 Programme as an immediate objective, the major features of the approach employed are as follows :

1. For reports of the Masagana 99 provincial technicians furnish information on farmer-co-orperators, credit support, planted/ harvested areas, technological inputs such as HYV seeds, fertilizers and farm chemicals, and such other information as extension services and marketing.
2. The information is sent to the Provincial Programme Officer (PPO) who will be directly assisted by the Bureau of Agricultural Economics provincial personnel in the summarisation of the reports.
3. Monthly summary reports for each province are transmitted via radio facilities to both the National Food and Agricultural Council (NFAC) and to the Bureau of Agricultural Economics (BAEcon) based on an agreed format for radio transmission purposes; mid-month reports on selected items of information are also transmitted in the same manner.
4. Provincial summary reports are prepared by the PPO with the assistance of BAEcon personnel for submission to the Office of the Governor. Copies of the said report are sent by mail to NFAC Secretariat and the BAEcon Central Office.

5. For specific work assignments in the monthly field data collection, the Masagana 99 provincial technicians cover the farmer-co-operators participating in the programme. The BAEcon provincial offices, on a sampling basis, cover all farms in the province and hire enumerators for data collection purposes.
6. Using the BAEcon survey information for the whole province, rough estimates are obtained for the areas that are not covered by the Masagana 99 Programme based on the reports submitted by the provincial technicians. Other items of information that can be drawn from the BAEcon sample provide checks on the reports that are submitted by the Masagana 99 provincial technicians.
7. National summaries on the items of information needed for management purposes are analysed by BAEcon and a report thereof submitted to the Secretary of the Department of Agricultural and Natural Resources on Scheduled dates. Other items of information are similarly summarised by the NFAC technical staff either for submission to the Secretary of Agriculture or for immediate adjustments necessary for the smooth implementation of the Masagana 99 Programme.

Population Commission Management Information System

I. Generalised Data Categories

Essential to the management and development planning of the national family planning programme are the following data categories:

Computerised :

1. Clinic Services—total new acceptors, total motivated and followed-up, acceptors by method, return visits, total caseload, clinics open.

Non-computer Based :

1. Project Monitoring
   (*a*) Training—number of trainees, schedule.
   (*b*) I/E/C—list of motivators, meetings conducted, education programme, number of referrals, type of information.
   (*c*) Research—type of activities, coverage, findings.
   (*d*) Services.
2. Regional Monitoring—workplan progress, regional FP conditions problems.
3. Finance—sources and uses of funds, budgets, cash balance, payroll.
4. Logistics—Logistics requirements and utilisation.
5. Policy Guidelines—clinic operational guidelines, sub-agreements, general policies.

II. Data Sources

1. Clinic Services—clinics, PER, P & O.
2. Project Monitoring—agencies, Plans, and Operations, PER.
3. Regional Monitoring—ROIC's.
4. Finance—Finance Division, agencies.
5. Logistics—Logistics Division, agencies.
6. Policy Guidelines—POPCOM.

III. Data Processing and Reports

Both computerized and manual processing of data are utilised.

Policy guidelines, regional monitoring reports, and project monitoring reports are manually processed. Regional and project monitoring reports are prepared by the respective regional offices and agencies concerned. These are submitted to the Head Office (POPCOM) and are consolidated to provide management information regarding regional operations and project performance. On the other hand, policy guidelines are originated from POPCOM Head Office and disseminated to all concerned.

Both Logistics and Finance information have only part of their processing computerised, since systems are still in the initial stage of development and implementation. The Finance system involves the computerised processing of payroll for the personnel of some agencies. Non-computerised information processing for finance involves the processing of sources and uses of funds, budgets, and financial reports.

The main bulk of information on clinic services is processed electronically. Input is based on the forms submitted monthly by clinics to the National Computer Centre. Form contains individual acceptor information (method accepted, source of information, status, etc.). From 3 contains information on sample number of return visits for the month and status of clients returning. Form 4 contains information on the caseload of the clinic for the month. Form 5 contains a summary of clinic services information, including manhours spent, personnel, etc. Form 6 and 6A are new forms which give information on the performance of motivators and on the number of follow-ups of the clinic.

The information from these forms are encoded at the computer centre and provide a data base at NCC for the reports which are put out and used for the evaluation of the programme performance. This involves the monthly report in the number of new acceptors, caseloads, and reporting clinics by agency, the percentage distribution by method, the motivation and follow-up performance, the ratio of return visits to total acceptor, and pill cycles dispensed versus pill caseload. Quarterly reports give the clinic by clinic number of new acceptors recruited, summary of acceptors by agency, total and average acceptors per province and region, ratio of cumulative acceptors to estimated eligible women per province, statistical cross-tabulation of acceptor characteristics and estimated current users of a method. Yearly, cross tabulations of acceptor characteristics are also prepared.

IV. Administration of the System

Each division has its own role in the smooth flow of information in the system. The logistics and finance division are responsible for the administration of their respective system of information. The plans and operation division takes charge of the processing and evaluation of project monitoring reports. The programming, evaluation and research division is in charge of the service statistics. The administrative division and the office of the executive director (together with the rest of POPCOM) are in charge of setting policy guidelines and regional monitoring of ROIC activities.

A study and redesign of the management information system is contemplated by the programming, Evaluation and Research Division, which is in charge of the overall administration of system.

Service Statistics are the more crucial category of data in the system for, these provide the picture of the overall performance of the programme. As such, the PER division is responsible for the proper consolidation and dissemination of these report to all concerned.

The National Management Information System

SYSTEM TITLE : *Monitoring of Vital Efforts and Reforms (MOVER) System :*

1. OBJECTIVE : The objective of the MOVER System is to monitor the progress of the implementation of vital development projects. This information system is primarily established to support the speedy decision-making required of Programme Project Management at all levels and to provide effective Presidential control.

2. USERS :

(*a*) The President.

(*b*) The National Economic Development Authority (NEDA).

(*c*) The Executive Office/DMS.

(*d*) Department Secretaries and Heads of National Agencies.

(*e*) Coordinating Officers for Programme Execution (COPE).

(*f*) Regional Officers/Supervisors/ Co-ordinators.

(*g*) Presidential Regional Officers for Development (PROD).

3. DESCRIPTION : The MOVER System is made up of programme project information sub-systems under the supervision of COPEs. The

formats of the reports of project officers vary in accordance with the information required by national programme managers/COPEs and the nature of specific projects. Status reports regarding projects belonging to different national programme are forwarded to the National Computer Centre (NCC) for file build-up/maintenance and summarisation for the use of Project Managers/COPEs and integration of the data of various National Programmes for the use of the President. The MOVER System also provides for the reporting of problems requiring immediate action from higher authority.

4. APPROACH :

(*a*) The COPEs define their respective programmes based on the Information Systems Development Guide and forward the definitions to NCC for report forms design.

(*b*) NCC forwards suggested input/output forms to COPE together with the report gathering scheme.

(*c*) COPEs establish and initiate the reporting system. PRODs follow-up reports.

(*d*) NCC receives reports, implements data processing, and forwards output reports by programme to the respective Programme Managers/COPEs.

(*e*) NCC integrates data of different programmes and submits integrated management report at national level to the President and at regional level to PRODs.

(*f*) The PROD-Grams are used by PROD to request immediate action from higher authority in order to resolve problems.

(*g*) National Programme Managers/ COPEs use Programme Project Assessment Form to report to the President their evaluation of the progress of their respective programmes and the actions they have taken to correct deviations and/or speed up the completion of projects. (Free Format).

(*h*) Forms required :
1. Project Status Report Form.
2. Problem-Action Request Form.

SYSTEM TITLE : *Presidential Information for Management Evaluation (PRIME) System :*

1. OBJECTIVE : The objective of the PRIME System is to integrate secondary data from primary data processing agencies into an information base with design orientation towards provincial/ regional/national profile in support of regional/national planning and evaluation.

2. USERS :
(*a*) The President.
(*b*) The Executive Secretary/DMS.
(*c*) Department Secretaries and Heads of National Agencies.
(*d*) Co-ordinating Officers for Programme Execution (COPE).
(*e*) Regional Officers/Supervisors/Co-ordinators.
(*f*) Presidential Regional Officers for Development (PROD).

3. DESCRIPTION : The PRIME System consist of basic elements of information showing provincial profile—Geography demography, infrastructure and industry. The system does not duplicate the functions of primary data gathering agencies but instead supplements their functions by integrating the secondary data they publish in support of regional planners.

The data of the system are slow changing data. The fastest turnover is one (1) year.

4. APPROACH : (*a*) NCC gathers the secondary data contained in the publications/reports of primary data gathering agencies like the Bureau of the Census, the Bureau of Forestry, etc.

(*b*) NCC builds up a data base classified by province, processes the data, and presents the information in a form suitable to the regional planners.

II

Communication and Grassroot Institutions

Co-operatives are being used in many countries as tools to accelerate the pace of progress. But the impact when viewed cross-culturally is fairly uneven. The author discusses the problems and prospects of co-operatives as a means to achieve development. The role of communication in the development of co-operatives is considered vital. Nevertheless, the necessary infrastructure of co-operatives has to be created and organised on a sound footing before communication can play positive roles. There are more chances of success than failure of such an approach is adopted.

Communication is both an art and a science. It can be used in a sophisticated or spurious manner. It can serve the cause of co-operatives well only if it is handled carefully; if not it may well spell the demise of a movement which has great social and economic possibilities.

It may be worthwhile to discuss at the outset, some thoughts on the co-operative movement—its successes and failures, its shortcomings and its adversities—and then proceed to the role of communication for communication in itself is a many-faceted phenomenon.

Many has been said and written about the cooperative movement. Seminars and Conferences have produced reports which have added to our knowledge of the problems and perplexities that bog the co-operative movement. Though they make interesting reading, practicalities seem to have been overshadowed by the welter of theoretical dissertations and philosophical treatises. Scientists and economists have also had their fair share in the realm of co-operatives but their work has been bogged down to a theoretical morass. We know, for example, that the co-operative movement has prospered and flourished in Germany and Sweden but Britain is facing difficulties. We know the spectacular success of the co-operative movement in Israel through the Histraudaut, although the Israeli experience is a special case, if not completely unique. But we can ask legitimately why in some affluent countries in the West the co-operative movement has succeeded whilst in others it has faltered, if not failed. I am quite sure that there are answers to these questions, but these answers, if any, are lost in the abstract theories on co-operation. Roger-Kerinect, Vice President of the International co-operative Alliance, has stated that co-operatives in the affluent world are no longer considered vital necessities for the majority of the population, and, certainly, do not give the economy the same advantages they provided because of greater efficiency of capitalistic consumer enterprises. Are we, therefore, to assume that the problem of obsolescence through affluence is one which at some time in the future will bedevil the co-operative movement? Could we take it then that the span of life of co-operatives and their influence on the national economy could be curbed when affluence finally catches up in the countries of the developing world?

Let us look at the developing world. Bert Oram, Co-ordinator of Development programme for the International Co-operative Alliance, in a paper delivered in Israel on "The Role of Co-operatives in Developing Economies" describes the needs of the developing world as :

(i) the indigenous accumulation of capital and widespread disposal of its ownership;
(ii) the need for a self-reliant market economy;
(iii) the need for industrialisation by methods appropriate to village communities;
(iv) a new approach to literacy and education and particularly the need to relate them to everyday living in peasant communities;

(v) the development of new forms of democracy which are suited to the third world and which ensure economic and social suffrage and not merely political representation;

(vi) the need for employment policies and labour protection organisations appropriate to the needs of the rural communities; and

(vii) the need for family planning policies.

Oram, said rightly that these are Government problems and that without Government's help, co-operatives may not succeed. Governments, in other words must first lay down the economic and social infra-structure on which co-operatives can find a safe and sound launching pad. And I suggest, that one of the reasons for the ills, pains and morbidity of the co-operative movement in several parts of Asia might be the lukewarm support from many Governments. Indeed, without Government's infra-structural facilities, co-operatives will not possess that ballast that would boost them towards successful evolution. Oram's assertion that co-operatives play a significant role in developing effective population programmes, employment policies, education, manpower utilisation and democratic principles are fine theories in themselves; but, in my opinion, theories alone do not provide practical recipes for co-operative development. Firstly, let us ask what are the central problems that still bedevil co-operative development? How do we tackle them in a practical manner? How do we get off the ground? Once these questions are answered and once we get off the ground, Oram's fine proposals can be translated into reality.

The developing countries, unfortunately, have been for a long time, the slaves of ideas and ideas propounded by the Rochdale Pioneers. Adherence to the ten Rochdale principles were, perhaps, appropriate to the political and social conditions prevailing in England of the 19th Century. The ethos of existence and survival is different in Asia; it dominates our whole life style. As such in Asia, political and social systems have evolved differently and are still evolving as modifications to the political systems grafted from the West.

Earlier, we referred to Roger Kerinect's paper. Let me trace my way back to this paper, although in this paper he dwells on

"The Role of the Co-operative Movement in an Affluent Society". He appears to conclude that the co-operatives could survive by knowing their members better, giving them better information on co-operative, matters and by providing them protection by assuming the role of Consumers' Associations. To me, this implies that communication is vital for co-operatives, not just to survive but to find a niche in the general economy of the country and to evolve successfully into an institution that brings to the people all the benefits that spring from co-operative endeavour. But first of all, let us consider what pre-requisites are required to make communication an effective instrument of evolution, change and improvement. Communication with and between literate and educated populations is not a formidable task, for literacy and education in themselves provide the very means to achieve the ends that we seek. But in the Asian rural societies, large concentrations of people are still illiterate. Basic education facilities are sparse, if not completely absent. The past, in other words, engulfs them, and religion and superstition are the codes on which their lives continue to be patterned. In such a context, communication towards the development of co-operatives or any other institution, becomes a most frustrating and, sometimes, an impossible task. The question to be asked, therefore, is what must precede institutional organisations in such societies.

It is our view that basic education must precede everything else, for without literacy no idea in the world can be sold to anyone. But what would be the response if an education programme is introduced? Would the rural folk sally forth in enthusiasm, and would there be teachers who understand the cultural and social make-up of those whose lives are more conditioned by the past than the ever-advancing present? It would be futile to speak of co-operative education in the absence of basic education and literacy which are among the most important requirements for communication. Effective communication must serve four functions, namely, informing, instructing and directing, evaluating someone or something and influencing other's thoughts or behaviour; and we can do all these if we can communicate with the rural masses. Indeed, the two terms "Co-operative" and "Communication" have deep-rooted educational connotations. The Director of the International Co-operative Alliance states "it has been said that co-operation is an economic movement employing educational action. The statement would be no less true if it were reversed. The co-operative is an educational movement employing economic action". How true this is, but this wise thought escapes through the prolific perforations in the general education system, which as I stated earlier, forms the grass-roots of communication. In this connection, perhaps, it would be pertinent to cite the Comilla experiment in Bangladesh which has been described as the only "high-impact" rural co-operative in Asia. One of the main reasons for its success was that women and religious leaders, who in rural societies have a profound influence on the people, were also taught the rudiments of co-operation. All the co-operative members agreed to send their children to schools and to guarantee their regular attendance. School lessons were adapted to the programme of rural organisation. What this really implies is that, even in a backward society, if some basic requirements are established then communication becomes a reality and a means for developing the co-operative movement.

Our experience in Singapore might help in the development of rural co-operatives, though we are talking in terms of co-operative development in a predominantly urban society. The development of co-operatives through our trade unions is, probably, for most of us, the only way to ensure the viability of a co-operative movement. In Singapore, the movement is backed by the full resources of our trade unions and is encouraged by the Government with a view to ensuring that the co-operative movement gets the proper guidance and expertise from the trade unions which, fortunately, have the type of leadership that is alive and amenable to the changing scene in the Republic's economy. What we have done is suitable for Singapore, which has a commercially oriented economy slowly being converted into an industrial economy. It would be disastrous to carry the methodology used in Singapore into a substantially rural economy. Nevertheless, we would suggest that there is no reason why the principles applied by us cannot be adapted to suit the conditions prevailing in a rural economy. For example, the raising of capital in a depressed economy might be solved if the urban trade unions with small capital resources available were to make these resources available in the rural sector for projects which would be mutually advantageous. We would further add that if accepted principles have to be jettisoned for viability, throw them overboard. In other words, let there be a re-thinking of policy and purpose in a practical manner. We would say that when run in co-operation or in conjunction with trade unions or other spontaneous organisations which are representative of the rural communities, effective communication with the people will be enhanced. If there are no such representative organisations or institutions, the first task, we suggest, would be to have them created so that the rural folk will know that they are direct participants in what is being done. The social objectives which organisations such as the trade unions subscribe to are then achieved and communication with and between persons who belong to an all-embracing organisation will form the catalyst to further development of the socio-economic environment of which co-operative development is an essential element.

The role of communication in the development of co-operative is vital. But the basic pre-requisites mentioned earlier must first be created. A publication by the Co-operative League of the USA (1966) entitled "Moving Ahead With Coops" states "it (the co-operative movement) takes the right and wise approach. It takes complete understanding with the group. It takes treatment of everyone with dignity and respect. Everyone must share in making a co-operative idea, no matter how good, really work". It is my view that this state of affairs can become a concrete reality through effective and meaningful communication provided that the basic institutional conditions are first created, for the institutions in themselves with in-built advantages have the capacity to generate a two-way communication between the masses and the institutions under whose umbrella some lacunae could be found to slot in the co-operative movement as part and parcel of that institution. There are more chances of success than failure if such an approach is made and is accepted.

III

Problems and Prospects

The section outlines a profile of the Sri Lanka model and indicates certain hypotheses based on his direct personal experience and observations. He deals with Sri Lanka's social economic, political and cultural characteristics with a view to getting a clearer picture of the problem areas inherent in the model. The centrality of the rural sector, low per capita productivity, high incidence of literacy, widespread political participation, lack of communication strategy, ownership and control of institutions and lack of communication research—all problem areas—are subjected to Jayaweera's incisive analysis.

It will be necessary for us to start by outlining a profile of our model.

In its economic aspect our model reveals characteristics typical of post-colonial Asian societies. The dominant characteristic of the model is poverty—compounded largely out of causes internal to the society itself and of centuries of *exploitation* by rich countries. For 80 per cent of it national income it continuous to depend on the export of primary commodities to those very countries (during the last two decades they have been paying less and less towards their purchase). Its industrial sector is negligible and contributes only 13 per cent towards the gross national product. The small holding agricultural sector, which performs on the aggregate only slightly above subsistence level, sustains nearly 80 per cent of its population. A low per capita productivity, both in the industrial and small holding agricultural sectors, together with low rates of investment and slow capital formation, are pervasive. A persistent and irremediable adverse trade balance, causing critical foreign exchange difficulties, operates as a constant drag on development, while low per capita incomes and an all-round low standard of living constitute its regular manifestations.

The hypotheses advanced here have not been derived or tested empirically in the accepted sense. They are generalisations based on the experience gathered over many years, working firstly as an administrative head of a district in the rural sector engaged in transforming peasant societies, than as a mass media administrator directing the strategies of the national broadcasting network, and finally as a researcher. While these formulations stand in need of empirical testing they may not, however, lack a foundation in experience.

In its social aspect, our model reveals characteristics at once both typical and unusual in a developing society. Typically, an annual population growth rate of 2.5 per cent and the concentration of nearly 80 per cent of its population in the rural sector it shares common grounds with most Asian societies. The rural social structures, even though denuded of their monolithic and undifferentiated quality, continue to manifest an institutional network and value systems of a traditional nature and are resistant to change. Unusually, an extra-ordinary literacy rate of nearly 86 per cent and a daily media consumption of 56 per cent distinguishes the Sri Lanka model from the Asian stereotype and lends to it properties that can serve both as great potential and as serious constraints for any communication strategy.

The social characteristic that has the greatest bearing on the communication process, perhaps even to a greater degree than literacy and media consumption, is the division of the society into two distinct social groups differentiated on the basic of economic power and privilege. Admittedly, the Sri Lanka model does not exhibit that yawning chasm between the *haves* and the *have-nots* that generally characterise poor countries. During the past two decades the process of income equalisation, set in motion by fiscal policie and comprehensive welfare strategies, have helped to level down all major outcrops of economic and social power and raise the vast mass of the under-privileged who comprise nearly 90 per cent of the population. Whole new layers of society have been brought into a sharing of economic, social and political power. And yet, the energies that impel and sustain social change continue to flow out of the consciousness of class divisions and the conflicts it generates.

In its political aspect as well, the model manifests characteristics which render it both.traditional and modern at the same time. It shows classic traditional characteristics in that it has not yet been able to integrate all its races and cultures into a consciousness of a single polity. On the other hand, few societies in Asia have shown evidence of a degree of political participation to be seen in our model. Since independence was granted in 1948, through the exercise of the free vote, the people have voted out of office five governments — on one occasion returning to office a party it had overwhelmingly voted out nine years earlier. While participation in general elections has consistently maintained a level over 70 per cent since independence, at the last two general elections held in 1965 and 1970, as much as 82 and 86 per cent respectively, exercised their voting rights. This acute incidence of political participation and the deep-going political consciousness of which it is a manifestation have great significance, as we shall try to show later on in this paper, for communication strategies.

Problem Areas

Four elements in this model stand out sharply as constituting problem areas for communication strategies. These elements define the goals, the scope and the constraints within which every serious communication effort has to function.

The Centrality of the Rural Sector :

The first of these elements is the fact that the society is predominantely rural and may remain so for many decades to come. No communication strategy can, therefore, be realistic that fails to throw maximum resources into this sector.

There is now a realisation that the kind of industrial development that served as the basis for transforming western societies, and even a few Asian societies like Japan and Singapore, are now no longer practicable or even desirable in Asia, and that modernisation and the high standards of living that go with it can be, and indeed have to be, achieved through a vigorous renewal of the rural sector. The focus of planning has moved away from the urban and come to centre on the countryside.

The significance this shift has for communication is deeper than may appear on the surface. Communication efforts directed towards the countryside had up to now, to deal with a twofold problem. One was how best to transfer knowledge , information and technology to the *have-nots* in the villages—and the other, how knowledge recipients could be persuaded to act on this new knowledge and apply it to concrete situations. These two objectives, characteristic of all rural communication strategies, have now to be re-defined in the light of the new role conceived for the rural sector.

There is now a need not merely to convince the villagers of their importance in the development efforts but, in a sense, to reverse the direction of information flow. This requires, firstly, that values which attributed to white-coller jobs and urban life-styles an intrinsic superiority be worn down rapidly and that new attitudes and values which bestow upon agricultural pursuits and rural life-styles a new dignity be supplanted in their place. Secondly, this requires that instead of the urban elites talking all the time and the rural peasants listening passively, the communication process be reversed, if not to enable the rural sector to do most of the talking and the teaching and the urban sector, for once, to do the listening and the learning, at least to enable both processes to function simultaneously.

Up to now the only concession our communication strategies have allowed to the rural sector is to run farm broadcasting services or a rural magazine on radio and to saturate villages with handouts issued by the Information Unit of the Agriculture Department. Recognising the crucial role of the rural sector and reversing the information flow will require more than intensification of these tactics.

Low Per Capita Productivity :

The second element that stands out sharply, presenting a problem area for communication strategies, is the low per capita productivity throughout its industrial and domestic agricultural sectors.

Productivity is a function of a complex of interrelated factors. Two important factors in this complex, perhaps the two principal determinants of productivity, are those concerning the transfer and application of technology and motivation.

Productivity increases with the transfer and application of new knowledge. What sort of knowledge should be transferred., how best to transfer it, how the transferred knowledge may be conserved and multiplied at grass roots levels so as to obtain the widest area of impact, are all questions concerning among other things, communication. Whether the knowledge-purveyors be media practitioners, or bureaucrats and technicians working in the field, they are all engaged in the communication process.

What a communication strategy has to do in regard to knowledge transfers is to find out what sort of knowledge is required in order to increase productivity, whether the knowledge being transferred now is relevant to the needs of productivity, and how the parcel of knowledge that is brought to be transferred may be best co-ordinated at grass root levels to ensure its absorption by the intended recipients. Very often knowledge or technology that is beyond the capacity of a society, at its current level of development to absorb or manage, is sought to be transferred purely because such knowledge or technology is modern or is considered indispensable by the standards of another society. In such cases, productivity is impaired rather than enhanced. So, low productivity can result not only from the lack of knowledge and the absence of technology, but also from an excess of it and from its misapplication. These are all problems of communication.

If the transfer of knowledge is a necessary condition of productivity, so is motivation. Indeed, of these two factors, motivation is the more crucial. Its prevalence or absence decides whether the intended recipients of knowledge reach out to it and determine how they react to it when they are exposed to it, and whether or not they will treat new knowledge as so much irrelevant information or apply it, transmit it and co-operate in its lateral spread. Knowledge by itself is not a catalyst. It becomes alive and transforms itself into a vehicle of change only when it is linked to a system of motivations or some dominant and overpowering drive. Such a motivation may be supplied by simple price incentives, or by some sudden eruption of patriotic fervour (as when the survival of the society is threatened by an external aggressor) or by ideology. Traditional societies often lack an adequate pattern of motivation, and one of the primary tasks of a communication strategy is to determine the conditions under and the manner in which that deficiency may be remedied.

The problem of motivating a society can sometimes present itself not as a motivation-vacuum but as a system of existing and pre-set motivation working counter to the goals of the communication effort. For instance, when an industrial work force is intensely motivated by a class ideology, a communication effort, mounted by the establishment and directed towards ensuring productivity (as conceived by the establishment), will first have to neutralise the existing patterns of motivation which may be counter-productive when judged by the criteria of the establishment. Only then can it hope to motivate the workforce for securing productive goals. But when cast in such a negative role, the communication effort, far from supplying an adequate motivation, soon finds itself trapped in the centre of a class war, unable to convince its intended audience of its *bona fides* or *impartiality,* loses credibility, antagonises and alienates its target audience, and secures results completely contrary to its stated goals.

High Incidence of Literacy :

The other tow elements of our model that have a bearing on a communication strategy are the high incidence of literacy and the vigorous and widespread sense of political participation. Both elements are really manifestations of modernity and run counter to the traditional stereotype. Normally their occurrence in such a degree (86 per cent literacy and 80 per cent political participation), along with 20 per cent urbanisation and 56 per cent media consumption would have been regarded, in terms of the Lerner thesis, as proof of take-off into modernity. To that extent they should be looked upon as factors that help the communication effort. But in our model both literacy and political consciousness have not always performed this role. Rather, they have sometimes acted as constraints upon the communication effort.

This has to do not with the strengths and infirmities intrinsic to these phenomena, but with their origins and the historical circumstances under which they evolved in our society.

The educational system suited to meet the requirements of colonial administration, did not enhance the productivity of the society as a whole. The social structure, for the perpetuation of which that literacy had been conceived and fashioned, had begun to disintegrate. The newly emerging social and economic structures required a different kind of literacy to support them—a totally new set of values and objectives for their growth and consolidation. In this situation, a tension developed between the newly literate groups and the changing structures which had little to offer them. Burgeoning literacy then became a constraint on development.

This had implications for the communication effort in a fundamental way. Normally, when a community is literate it is easier to communicate with and within it. A communication effort directed at such an audience was lacking in literacy. But when that literacy conceals a set of values and objectives which is opposed to those which the communication effort is seeking to inculcate, and which depends for its fulfilment on a social and economic environment which is either disappearing or which the communication effort is consciously seeking to wear down, the positive relationship that one expects to find between literacy and communication breaks down. They become antagonistic phenomena working at cross-purposes.

The claim that literacy, of whatever quality or content, should exist in a counter-productive relationship to communication, is certainly an extraordinary one and is clearly heretical. One must, therefore, limit and sharpen its application.

Literacy on a mass scale made such demands upon the existing environment and exerted such enormous pressures as were clearly, beyond the capacity of the existing structures to contain, that even without a conscious communication effort to aid in its dismantling, a disintegration of the social and economic order became inevitable. So, in the long run, literacy did perform its traditional role as a catalyst and a solvent only, in the short-term, there was a failure of convergence between the values supporting the new literacy and the values sought to be inculcated by the communication effort.

Widespread Political Participation :

Political consciousness is generally a function of literacy. In our model it was largely the product of universal franchise and the working of the parliamentary process in an unbroken tradition for over 40 years. When a society is politically conscious it seeks to do two things, among a number of other things. On the one hand, it seeks information, even though it selects such information as will reinforce views and attitudes it already holds. On the other hand, it seeks to transmit information. The impulse to express opinions, persuade dissenters, debate issues and attack and defend policies, is a characteristic common in societies that are politically conscious. Both the search for information and the impulse to transmit information are manifestations of communication. Political consciousness is then both a consequence and a multiplier of communication.

But there is a point at which political consciousness can pose a serious problems for a communication strategy and work even counter to its total effort. When we talk of the political consciousness of a society, we somehow assume that its prevalence is *per se* a good thing and that must necessarily work towards and result in the preservation and enrichment of those institutions, assumptions, concepts and values which constitute the political frame of that society. For example, the two-party systems of the United Kingdom and the United States of America work within a framework of certain assumptions which are never seriously brought into question. In UK, the role of the Queen and the Sovereignty of Parliament, the place of the Rule of Law, the independence of the Judiciary and the Liberties of the Individual are taken as the invariable and constant factors of that society's political life. Similarly in the United States, the supremacy of the Constitution, the institution of the Separation of Powers and the concept of Fundamental Rights, command allegiance from all contenders to political office. At the most, debate is confined only to questions concerning their infringement but never extended to undermine their validity. Indeed, in both these societies, maturity of political consciousness is measured in relation to the extent to which it tends to preserve and enrich these basic assumptions.

In such a society, the task of the communicator should be a fairly straightforward one. It would consist of affording a platform or forum for the continuing debate and imparting information that will help enrich its quality. However, at the back of the communicators, politicians and the people and underlying all dissent, there will be a unity of purpose derived from a common sharing of basic palitical assumptions.

We often tend to assume the universality of this monolithic political model when we discuss communication strategies in Asian societies. A dominant characteristic of the politics of developing countries is the polarisation of their societies into two broad groups. On the one hand, there are the western educated elites saturated with values and assumptions of western political models and enjoying a level of affluence and economic power not generally diffused through all layers of the society. On the other, are a vast mass deficient in economic power and lacking the means for acquiring it in the ordinary course, for whom the prevalent political institutions appear only as instruments of a ruling class designed for perpetuating its own hegemonic interests, and for whom political action consist primarily of the obligation to erode the economic and political basis of that hegemony, and supplant in its place its own ascendancy.

A society afflicted by such a deep-going class cleavage presents a serious problem for a communication strategy. On any given issue, people tend to divide and respond not on the basis of facts objectively determined, but on the basis of their class allegiances. Seemingly, non-political issues come to be invested with profound and far-reaching political implications. Where a communication effort tends to assume that given the facts people will respond *rationally*, it finds itself confronted by emotions which do not lend themselves to validation by reference to objective criteria and which for that reason remain outside the capacity of media to cope with. And such emotions evading interaction with the normal communication process, often prove themselves far more effective determinants of societal change than the best directed communication effort. In such situations, not merely the content of facts but even the very concept of *fact* as objectivity is questioned. There are no *facts* as such. There are only *class facts*. The concept of *objectivity* itself undergoes a semantic transformation. What is *objective* and *impartial* to the purveyor is *subjective* and *biased* to the recipient. *Facts* are objective or subjective only as they promote or vitiate class interests. In this way a communication effort can be reduced, whatever *bona fides* are back of it, to the role of a protagonist in the class struggle.

Some More Problems :

To appreciate the deeper significance of the four major problems described above, we should consider them in their total setting, within the tensions of a highly literate and politically divided society trying to work through democratic institutions and still adhering to concepts and values borrowed from western models.

Lack of Communication Strategy

The first of these problems was that there was never a consciously formulated strategy encompassing all the available communication channels or even a sense of the need for one. A communication strategy should be considered as a sub-system of the overall development plan, one element in the total engagement for growth. However, professional economists and planners have tended to consider development to be the function only of conventional growth factors such as savings, investments, entrepreneurship, management, productivity and so on, and have generally ignored communication as an important determinant. The tendency has been to limit the application of the communication concept to information and publicity and confine it to the parochial concerns of the Ministry of Information.

At the Ministry of Information the communication concept undergoes further metamorphosis and issues either as a series of campaigns directed at specific short-term objectives which may not be even developmental in character or may deteriorate into straightforward publicity gimmicks for persons and programmes. At this point, communication strategy deteriorates into publicity tactics.

The lack of overall communication strategy was seen not only in the failure to feed media intelligently but, even more, in the failure to exploit the vast communication network available to the government through its far-flung bureaucratic apparatus, reaching down to every village in the country. A vast army of divisional and village level government officers interact with villagers daily. They are all communicators, purveyors of knowledge and agents of change. But their activities remained uncoordinated at the village level and their communication potentials unexploited and wasted.

The lack of a strategy was further seen in the failure, until very recently to provide institutional devices for harnessing the vast potential of privately-owned and very powerful private newspaper organisations which, together with radio, reach almost 56 per cent of the country's adult population daily. Private newspaper organisations have been allowed over the past many decades to try to determine the aspirations and influence the values of society entirely according to their private perceptions and prejudices.

This arrangement was justified and preserved on the ground of 'freedom of speech', but it never worked for advancing the development goals of society as a whole. Had there been a conscious communication strategy, it would have been possible to harness the enormous potential of the newspaper media in a manner that would have secured the development goals of the community and at the same time preserved the liberties of the individual as well. The National Press Council that was set up recently in Sri Lanka provides an institutional device for achieving these ends.

However, the provision of an institutional device does not by itself achieve much. If it is to play a positive role in the transformation of societal values and aspirations, it must be backed up by and manifest in its decisions, a comprehensive policy of communication related to long-term development goals. Otherwise it runs the risk of being transformed into an instrument of oppression, a device for perpetuating a ruling clique, defeating the very purposes it was intended to achieve.

Ownership and Control of Institutions

Before development goals can be diffused through the various layers of society and their members persuaded to lend their weight for their fulfilment, there must be a sharing of these goals at the level of those in authority over media and an acceptance by them of the strategies and techniques to be followed.

In the absence of an overall strategy, such a sharing of goals and techniques could not have been, and was never, achieved. Thus, the formulation of communication goals was left to the individual insights of persons and boards in charge of media institutions. Very often their insights did not correspond with those of the planners responsible for formulating development goals. In any case, it was inevitable that, given a multitude of media institutions, both government-controlled and independent of government control, there should emerge a whole range of goals and strategies out of alignment not only with the overall goals of the planners but also with each other. So that where there should have been a concerted communication offensive directed from a single centre and focussed on clearly defined goals, all we had was a babel of discordant opinions and voices.

It was as if a major military campaign was left to the strategic capabilities of individual platoon commanders, acting independently of each other, to execute. Under the circumstances, the results on the media field were about as glorious as they would have been on the battle field!

While this argument shows up the futility of allowing media and other communication channels to act independently of each other and emphasises the need for some measure of central direction, it also raises the important question concerning ownership and control of media. While there is a great need in developing societies for the optimum utilisation of media potential, the central direction of strategies that this need entails must not be conceived to include the total ownership of and dominion over media.

Actually, the more cogent arguments against a government's total control over media rest not on a *priori* first principles touching on individual liberties, but on a *posteriori* and demonstrable principle of expediency. Unless we have a totally regimented society organised around a monolithic ideology, and given a society that is highly literate, intensely political and habituated for many years in the exercise of the free vote, it becomes clearly inexpedient for any government to seek a total hegemony over media. In a literate and politically conscious society, media totally dominated by government suffers a serious loss of credibility. It not only fails to carry the message and convince the audience, but also generates a disbelief that the facts themselves, on their own merit, could not have earned. More importantly, it insulates the government from its own mistakes and denies to it the corrective benefits of popular pressures and criticisms which, failing to obtain expression through normal media channels, can find manifestations destructive of the government as a whole and injurious to the wider society's development goals.

Then the task for a communication strategy is to evolve a conceptual and institutional framework within which this conflict can be kept in equilibrium and whereby the need for providing an integrated communication support for development may be kept in tension with the need to preserve the integrity and credibility of media, without causing violence to either. It is important that this tension should be kept going. It could very well be the condition of securing development goals and preserving individual liberties at one and the same time.

Lack of Communication Research

The lack of communication strategy resulted not only in the failure to co-ordinate and direct media but more importantly in the lack of a desire to find out what communication was all about. The lack of strategy rendered research unnecessary and the absence of research reinforced immunity to strategy. They were supportive of each other.

The need for research exists at two levels : (1) at the level of mass media; and (2) at the village level.

There is a notion popular even among practitioners that mass media are performing a communication function when they carry large doses of development material in the form of speeches by ministers on radio or as lengthy feature articles issued by the Information Department in newspapers. Any practitioner who has, even marginally, a feel of his medium, knows how ill-founded these beliefs are. Far from achieving the goals they set themselves, these techniques serve to build resistance to the message and succeed only in undermining the medium itself. But this practice tends to perpetuate itself in the face of accumulated wisdom on the subject.

One of the reasons for the perpetuation of this folly is that there is no on-going research on media performance and impacts. A considerable volume of research on the effects on mass media has been carried out in modern societies but the conclusions they have thrown up do not always bear application in our societies. The magnitude and content of the media, the quality of the audience and the whole ecology of modern and post-industrial societies are so dissimilar to ours that the lessons learnt there can have only an academic interest with us. What is required, therefore, is particularised research within our own environments.

A hypothesis that suggests itself as deserving of study is the limitations of mass media as a catalytic agent in a society strongly divided along class lines. Although mass media reaches 56 per cent of the country's adult population daily, their proven capacity to influence the drift of political change and to determine its character has been only peripheral. The political, socio-economic and cultural aspirations of our society have been influenced overwhelmingly by massive social forces which were brought to life and sustained not by mass media but by politicians, trade unions, university teachers and Buddhist priests, acting most of the time in *opposition* to mass media. These social forces developed not only in spite of mass media but in a sense because of them. They represented the counterblast to mass media. The more intensively mass media tried to push goals that they conceived to be desirable or necessary for national development, the more swiftly social forces mobilised against them.

In Sri Lanka, after the emergence of literacy and political consciousness as powerful determinants of development, mass media have seldom decided the direction of societal change. At best they only deepened and consolidated the work of social forces, and that too only when they clearly lined themselves up behind them.

This hypothesis naturally diminishes the assumed role of mass media as an independent factor in societal change. It allocates to media a clearly subordinate role.

We are not linking this hypothesis to value judgments. Whether an independent role for mass media is better than a subordinate role is not the question. The question is, what is functional and what is not functional; what is realistic and what is illusory.

What we have set out in the preceding paragraph is in a sense more than a theoretical generalisation. It is a narration of what actually happened within our model. What research can do is to find out whether, and to what extent, this experience may be constructed into an empirical hypothesis.

To more critical research vacuum is in the village area. Governments and media authorities often confine the communication concept to the operations of mass media, ignoring the whole phenomenon of rural communication which, at least within the village, probably handles a larger volume of information and knowledge than mass media and whose impacts on rural values and life-styles, though less spectacular in the short term, are more enduring and pervasive. The fact that the rural communication phenomenon is almost an independent system with a dynamics of its own, and that its operations can modify and seriously distort mass media inputs is rarely recognised.

The rural sector is already chocked with communication channels. These are, firstly, the mass media disgorging daily a flood of information. Then there are hordes of government official bringing new knowledge and new technology and trying to persuade the people to adopt them. Then there are the politicians, the political platforms, the elected bodies, the participatory institutions and so on, all ostensibly bent on the same purpose—trying to give the people a better and fuller life, or at least trying to afford to them the conditions under which their attainment may be rendered possible. And then there are the traditional channels—the priest in the temple, the village school master, the gossip in the *bazaar* (market), the folk-play and so on, all making their contributions, consciously or unconsciously, towards change. This interlocking communication system represents a medium in itself, and we know very little about its behaviour.

We want to know whether there is in fact an excess of knowledge flow into the village—whether knowledge transmitted by channels acting independently of each other and along parallel lines does not actually succeed in neutralising one another. We want to know what knowledge needs remain unsatisfied and how they can be met. We have to find out how knowledge that gains entry into the village communication system flows within it, is modified in the process and how it eventually manifests itself in the recipient's mind. It is important to know what sort of overt and submerged resistance operate against information inputs. Is there a feedback of knowledge from the recipients to the purveyors? How does this mechanism work? Are there any institutions within the village— knowledge centres similar to the Land Grant Universities of the United States —that can generate, conserve and transmit knowledge of a regional character so that every village can build up for itself a reservoir of knowledge and technology relevant to its needs? Most importantly, why is it that in spite of the extraordinary incidence of literacy, widespread political consciousness and a tradition of intensive and sustained rural construction programmes, we have been able to achieve so little in the way of rural transformation and rural productivity? We have to find answers to all these questions before we can hope to transfer the weight of the national development effort to the villages. This is initially a matter of research.

Generally, governments are impatient of research. They want instant solutions and are content with *ad hoc* measures that will help them tide over some immediate crisis. In these circumstances, the burden of research has to be borne more and more by Universities, Foundations and private research institutions.

Conclusion

This paper makes no claim to being a research document. That is self-evident. It sets out generalisations which have not been subjected to the rigorous disciplines of empirical research. Some of these generalisations may find support in the findings of research studies carried out elsewhere, but others cannot lay claim even to that. However, what all the generalisations contained in this paper do claim is that they are derived from experience accumulated at the points where the action took place. That is the main reason for stating them.

Appendix

A Media and Communications Factsheet

INTRODUCTION

As a starting point for such a discussion and to show the present state of telecommunication, and hence the basis for our arguments, we present a survey of the factual background.

Clearly we shall not attempt a factual or technical description. Such descriptions are better provided by technical experts familiar with present telecommunication systems and future trends.

Our description is more a *functional* description based on typical examples of telecommunication services. It is, of course, not exhaustive and is to a large degree designed especially for the purposes of this report. Categories are defined not solely with reference to technical characteristics but also having regard to their interest from the legal standpoint. In discussing each category both technical and legal characteristics are indicated without, however, going into detail.

The categories fall into two groups, one concerned with communication and the other with application related services. In the first group there are four specific categories of services : "electronic mail", "EFT", "information retrieval", and "teledoc". In the second group there are three specific categories of services: "information management", "processing", and "data services".

Attempt have been made by others to construct a similar classification. Hogrebe in particular has introduced a classification scheme for similar purposes to those pursued in this report. His scheme is perhaps more systematic and is certainly different. As an example of an alternative classification of telecommunication services by categories, his classification is summarised in the Table below, while our corresponding categories are indicated in the right hand column.

Classification of Telecommunication Services

Category of communication	*Mode*	*Communicators*	*Corresponding category*
I Distribution of information	One way	From systems to individuals, groups, masses	Information retrieval
(1) local access to information			
(2) remote access to information			
II Electronic transaction	One way	From individuals to systems	EFT MIS
III Person-to-person communication	Two way	Between individuals	Electronic mail
IV Multiperson communication	Two way	Among numerous individuals/groups	Teledoc
V Man-machine communication (1) intelligent man-machine (2) Complex man-machine communication	Two way	Between individuals and systems, programmes or processes	Processing services

Source : Hogrebe Edmund, "Dangers and Opportunities of Digital Communication Media", Instituto latinoamericano de estudios transnacionales, Mexico City, 1980, p. 83.

There is of course, no category by category correspondence between Hogrebe's classification and that discussed in this report. Hogrebe maintains that his classification is pragmatic and our's is perhaps even more so although the frame of reference is slightly different.

A second alternative is presented in a Japanese proposal to the Expert Group on Transborder Data Flows, where flows are classified into two broad main categories :

1. international remote processing and data bank services, and
2. telecommunication and information system within enterprises.

We have mentioned the alternative structures to show that the classification adopted in this Annex is only one of several possible ways of distinguishing computerised telecommunication facilities and is no more than a modest contribution towards describing them. To some extent we will refer to the categories in the discussion (Chepters III and IV) of legal problems and principles.

We have classified services into two main categories. The first category—*communication related services*—includes those services where the main characteristic would seem to be one of communicating data from one point to another. Computers are usually employed in some way either to identify data to be communicated (as in information retrieval), for routing and intermediate storage of messages (as in electronic mail or teledoc) or to receive the message and act upon its content (as in several EFT applications).

The second category concern *application related services*, where the communication is not really the major functional characteristic of the service. This is rather evident in processing services where the telecommunication network is only one of several alternative channels for presenting input and receiving output to and from a certain system. It is likewise characteristic where the service is based on data maintained by a computer and the customer manipulates these data or combines them with his own. This is perhaps less characteristic of management information systems, among which we have included major examples such as airline ticket reservation systems. The main characteristics, however, would seem to be the maintenance of certain data structures rather than communication, although communication is a prerequisite to the necessary correspondence between the real world and the data structure.

The distinction made in this report between communication related services and application related services does not correspond to that made by the United States Federal Communication Commission (FCC) between basic and enhanced services, a distinction of convenience made by the Commission for its application of the Communication Act. Basic services would correspond fairly closely to a sub-set of what in this report is termed electronic mail, a term used differently by the FCC. The categories below will therefore mainly be examples of enhanced communication.[1]

CATEGORY I—COMMUNICATION RELATED SERVICES

1. Electronic Mail

"Mail" is a word used to describe the physical transport of a document from one point to another (*see* Chapter II. D). "Electronic mail" is therefore to some extent a misnomer since it only functionally imitates conventional mail services.

Basically, this service is the communication of a computerised text from one point in a computer network to another point in the same or a linked network. In its simplest form, electronic mail is represented by the messages sent from a user of a computer terminal to the operator of that computer or to a user of another terminal of the same computer.

It is only a slight extension from this point of departure to those situations where the computer is part of a network where the users are geographically far apart. In such a situation, electronic mail becomes an alternative to conventional mail, telegraphy or telex for users of that network. Functionally, electronic mail is identical for example with telegraphy so that possible infringement of a national telegraphy monopoly may become a legal issue (*see* Chapter II. B.).

Systems of electronic mail may offer special facilities, such as sorting mechanisms and facilities for intermediate storage where the user is not on the network, etc.

Systems may also contain conventional elements. An example is the E-COM service to be introduced by the US Postal Service. Employing telecommunication links subscribers may send messages to approximately 25 specially equipped post offices, where the message is printed, placed in an envelope and delivered in the conventional way.[2] This may be seen as a response to services offered by special delivery companies where the printed massage is delivered locally by car.

As indicated, electronic mail covers a broad range of services: from the exchange of simple messages to regular postal services. It should be emphasized that the message communicated may be very brief (as in a telegram), medium (as in a telex) or very long. An example of "letters" communicated by electronic mail and consisting of rather long texts would be documents, reports, etc., sent from one word processor to another for distribution, processing, or simply as part of a division of labour (a report may, for example, be proof read at another location).

The last example is probably a sector of electronic mail which will expand fairly rapidly into a "super-telex" service. Public data networks will probably be developed to accommodate this type of electronic mail.

The legal aspects of this service are mainly a consequence of the fact that conventional services such as mail, telegraphy, or telex are regulated. Electronic mail must therefore find its place in the national and international regulatory environment. These problems would, however, seem mainly to be matters of adjustment.

Electronic mail is—as its name indicates—functionally equivalent to conventional mail (and to some telecommunication services such as telegraphy). As in the case of the conventional services, communication is mainly point-to-point between individuals, though of course one individual sender may address a number of individual addressees.

2. Electronic Fund Transfers (EFT)

EFT is defined by the US Electronic Fund Transfer Act of 1978,

Section 903(6) as :

> " .... any transfer of funds, other than a transaction originated by cheque, draft or similar paper instrument, which is initiated through an electronic terminal, telephonic instrument, or computer or magnetic tape as to order, instruct, or authorise a financial institution to debit or credit an account. Such term includes, but is not limited to, point-of-sale transfers, automated teller machine transaction, direct deposits or withdrawals of funds and transfer initiated by telephone...."

By this definition EFT is basically a transfer of funds authorised by a computer message and taking place within a financial institution. This message may originate in a point-of-sale terminal. The transfer from one account to another, from the customer's to the seller's, takes place in a bank or other financial institution to which the terminal is connected.

There are strong similarities between EFT and the more trivial electronic mail services. In both cases a message is communicated from one point to another, and the addressee acts upon the message.

In this report the term EFT is used in an even broader sense then that given by the above definition. Two other major categories are included.

One category includes those cases where a computerised message replaces a conventional legal document, *e.g.*, a negotiable instrument such as a promissory note or bill of lading. The legal rules traditionally applied to paper instruments will then operate, particularly as regards the authentification of the message. This implies that the message retains the functions of the paper document and that the legal rules do not themselves require a traditional paper document. Only certain functions of the document are required and may be fulfilled by a computerised document. It is interesting to note that a number of international trade agreements are currently being amended or drafted in such a way that computerised systems will be permitted within the framework of the instrument.

The second category includes those cases where the regulatory environment is changed to accommodate a computerised rather than a paper-based system. This may be done by replacing one set of legal rules by another, while retaining the functional aspects of the legal regime. For example, statutory rules on negotiability may be replaced by explicit contractual provisions which retain the legal functions of the paper based system.

A computerised system to replace the conventional system of paper bills of lading, where the computerised system is functionally equivalent to the present system, but where statutory rules on negotiability, etc., of bills of lading are replaced by contractual terms, has been proposed by Reinshou.[3] In this system public key encryption systems are used for authentification.

A more drastic way of introducing the new regulatory framework would be to amend existing legislation to accommodate computerised systems rather than paper based systems. An interesting example is the Securities Centre, set up by a Danish Act of Parliament, which issues and registers dealings in securities quoted on the Copenhagen stock exchange and whose maintained registers have been given legal consequences by statute.

In spite of the close similarity between electronic mail and EFT it seems more appropriate in this report to identify EFT as a separate service. These transactions do by definition have a legal function and give rise to problems in regard to the present law on negotiable instruments and other types of legal document. They also represent transfers of funds and this creates a special need for data security and to determine the identity of the sender, his authority, etc.

As with conventional transfers of funds, the communication is mainly point-to-point, from a customer to a financial institution or *vice versa*, or between two private parties (perhaps with a financial institution as an intermediary).

3. Information Retrieval

The term "information retrieval" is used to describe a situation where a provider offers a data base to customers for retrieval. The data base is pre-recorded and kept up to date by the provider. Data is retrieved by the customer on request from an on-line terminal. The customer is billed for his use of the system and, occasionally, for an additional charge per documentary unit, a charge which may be royalty to a copyright holder. Data provided is not processed by the user, except for processing to retrieve and sort, print or otherwise make available the retrieved documents.

Information retrieval is traditionally divided into "fact" and "reference" retrieval.

Fact retrieval is a situation where the customer wants to retrieve a fact, a data element he is well able to define. It may be the population of a country, the ships available at a certain port, etc. Since his information needs are well defined, he is also in a position to make a clear relevance assessment. For fact retrieval, data bases with well structured records are generally provided. The search request will then identify which field of the record is to be searched and what values within these fields will be acceptable.

Reference retrieval is a situation where the customer has a problem and wants information which may shed light on this problem. He may, for example, be lawyer looking for case law pertinent to a certain legal problem. In such a case the information need is not well defined and the structured data bases may be less appropriate. To facilitate reference retrieval, text retrieval systems have been introduced where the data is not structured and where documents may be retrieved from any word or combination of words occurring in the document. These systems tend to contain rather long documents and often reproduce the original document word by word. The main area of application has hitherto been legal documentation.

Information retrieval has two aspects of interest for this report. Firstly, the provider of the data base often has a contractual arrangement with authors or owners who have rights over the documents. This may impose obligations on the use of data provided which will influence the second aspect which is the relationship between the provider and the customer, which is also of a contractual nature.

A typical legal issue is that of copyright in documents provided through the retrieval system. These rights may impose restrictions in regard to what may be provided and the terms on which documents may be offered. More generally, the same is true of all limitations resulting from the contract between the provider and the parties supplying him with documents.

A working party of the Committee of Legal Data Processing at the Council of Europe is at present looking into the relationship between providers and users of legal information services. This study also deals with the problem of liability where errors in the data base entail a financial loss for the user.

The close link between information retrieval land modern reproduction methods must be stressed. Indeed, information retrieval services and on-demand publishing services are loosely associated. So far, bibliographical data bases (like Lockheed's) have only contained bibliographical data, while the source document was obtained by conventional systems. New technology like video-discs, telefax systems, rapid local printers, etc., may make alternative modes of access to the source document more attractive, making tele-publishing the rule rather than the exception.

The legal interest of this category is pointed out above, with the copyright issue as an example. Other and perhaps more general problems are associated with the protection of data bases as such.

UNESCO and WIPO have pursued some activities in respect to "copyright problems arising from the use of computers for access to or the creation of works".[4]

Data from the provided base is usually communicated in response to a search request, which may mean a rather longish dialogue. Communication is point to multi-point; messages are generated by the information service at one point and communicated to a number of users at their various locations.

4. Teledoc

"Teledoc" is a term used in Sweden to describe systems with a number of features discussed above, particularly those of "electronic mail" and "information retrieval". In this report it will be used to denote complex systems with a number of users who are communicating with each other and with data bases offered within the system. It will be broken down into two main categories.

The first category covers the "teleforum" systems. Such a system is established between the members of a group: the subscribers. In some instances subscribers have to meet certain qualifications to become members; in other cases it is enough to open an account with the system. Members may communicate with each other through they system which supports electronic mail functions. Messages may also be stored in common areas, creating a forum for discussion or comment. Teleforum systems may be established for closed user groups to facilitate communication between members of a team working on a common report, and to facilitate commentary on drafts by the members as they proceed. The teleforum system may also include one or several data bases, offered by the provider of the service or by the users, for retrieval of data by one or more other members of the group.

This type of system has given rise to legal problems; in Sweden both data protection and public access to government files have been issues in relation to one teleforum system, the DOM 79 developed by the National Defence Research Institute.

The second category contains the teledata or view-data type systems. At first sight these seem rather different from the teleforum systems, but it is probably a question of emphasis. While teleforum systems stress the electronic mail angle, the teledata systems stress the information retrieval aspect. The teledata system is operated by an organisation, often associated with a carrier or a PTT, and the data bases are offered by private and public organisations on contract with the teledata organisation. In addition, the teledata system offers facilities for the communication of messages and data bases created by subscribers for their own or closed group use, etc.

Teledata services are emerging as new mass media, to an even greater extent than the teleforum services; but for both these types of services, generally available to the public at large or to large loose-knit user groups, the same problems arise as those related to conventional mass media. One problem is related to responsibility—the rules governing civil and criminal liability of editors and technical personnel as regards publishing and broadcasting have to be adapted to the new environment. Another problem is that of "programme policy". For example, should advertising be restricted in teledata or teleforum services as they are in certain national broadcasting services? Should anybody be free to offer data bases through such services ? Or should the organisation operating the service enforce quality control standards? Such systems also present a problem due to their public nature (*see* Chapter II. F.).

Indeed the very nature of these types of systems may be questioned. Teledata systems typically rely on existing cable networks meant for television transmission and, where national broadcasting legislation covers transmission by cable, the service may be caught by the definition of the special type of telecommunication known as "broadcasting" which may well be subject to special regulation (*see* Chapter II. C.).

Communication in these systems is typically multipoint to multipoint, from a number of data base providers or users to a number of users. It might best be seen as a communication network with added facilities for storing and retrieving data.

CATEGORY II : APPLICATION RELATED SERVICES

1. Management Information Services

A wide spectrum of different computerised services is used to co-ordinate the activities of an organisation. The systems usually pivot on a data base which represents the state of the activities of the organisation at a given moment. In real-time systems this moment is the present. The systems also generate aggregated data for more general management purposes.

Such systems will perhaps most frequently be in-house systems, for instance for supply or acquisition control. In decentralised organisations, however, such systems have sometimes become very important, the typical example perhaps being airline booking systems.

There is sometimes a close link between such systems and information retrieval, particularly when information retrieval is based on a structured data base. There is, however, a characteristic difference. In management information services the data base is constantly being changed by the users.

They do, of course, retrieval information, for example, on seats available on a certain flight. The main object, however, is not just access to information, it is to enable the user to book a seat and, by so doing, change the state of the data base and make co-ordination with other users at other locations possible. The main characteristic is not solely information retrieval from the data base but the way an organisation communicates through the system.

For EFD services management information services may also be a prerequisite. Only through a system co-ordinating the different transactions between accounts can the position at any one time be determined and, for instance, an overdrawn account closed for further transactions. In teledoc systems management information services may be used by groups, for example, to co-ordinate job rotation or studies. Special management information services may also be offered by service bureaux rather than operated by the organisation itself. An example might be a system providing information on transport availability, to which ship brokers could have access for identifying an appropriate carrier for their clients.

This category of services is of legal interest due to its close association with decision-making. Data protection may easily become an issue when systems contain personal data. Trade unions may have an interest in influencing the design of the system in view of the close relations which it creates between individuals and the employment situation and organisational structure.

Under Norwegian law employees have a statutory right to participate in the planning and design of such systems, and the right to have a representative specialising in management problems participating in study groups , etc., (*cf.* Job Environment Act 1977, 4, Section 12, especially No. 3). It may be noted that under Brazilian law steps have been taken to ensure that information services, including management information services such as airline booking systems, are not offered by a facility located outside Brazil so far as national reservations are concerned.

Communication is typically multi-point-to-point, from a number of users to a centrally located system which co-ordinates their activities.

2. Processing Services

The traditional service offered by a computer service bureau is the processing of a customer's data by application programmes provided by the bureau or by the user himself. In this way bureaux have offered accounting programmes, invoicing programmes, mailing programmes, etc. The customer may enter his data in a number of different ways, but no-life communication is the most common one.

For the customer the service offered by a computer service bureau may be one of several alternatives to solve a particular problem. For standard services such as accounting, stock management, etc., there will be other alternatives like specialised micro-computers operating without supervision. In these cases the user will choose the bureau only if it is more economic and this share of the market may actually be declining.

The customer may, however, choose a service bureau for other reasons. The service bureau may, for example, offer a programme not otherwise available , or , rather than a programme, it may offer a service not readily obtainable elsewhere. A simple example would be the production of microform documents, which would presuppose access to COM equipment. In this way, service bureaux will compete in terms of programmes and special services rather than in terms of prices.

It may be mentioned that the distinction between processing services and production of products is not always easy to make. In Norwegian administrative practice there have been two decisions. One relates to market analysis for a few clients, where results were distributed to clients as listings at a price of about $2,000. This was held to constitute data processing services for tax purposes. Another decision relates also to market analysis but in this case there was a somewhat larger number of clients and results were distributed as offset copies of listings at a price of around $150. This was held to constitute publication, *i.e.,* the production of goods, for tax purposes.

Since users communicate with service bureaux through telecommunication lines, the development of international data networks may have a significant impact on this sector. An international market for processing services is indeed emerging, and in this market bureaux will complete not only by pricing their services but by offering specialised programmes and services which will be competitive in terms of quality.

With regard to the quality of a service, account has to be taken of the contractual relationship between service bureau and customer. Where a bureau accept extensive liability it will give the customer a degree of financial security, a factor which may well be decisive in the customer's choice of bureau.

This also demonstrates the legal interest of this category of services, since the contractual relationship between user and bureau, the allocation of risks and liability between them, are elements of potential use in promoting the services of a given bureau.

Considerable political and legal interest also attaches to problems of the international market created by such services. For example, these services are generally subject to VAT and different VAT rates in different countries may affect the prices a customer has to pay . Customers may also usually import data processing services through telecommunication facilities without paying national VAT but will have to pay VAT to the bureau—in contrast to the position in regard to the import and export of goods (*cf.* Chapter IV. D). The fact that foreign service bureaux may come to compete with national bureaux may give rise to political concern.

Communication is typically point to point, from one customer to the computer service bureau.

3. Data Services

"Processing services" are an area traditionally assigned to computer service bureaux, although services offered are rapidly changing and expanding. One typical example of this change is the shift of emphasis from processing and programmes to data.

Although some bureaux offer the customer rather standard programmes, they combine this with possible access to data maintained by themselves. For example, the results of a market analysis on the basis of sampling conducted by the bureau would be retained by the latter. Any producer of consumer goods could then use the data from the surveys to assess the impact of his own brand on the market. Although the bureau of course provides the processing power and necessary programmes, the emphasis is on the data provided for analysis.

This service is related to information retrieval, but is characterised by the fact that data are not only retrieved but also actually processed according to the instructions of the customer. It is also related to management information services but differs insofar as the data are maintained by the bureau rather than by the customer .

Data services may therefore be seen as an extension of the category "processing services" but with a slight shift in the emphasis. However, the same considerations also apply to the development of the international market. They are perhaps even more relevant in this case since there will be an increasing number of potential customers for whom it may be financially advantageous to purchase data services offered by a bureau.

Consequently, the same legal considerations are relevant as those for processing services so far as contractual relations and international market aspects are concerned. it will be noted that in respect to data services, the problem of marketing requires special attention : this is obvious in regard to personal data but is also relevant in regard to data bases which may involve copyright, trade secrets, etc.

Communication is typically point to point, from a customer to a computer service bureau.

BIBLIOGRAPHY

Bender, David, *Computer Law : Evidence and .procedure;* Bender, New York, 1979.

Bequai, August, *Computer Crime,* Laxington, 1978.

Bing, Jon, "Merverdiavgift, investeringsavgift og datamaskinprogrammer", *Lov og rett,* Oslo, 1976, pp. 100-112.

Bing, Jon, "The Computer in Private, International Law", in *Computers, Contracts and Law,* On-line Conferences, Uxbridge, 1979, pp. 39-49.

Bing, Jon, "Regulating International Computer Services : The Problem and a Possible Solution", in *IBI World Conference on Transborder Data Flow Policies,* IBI, Rome, 1980.

Burhenne, Wolfgang E./Perband, Klaus, *EDV-Recht,* Schmidt, Berlin, 1970.

Freed, Roy N., *Computers and Law—A Reference Work* (4th ed.), Freed, Boston, 1973.

Freese, Jan, *International Data Flow,* Studentlitteratur, Lund, 1979.

Forsberg, Petter, "Legal Regulation of Laser and Fiber-optics", in Bing, Jon and Selner, Knut S. (ed.), *A Decade of Computers and Law,* Norwegian University Press, Oslo, pp. 432-439.

Gottlieb, A./Dalfen, C./Katz, K., "The Transborder Transfer of Information by Communications and Computer Systems : Issues and Approaches to Guiding Principles", in *The American Journal of International Law*, 1974, pp. 246-248.

Greguras, Fred M./Sykes, David S., "Authentification in EFT : The Legal Standards and the Operational Reality", in *Computer/Law Journal*, 1980, pp. 67-86.

Gronfors, Kurt, "Transport Documents and Computerisation", *Marius*, No. 22, 1977.

Henriksen, Roger, *Legal Questions of Security*, Nordic Legal Committee, Oslo, 1981.

Hogrebe, Edmund, *Dangers and Opportunities of Digital Communication Media,* Instituto Latinoamericano de estudios transnacionales, Mexico City, 1980.

Keplinger, M.S., "The Case for the Invisible Copies", in *Revue internationale du droit d' auteur*, October 1980, pp. 3-31.

Logica, *The Usage of International Data Networks in Europe*, OECD Paris, 1979.

Niblett, Bryan, *Legal Protection of Computer Programmes*, Oyez, London, 1980.

Nora, Simon/Minc, Alain, *L' informatisation de la société*, La Documentation Franchise, Paris, 1978.

Ploman, E.W., "Transborder Data Flows and International Regulation of Information and Communication", in *IBI World Conference on Transborder Data Flow Policies*, IBI Rome, No TDF 021, 1980.

Nygaard, Erik, "To datarettslige arbeider : toll og ansvar", *Papers on Computers and Law*, No. 47, Oslo, 1981.

Ripper, Mario Kias/Wanderley, Jorde Luiz Cesario, "The Brazilian Computer and Communications Regulatory Environment and Transborder Data Flow Policy", in *IBI World Conference on Transborder Data Flow Policies,* IBI, No. TDF 001, Rome, 1980.

Renschou, Knut Helge, "Konossementer og EDB", *Marius*, No. 50, Oslo, 1980.

Robinson, Peter, "Scientific and Technological Information in Transborder Data Flow", Toronto, 1980 (ms.).

Schjolberg, Stein, "Datamaskinassistert Kriminalitet", *Papers on Computers and Law*, No. 42, Oslo, 1980.

Seipel, Peter, *ADB och juridik—en problemoversikt*, Finansdepartementet, Stockholm, 1975.

Seipel, Peter, *Computing Law*, Liber, Stockholm, 1977.

Selmer, Knut S., "Transborder Da Flows", Monte Carlo, 1980 (ms.).

Sitre, Ingre Marie Dons, *Bankgiro. Saerlig om ansvar og tilbakekall*, Institutt for privatretts stensilserie, No. 48, Oslo, 1976.

Stromholm, Stig, "Några rättsfrågor kring bestallning av konstverk", *Tidsskrift for rettsvitenskap*, Olso, 1980, pp. 582-600.

Tapper, Colin, *Computer Law*, Longman, London, 1978.

Wilhelmsen, Jan-Fredrik, "Publikums adgang til forvaltningens presedenser", *Papers on Computers and Law*, No. 30, Olso, 1978.

Journals

Transnational Data Report : monthly, published by G. Russel Pipe, Amsterdam.

AFIPA, *Washington Report*, 1980.

References

1. *See* AFIPS, *Washington Report*, 6/1980, pp. 1-3 and 12/1980, pp. 3-4.
2. AFIPS, *Washington Report*, 10/1980.
3. *Op. cit.*
4. *See* the reports of the Committee of Government Experts on problems arising, as regards copyright, from the use of computers, UNESCO/WIPO (1979) and of the Committee of Government Experts on copyright problems arising from the use of computers for access to or the creation of wroks, UNESCO/WIPO (1982).

Modern Communication Glossary

Analog Computer : A computer in which numerical data is manipulated, using especially calibrated electrical signals, scales, etc., to represent an analogy or physical model of that which is being studied. A slide rule is an example of a simple analog computer, wherein marked logarithmic and trigonometric scales, are used to perform multiplication, division and trigonometric functions. The "scale" or model in an analog computer is "continuous". Thus, answers derived from the computer can only be approximated to the degree of precision of the model or scale.

Analog Modulation : A process of continuous changing of a signal (usually a radio wave) to convey a message. Typically, the amplitude or frequency of a radio carrier wave as in amplitude modulation (AM) and frequency modulation (FM) is continuously changed so that a receiving crystal will be able to re-create the original sound or pattern being imitated by an analog model. This could be a voice, music, television picture, etc.

Analog Transmission or Analog Communication : Continuous sending of an analong modulated signal through an appropriate medium, such as cable radio transmission, telephone or telegraph wire. Although analog transmission is predominant throughout the world today, digital transmission (q.v.) will be predominant within the next 20 years.

Arcology : A new discipline that seeks to combine the fields of ecology and architecture.

Bit : The smallest unit of information in digital computer language. A bit is a single character in a binary language wherein there are only two characters—the binary digits of 0 or 1. All numbers can be written in binary code, using the base 2 system, although it requires more characters than the base 10 system with which we are more familiar.

Bit Error Rate (BER) : The number of errors made in a digital transmission as compared to complete accuracy. Today a typical range of accuracy is between one error in one million (BER = 10^{-6}) to one error in a billion (BER = 10^{-9}).

Bit Rate : Rates at which digital information can be sent over transmitting systems. Advanced satellites and fiber optic system can send data at the rate of 1 billion bits per second.

Byte : Eight bits of information. Term used in computer field particularly in reference to memory capabilities.

Carrier Wave : An electromagnetic wave that can be modulated in frequency, amplitude, phase or otherwise to transmit information. Frequently in telecommunications a large carrier wave will package a number of sub-carriers within it to achieve greater efficiency.

CCIR : Consultative Committee on International Radio of the ITU. Recommends global standards and procedures for radio and television communications and broadcasting.

CCITT : Consultative Committee on telephone and telegraph of the ITU. Recommends global standards and procedures for telephone, telegraph, data, facsimile, electronic mail, etc.

CEEFAX : Trade name for a videodata system in the United Kingdom. CEEFAX sends text information to television viewers of the Independent Television Authority by using the subcarrier of the television signal. Information sent in this manner is frequently updated and includes weather, entertainment and travel information.

CELTIC : Name of French digital compression equipment for telephony. Uses voice activation to assign active channel only when party is speaking. (*See* DSI and TASI-D).

CODEC : A piece of electronic equipment that is used for coding or decoding digital signals from or into the analog mode. (*see* Also Source Encoding.)

Companding : A modulation process that manipulates (through compression and then later expansion) the amplitude of a telephone signal. This is done to improve the ratio of the wanted signal to the unwanted noise in the circuit. In digital systems this means a voice signal can be transmitted at lower bit rates, *i.e.*, about 40 kilobits per second rather than typical rates of 56 kilobits per second. The companded circuit has an amplitude *compressor* at one end and an amplitude *expander* at the other end—thus the term "compander".

Computer Output Micrographics (*COM*) : Direct conversion of type characters stored on computer tapes or discs into microfiche or microfilm rather than printing out the information in hardcopy form on paper. This is an important aspects of the paperless office of the future.

Cyberspace : An imaginary void which is the "housing" for the paths of interconnecting computers worldwide.

Data Packet : A packet of data that typically contains one hundred or so bits of information. A data packet contains part of a message plus an "address" indicating where the information is to be sent. By dividing messages into packets for sending through a large, switched digital transmission network, a higher efficiency can be achieved throughout the network. This is true because parts of the message can go by different routes. Route selection is determined by selecting the route least loaded at a particular millisecond interval.

Decibel (*dB*) : Measurement in communications field of power level of a signal expressed as a logarithmic ratio. An increase in power of 3dB is about a 10 fold increase.

DGT : Directorate General of Telecommunication, name of French Ministry of Post & Telecommunications.

Digital Compression Techniques : Techniques to send more information over a channel by processing or manipulating digital codes. This is most productive for television transmission, and for reasonably productive telephony (*see* Digital Speech Interpolation).

Digital Computer : A computer that performs calculations or operations wherein information is translated into code that is represented electronically as digits in binary language, *i.e.*, as 0's and 1's. Most logic functions of the digital computers are based upon Boolean Algebra or "syllogistic reasoning", wherein choices are made between the options of : (a) "and" (*e.g.*, addition) : (b) "not and" (*e.g.*, subtraction); (c) "and/or"; and (d) and "not and/or".

Digital Modulation : A technique use for transmitting information by encoding an analog message into a series of discrete or precisely separate pulsed signals. The code is constructed by altering the amplitude or phase of a radio or light wave carrier between pre-established levels or angles.

Digital Speech Interpolation (*DSI*) : A technique used in transmitting digital voice signals to make more efficient use of the telecommunications channel. The main advantage of this technique is to make active use of the transmission channel only when someone is talking. On the average, both speakers talk 40 per cent of the time and there is 20 per cent silence. By continuing sampling of speech at millisecond intervals and switching off the listener, an increase in capacity of 2.4 to 3.0 times thus can be achieved.

Digital Transmission of Digital Communications : The Conveyance of information of any nature between two or more points by means of discrete pulses as opposed to continuous, analog signals. The telegraph was the first digital communications system.

Diode : An electronic device that restricts current flow chiefly to one direction. Typically, in today's applications, this semiconductor device with cathode and anode terminals is used to rectify an electronic signal. Solid state diodes have replaced radio vacuum tubes in most electronic devices.

EIRP : Effective Isotropically Radiated Power. Measurement in communications field of the quality of signal. The effective power is thus the gain or power of the signal (measured in decibels) compared to the interference in the channel experienced with regard to the wanted signal (measured in degrees Kelvin). This is also known as the Signal-to-Noise ratio.

Encoding : (*see* Source Encoding.)

Extremely High Frequency (*EHF*) : Radio frequencies in the 30 Giga-Hertz to 300 Gigabits range (Millimeter wave region).

Facsimile : A method of transmitted images or printed matter by electronic means. Electronic dots are concentrated together typically at a maximum density of one per quarter of a millimeter to create the image over a grid. Dark shadows or light images are created by changing the density of the dots on the grid. This is the basic concept on which television is based.

Feed : The active electronic part of a radio or radar antenna where the signal originates or where the antenna reflector concentrates the signal for reception. Multiple electronic feeds can be combined to create complicated signal beam patterns.

Feedback : The return of a portion of the output of any process or system to the input, especially when used to control or maintain the output within predetermined limits. Feedback is the essential element in the field of cybernetics, automatic control and robotics.

Geosynchronous Orbit : An orbit 22,300 miles from the earth's surface wherein a satellite's speed will be sufficient to both sustain its orbit indefinitely while completing a revolution around the earth exactly every 24-hour day. This means that a satellite will remain as if fixed above a predetermined spot on the earth's surface. A network of three such satellites can thus provide continuous global coverage.

Giga : A billion. A gigabit is 1 billion bits of information and a Gigahertz is a billion cycles per second.

GHIUD : Global Human Information Use Per Decade. Equivalent to 1.2×10^{19} (12 quintillion) bits of information.

Heinsenberg Uncertainty Principle : A principle of physics, discovered by Werner Heinsenberg, that indicates that no physical phenomena can be measured with absolute certainty, because of the limitation of measuring devices, the interference of the measuring process with the phenomena being measured, and the randomness of events at the atomic and sub-atomic levels.

Hertz : Scientific name for cycles per second.

High Frequency (HF) : Radio frequencies within the range of 3,000 to 30,000 Kilo Hertz. HF radio is also known as shortwave.

Holography : The technique of producing images by wavefront reconstruction, especially by using lasers to record on photograhic plates the diffraction pattern from which a three-dimensional image can be projected.

Holographic Transmissions : Transmission of a holographic image. To achieve near instantaneous transmission of holograms at speeds comparable to those for television would require gigantic telecommunications capabilities well beyond those now known. This rate (25 trillion bits per second) is some 25,000 times greater than today's most advanced telecommunications systems.

INTELPOST : Name of the international organization created to conduct experimental electronic mail transmissions using 9.6 to 64 kilobit/second facsimile transmission. Initial membership U.S., U.K., France, Germany, Netherlands, Argentina.

INTELSAT: International Telecommunications Satellite Organization. INTELSAT provides 60 per cent of the world's overseas telecommunications traffic on its global satellite system.

Intersatellite Link (ISL) : The transmission of messages between satellites in space. EHF and SHF frequencies in the millimeter wave and light wave regions are reserved for this purpose.

INTERSPUTNIK : International communications satellite system that essentially serves Soviet Bloc countries.

ITU : International Telecommunication Union. U.N., specialized agency concerned with regulating and co-ordinating communications activities on a global basis.

Japanese Metabolism : A school of architecture founded in Japan that uses biological models and growth patterns as their inspiration for architectural design.

Kilo : A thousand. A Kilobit is a thousand bits. A Kilohertz is a thousand cycles per second.

Laser : Light Amplification by Stimulated Emission of Radiation. A device that converts incoming electromagnetic energy of mixed frequencies (incoherent source) into a highly amplified and coherent light source of a single frequency.

Laser Communications : Communications using a modulated laser as the carrier medium. Laser communications can be transmitted through glass optical fibers or through space. Lasers are greatly attenuated by atmospheric interference and thus lasers will be first used for intersatellite links, rather than space-to-earth-to-space communications.

LED : Light emitting diode. LED's can be used to modulate signals for light communications. LED's can be thought of as cheap and unsophisticated lasers.

Maser : Microwave Amplification by Stimulated Emission of Radiation. (*see* Laser).

Mega : Million. A Megahertz is 1 million cycles per second. A megabit is I million bits of information.

Modem : Equipment for modulation and demodulation of a telecommunications signal. Sometimes this equipment is known informally as MUX and DEMUX gear.

Murphy's Law : If something can go wrong, it will go wrong and at the worst possible time.

Nano : One billionth. A nanosecond is thus one-billionth of a second.

Narcotic Dysfunction : Psychological reaction to being overloaded with information. Typical reaction tends to be apathy.

NTSC : RCA/NBC-developed colour television standard. Initials stand for National Television System Committee. NTSC is used primarily in the U.S. and South America. European countries have developed the derisive nickname : "Never Twice the Same Colour." (*see* SECAM and PAL).

Office of the Future : Business office equipped with new automated electronic equipment. Also called the Paperless Office. Word processing, computer output microfilm, intelligent PABX, optical character recognition, interactive computer terminals are some of the types of equipment that are involved.

Optical Character Recognition : Equipment designed to recognize written characters and convert them to impressions on computer tapes or discs.

Optical Fibers : High purity glass fibers with reflective coating that can be used for transmitting laser communications.

ORACLE : Viewdata or teletex system similar to CEEFAX, operated by the British Broadcasting Corporation (BBC) in the United Kingdom.

PABX : Private Automatic Branch Exchange. The installation of computerized or "intelligent" PABX equipment in the office can allow complex intraoffice, as well as interoffice, telecommunications.

Packet Switching : A digital telecommunications process, wherein independent data packets are sent over a switched network and recombined into a complete message at the receiving computerized terminal.

PAL : Phase Attenuation by Line. The colour television standard developed by AEG-Telefunken of Germany. One of three colour TV standards used world-wide. (*see* NTSC and SECAM).

PCM : Pulse Code Modulation. A modulation technique wherein an analog signal is sampled and quantized and then converted into a stream of coded binary bits.

Pelton's Perversity Principle : The news coverage of an event tends to be ,inversely proportional to its success and long term social significance.

Photonics : The application of light energy (whose basic unit is a photon) to discharge a wide range of functions, similar to those previously performed by electronics.

Photovoltaic Device : Semiconductor devices (frequently silicon-based) that are excited to a higher energy state by exposure to light or solar energy and thus generate electrical current. Commonly known as solar cells.

Pico : A trillionth. A picosecond is thus a trillionth of a second.

PRESTEL : Tradename for the U.K. Post Office Corporation's viewdata or teletex service. Prestel allows telephone access to large computer data base. Data is displayed on a television screen that has been equipped with an electronic attachment supplied by the Post Office.

PSK : Phase Shift Keyed. The discrete variation of the phase of a carrier by a digital signal.

SECAM : The French-developed colour television standard. SECAM (which stands for Séquential á Mémoire) was developed by the Franch firm of CSF and the patents are now controlled by Thomson-CFS. (*see* NTSC and PAL).

Semi-conductor : A material capable of conducting electricity whose resistance unlike that of metals, decreases with rising temperature and the presence of impurities. Use of the characteristics of these materials, (most frequently this is silicon), circuits can be etched in the material to create transistors.

Shannon's Rate/Distortion Boundary : A theoretical boundary derived by Claude Shannon demonstrating the efficiency limits for the transmission of information over a telecommunications channel.

Specialized Carrier : See Value Added Service.

Silicon Chip : Small wafer of high-grade silicon that can be designed and fabricated to perform a number of functions, including that of solar cell, computer memory and. microprocessor. The elector-chemical qualities of silicon (a semiconductor of electricity) makes it well suited to these tasks. Semiconductor material research is currently the number one materials research in the world. (*see* Semi-conductor).

Source Encoding : The process of converting an analog signal to a digital signal and doing it in a manner so as to achieve maximum transmission efficiency. This is done by eliminating redundant data bits, in order to allow fewer bits of information to be transmitted. Thus source encoding allows the transmission of the same information with the same fidelity, but at lower bit rates. The "rate of encoding" is the ratio of the number of information-carrying bits to the total number of transmitted bits.

"State of the Art" Technology : Technology under development in advanced research and development laboratories that is likely to be implemented in the next generation of high-technology products, such as computers, satellites, etc.

Super High Frequency (SHF) : 3,000 to 30,000 megacycles (Microwave region).

TASI : Time assignment speech interpolation. An information compression technique for voice transmission developed by AT& T. The most advanced system, TASI-D, uses digital compression technique (*see* DSI and CELTIC).

TDMA: Time division multiple access. Digital transmission technique that divides transmission capacity among terminals in the network in terms of time slot allocations, rather than by frequency division. Data is sent in short bursts in accordance with a predetermined time sequence.

TERA : A trillion. Thus, a terabit is a trillion bits of information.

TELEDACTYL : Voice recognition equipment that can transcribe a human voice to written characters and which can also be combined with a telephone for purposes of receiving remote dictation. This equipment is presently only 90 per cent accurate.

TIUPIL : Typical information use per individual lifetime. This is equivalent to 20 billion bits of information.

Transistor : Transfer of an electrical charge across a *resistor;* a small device made of semi conductor material used to amplify electrical current in a similar manner to vacuum tubes or valves.

Ultra High Frequency (UHF) : Radio frequencies in the range 300 to 3000 megacycles.

UNESCO: United Nations Educational, Scientific and Cultural Organization. This has been the prime forum for international debate concerning the need for a New World Information Order.

Value Added Service or Value Added Network (VAN) : Networks or services that are provided through an existing telecommunications network. Typically the VAN uses more efficient modulation or coding techniques so that more information can be sent by a regular customer. VANs are also known as specialized carriers.

Very High Frequency (VHF) : Radio frequencies in the range 30 to 300 megacycles.

VIEWDATA : Generic name for a home information system that transmits data by means of television, radio or telephone signals to be displayed on a home television screen. Systems developed to data include : France : TELETEL and ANTIOPE; United Kingdom : PRESTEL, ORACLE and CEEFAX; Canada : TELIDON.

Voice Recognition Equipment (VRE) or Speech Recognition Equipment (SRE) : Equipment that recognizes spoken words. Industrial robotics equipment currently has vocabularies of 50 words or less. Advanced systems will be able to understand a much larger vocabulary and in several languages.

Voice Programming : Computers with voice recognition equipment that can be verbally programmed to perform tasks.

WARC : World Administrative Radio Conference. Worldwide conference held by the ITU to allocate the world's radio frequencies and to establish rules governing the use of the electromagnetic spectrum.

World Processing : Technique of keyboarding text onto a computer tape or disc in order that the stored information can be used conveniently and efficiently in one of the following ways : editing; producing multiple copies of "personalized letters", sending electronic mail; receiving comments and revisions from others with CRT terminals; reformatting text for printing; producing microfiche records (COM).

Index